AMERICAN HOMO

AMERICAN HOMO

HOMO

Community and Perversity

JEFFREY ESCOFFIER

UNIVERSITY OF CALIFORNIA PRESS
Berkeley   Los Angeles   London

University of California Press
Berkeley and Los Angeles, California

University of California Press, Ltd.
London, England

© 1998 by
Jeffrey Escoffier

Library of Congress Cataloging-in-Publication Data

Escoffier, Jeffrey.
    American homo : community and perversity / Jeffrey Escoffier.
        p.   cm.
    Includes bibliographic references (p.) and index
    ISBN 0-520-20632-0 (cloth : alk. paper).—ISBN 0-520-20633-9
(pbk. : alk. paper)
        1. Homosexuality—United States.   2. Homosexuality—Political
aspects—United States.   3. Gay and lesbian studies—United States.
4. Gays—United States—Identity.   5. Lesbians—United States—Identity.   6. Gay men—United States—Political activity.   7. Lesbians—
United States—Political activity.   I. Title.
    HQ76.3.U5E83   1997
    306'76'6'0973—dc21   97-16513
                                                                     CIP

Printed in the United States of America
9 8 7 6 5 4 3 2 1

The paper used in this publication meets the minimum requirements
of American National Standards for Information Sciences—Perma-
nence of Paper for Printed Library Materials, ANSI Z39.48-1984.

To those friends and comrades who shared my years at SR,
the History Project, and *OUT/LOOK* and who helped
to create a wonderful and exciting intellectual life outside
the university.

CONTENTS

ACKNOWLEDGMENTS

It is daunting but nonetheless pleasurable to acknowledge those who, for more than a decade, have helped me think more creatively and write more clearly about the historical and social conditions of gay and lesbian life. When I first began writing these essays, an extraordinary group of friends and colleagues offered encouragement and support— as fellow editors at *Socialist Review,* as members of the San Francisco Lesbian and Gay History Project, as editors at *OUT/LOOK,* and as friends and lovers. That group includes Dorothy Allison, Tomas Almaguer, Allan Bérubé, E. G. Crichton, Lisa Duggan, Jackie Goldsby, Amber Hollibaugh, Bo Huston, Mark Leger, Donald Lowe, Esther Newton, Ilene Philipson, Gayle Rubin, Michael Sexton, and Howard Winant. Their initial endorsement, emotional nourishment, suggestions for further reading, and sharp criticisms, as well as their own essays and books, have helped make my social and political analysis more honest, meaningful, and useful.

These essays were written over the course of twelve years, and for different audiences, each of which had a distinctive set of operative assumptions. I published the first of them in 1985 and the most recent in 1997. Although not consciously undertaken to explore any one perspective on identity politics, the essays nevertheless have thematic links and overlapping arguments. One recurring theme is the vicissitudes of homosexual identities in the post–World War II United States through the interplay of cultural politics and economic forces. In additon, the essays often stress the role of lesbian and gay intellectuals in the development of gay and lesbian community, the elaboration of identity politics, and the construction of lesbian and gay studies as a form of social knowledge. Many of the essays also touch on the contingency of a collective identity that is always contested, unstable, and full of unresolved differences. Published together these essays interweave the history of sexual revolution, cultural politics, and capitalist development to offer what I hope is an interpretation of gay and lesbian life since the end of World War II. Writing on topics that are somewhat new and undeveloped, and which draw on concepts from across intellectual disciplines, is a difficult process, in part because the analytic frameworks are not yet thoroughly worked out. I have revised most of the essays included here—to update them and delete outdated references, to remove some of the redundancy between essays, and to eliminate any glaring inconsistencies—but it was impossible to blend them into one seamless narrative.

While writing these essays, I have had conversations with Rudiger Busto, Barbara Epstein, Lisa Hall, Leslie Kauffman, Caitlin Manning, Jim Shoch, William Simon, Judith Stacey, and Ara Wilson at crucial moments. I am also fortunate to have had excellent editors for several of my essays, among them Martin Duberman, Barbara Epstein, Amy Gluckman, Leslie Kauffman, Michael Rothberg, David Trend, and Elliot Weininger. At the University of California Press, my editor, Naomi Schneider, has encouraged me throughout the process. Scott Norton, the Press's production editor, and Eve Kushner, the manuscript's copyeditor, have worked hard to help me make this a better book.

Since moving to New York in 1993, I have relied on a circle of friends who, as I worked to assemble and complete this book, have routinely offered me encouragement, stimulating conversations, and extremely helpful criticisms and comments on my work. That circle includes Chris Bull, John Gagnon, Robert Hughes, Terrence Kissack, Regina Kunzel, Molly McGarry, Fred Morris, Kevin Murphy, Michael Rothberg, Matt Rottnek, and Andrew Spieldenner. Amber Hollibaugh and Loring McAlpin have sustained me through many dark moments and helped keep alive my intellectual vocation. Above all, I am deeply grateful to Matthew Lore, my partner and companion in complicated living. I thank him for his love, his sense of fate, his curiosity, and his intellectual passion. Without these things, I could not have written the most recent essays. He has read more of them than anyone else, and more times than anyone. He has critiqued my essays with grace, a sharp sense of style, and a clairvoyant sensitivity to the truth I sought.

INTRODUCTION

So we are taking off our masks, are we, and keeping
our mouths shut? as if we'd been pierced by a glance!

FRANK O'HARA, *"Homosexuality"*

No social study that does not come back to the
problems of biography, of history and of their
intersections within society has completed its
intellectual journey. . . . Perhaps the most fruitful
distinction with which the sociological imagination
works is between "the personal troubles of milieu"
and the "public issues of social structure."

C. WRIGHT MILLS,
The Sociological Imagination

Am I to become profligate as if I were a blonde?
Or religious as if I were French?

FRANK O'HARA,
"Meditations In An Emergency"

The desire to live honestly underlies the political emergence of lesbians
and gay men in our time.[1] Such honesty requires self-knowledge. The
moment of acknowledging to oneself homosexual desires and feelings—
the culmination of a process that, for many, intermingles horror and
excitement—and then licensing oneself to act, and perhaps to discover
anew one's vulnerabilities, is the central drama of the homosexual self.
That moment of self-classification, of self-naming, and of exile from our
natal culture is an emergency—sublime, horrible, wonderful—in the

I

life of anyone who must confront it. Although we become ourselves in that moment of recognition, we also discover the injunctions of the law, the punitive rule of normalcy, and the ferocity of social exclusion. We see that our *selves* are traversed by social processes that shape our lives.

That cathartic moment initiates three phases of homosexual emancipation. In the first one, we begin to narrate our autobiographies in new ways. Out of necessity, we start to theorize what has happened to us and seek to recreate our place in society. In our autobiographies, we find our responsibilities—to the realization of our desires.

In the next phase, we "discover" ourselves and begin to learn the social skills that enable us to share our desires, achieve bodily pleasures (perhaps even moments of bliss), and build fragile solidarities with others. In the course of our trajectory, which is one of emancipation from stigma and self-hatred, we strive to act as though we are "real" members of society. We say to ourselves, "I want recognition and acceptance of my difference."

In the third phase, we find out how complicated life is: that we are outsiders at the same time as we belong, and that although we may live like our putatively happy married straight friends and neighbors, we owe our independence to sexual perversity. Ambivalence and perversity constitute the sublime elements of homosexual life—by which I mean the mingling of the exalted, unimaginable, painful, and glorious. And we grasp the thought, "My homosexuality is an adventure."

This *adventure* starts with a drive for personal fulfillment, moves on to the building of communities, and almost inevitably ends with a division of communities. Differentiation separates and divides members from one another, sometimes quite acrimoniously, and leads to the creation of new communities for those who share issues and identities.

My essays on gay and lesbian cultural politics, written over ten years, explore the social significance of homosexual emancipation since the end of World War II and the political reaction that it has precipitated in American public life. Although I did not consciously try to articulate a coherent perspective on identity politics, several themes recur in these essays.

One theme is how homosexual identities have changed in the post–World War II United States because of the interplay of cultural politics and economic forces. It is impossible to separate the emergence of homosexual communities from the economic context in which most lesbians and gay men have found themselves. Usually in homosexual emancipation projects, the economic theme is only a subtext, but it is always an absolutely essential one.

A second important theme I return to again and again centers on lesbian and gay intellectuals. I am particularly concerned with their role in developing gay and lesbian community, elaborating identity politics, and constructing lesbian and gay studies as a form of social knowledge (and self-knowledge). As with the conceptualization of nationalism in the nineteenth century, the cultural construction of modern lesbian and gay "identity politics" is, in large part, the work of writers, journalists, activists, academics, and other intellectuals. Through the historical process of creating a "community," this diverse group—which I think of collectively as intellectuals—created a public sphere, including community newspapers, discussion and support groups, political groups, film festivals, historical societies, and community centers, all of which fostered wide-ranging dialogues. Participants in the public sphere constructed their lives around the values and norms that emerged from these conversations.

I have chosen to explore the political-cultural status of "homosexualities"—as varieties of behavior, as the basis of identities, and as expressions of desire—in the United States after World War II. I focus on lesbians and gay men, although they are not the only Americans who engage in sex with someone of the same gender—because by identifying themselves as gay or lesbian, they shape the context in which homosexuality is understood. Drag queens, bisexuals, those who engage in S/M, transgendered people, and other sexual minorities have always participated in homosexual communities and continue to play a role in contemporary gay and lesbian communities. Lesbians and gay men have taken the lead in organizing homosexual social movements, creating communities, and working to increase the visibility and viability of homosexuality as a way of life.

At the heart of this process of identity and community formation is what I call *American homo*, within which lesbian and gay politics and the economic-cultural organization of homosexual communities take place. I have tried to flesh out the complex social process by which individuals join and leave communities. This long journey starts with a drive for personal fulfillment, moves on to the individual's participation in the building of communities, and leads to a differentiation between the members that divides the community, sometimes quite acrimoniously, and spurs dissenters to create new communities. The autobiography that underlies these essays illuminates some of the assumptions that have shaped my writing. This historical trajectory from closeted individual to the dynamic of community building describes, I believe, a characteristic journey of the white, modern, North American homosexual. Perhaps more realistically, it epitomizes one particular generation's experience—my own. Maybe most accurately, it captures my own journey through the tangled politics of authenticity, identity, and community.

AMERICAN HOMO

Homoeroticism pervades American life. Among many other things, it provides the cultural context underlying the development of visible gay and lesbian communities. Homoeroticism exists as a long-standing structure of feeling in American culture. Such a structure reflects organized and relatively enduring relationships between homosexual desire, behavior, and cultural forms of expression.[2]

Homoeroticism as a reality in U.S. society has taken several forms over more than two centuries. Even before Europeans arrived in North America, many tribal societies sanctioned homosexual behavior, as distinct from what we conceive of as a homosexual identity. Early European explorers and colonists viewed some of these homosexual practices as belonging to a broad category of nonprocreative sexual acts. This does not mean that the Church or state approved of homosexual behavior or eroticism; Christians considered homosexual behavior, particularly sodomy, to be theologically unacceptable.

During the nineteenth and early twentieth centuries, opportunities for same-sex erotic activities varied by gender, class, and race. Within the white working class, both men and women were increasingly able to form same-sex attachments as more people worked outside the family economy. Homosexual intimacy was probably common among white wage-earning men. Such laborers, often dwelling in cities and large towns, had greater geographic mobility, more access to housing for those who were single, and higher levels of employment than did women, blacks, or even those who worked in agriculture. Same-sex social situations were extremely common in nineteenth-century America.[3] In such situations, male bonding—often an important aspect of social relations in those environments—may have blended with erotic experience. This is not to say that the nineteenth century was a "golden age" of homoeroticism. In the middle class, men had more opportunities than women for same-sex physical intimacy, although same-sex romantic friendships might have had a sexual component for both men and women.[4]

People feared erotic bonding on many levels; some nineteenth-century commentators believed that it (as well as masturbation) sapped entrepreneurial energies.[5] Christian theology and procreative ideology—which were often conflated—condemned homosexual behavior as sinful or detrimental to the survival of the species. Homophobia (as a phenomenon—the term was only invented in 1971) led people to stigmatize homosexuality and stirred up a fear of homoeroticism, causing many to define the emotional bonds within same-sex relationships in nonsexual terms.[6]

Homoeroticism and the passions of homosexuality have motivated men and women to embark on geographic expeditions; participate in antipoverty campaigns; initiate educational reform; fight for women's rights; propose reforms in the treatment of prisoners and juvenile delinquents; serve in the military as soldiers, sailors, and medics; and join in civil rights struggles. The lives of many of these women and men remain hidden or denied in American social history.[7]

Whereas there is direct as well as much indirect evidence of this repressed homoeroticism in diaries, letters, and legal documents, representations of homosexuality have also surfaced in American novels, plays, poetry, visual arts, and many forms of popular culture. Herman Melville's novel *Moby-Dick* includes one of the boldest representations in his account of Queequeg and Ishmael's sleeping arrangements and subsequent warm embraces. Walt Whitman's "Calamus" poems found many readers who recognized their deeply felt homosexuality; the poems also strongly affected a number of European intellectuals who campaigned for homosexual rights during the late nineteenth century.[8] Although widely celebrated literary and artistic figures—Melville, Whitman, Emily Dickinson, Willa Cather, Hart Crane, Langston Hughes, Greta Garbo, Gertrude Stein, Tennessee Williams, James Baldwin, and Allen Ginsberg—drew their inspiration from homosexual passions, that fact is routinely suppressed.

Homoeroticism is also a cultural semiotic, albeit a heavily coded one. It is a cultural formation, a system of meanings, signifying the potential intimacy, sexual pleasure, and sensibility of same-sex bonding that the hegemonic regime of compulsory heterosexuality prohibits.[9] For example, Michael Moon has proposed that "between American literature and homoeroticism there have historically been peculiar and intimate connections."[10] Moon has also noted, however, the extraordinary degree to which discourses dealing with abortion, contraception, prostitution, masturbation, and homosexuality have overlapped and affected social issues such as education, public health, housing and racial conflict, masculinity, and nationalism.[11]

This strong historic presence of homosexuality has its dark side—a virulent hatred and suspicion of the homoerotic. This antihomosexual paranoia—what we now call homophobia—arouses visceral anxieties of homosexual conspiracy, horror of sexual advances, the assumption of rampant sexual abuse of children, and panic about one's own homosexual desires.[12] The degree to which homoeroticism has been repressed or the way in which it has been stigmatized has varied quite significantly over the last two hundred or more years.[13] There have been periods of relative tolerance, such as the 1920s, and moments of cultural history imbued with homoerotic expression, such as the American Literary Renaissance of the 1850s, the Harlem Renaissance of the

1920s, and post–World War II art and literature. These, however, alter
nate and even overlap with episodes of persecution: Franklin D.
Roosevelt's 1919 investigation of homosexuality in the Navy; the Mc-
Carthy purges of the 1950s, which scapegoated homosexuals as security
risks; and, currently, religious conservatives' twenty-year crusade to
eliminate the open presence of lesbians and gay men from American
life.[14]

The interlocking structures of feeling—of homoeroticism *and* homophobia—have long been bound up with other social forces.[15] The
whole complex of attitudes and practices, both antagonistic and affirmative, that I identify by the phrase *American homo* draws on a deeply
ingrained "polymorphous perverse" sexuality in American culture.
Polymorphous perversity reflects sexuality before it is unified and narrowly focused on heterosexual intercourse. The libidinal energy of perverse desire, tirelessly tamed and harnessed by hegemonic social structures, repeatedly erupts to shatter dominant social patterns, identities,
and norms. It is a steady current throughout American history sustained by sexual subcultures and dissenters who resist the heteronormative organization of desire.

These deeply embedded structures of feeling and libidinal energies
are reconfigured through a long-term historical process of sexual revolution. In this revolution, social forces remapped the biological capacities of sexual and gender roles. During this process, the mapping repeatedly breaks down, partly because social groups' actions reshape
roles and institutions but also because of those actions' unanticipated
consequences. Thus, the gay movement, by encouraging the public disclosure of its members' homosexuality, has provoked the political mobilization of religious conservatives.

Since the mid-1970s, American homosexuals have been poised to
break through into public life. Many straight people, however, hesitate
to include homosexuals openly in American life. Homosexuals' enlist-
ment in the military, gay and lesbian marriages, and representations of
two women or two men kissing on a prime-time television show—these
actions provoke anxiety, perhaps even fear and loathing. The Religious
Right arouses and channels these anxieties, depicting homosexuals as

the symbol of American decadence, the illustration of the decline and fall of the American empire.

Ironically, since the advent of the AIDS epidemic, homosexuality has directly entered mainstream American political discourse, while at the same time the Right has launched a momentous campaign to reshape American values. This campaign aspires to be as far-reaching as the restoration of traditional values attempted at the end of World War II. At that time, young white women were pushed out of the labor force and back into the family; communists were arrested, blacklisted, and forced to flee; and the mass media, big corporations, and the power elite encouraged cultural conformity.

The culture wars of the present are, as Irving Kristol has said, a new cold war. Now, instead of containing "the communist threat," American conservatives seek to crush the "homosexual threat" to America's so-called traditional family values. *Homosexuality*, along with *abortion*, is the code word for the threat to American society. Implicitly (because it is no longer acceptable to "blame" most of these groups publicly), the Right also refers to African Americans, Jews, Japanese, and Mexicans as threats.

Contemporary Americans face a prolonged political-cultural war over the acceptability of homosexuality. Neither side has a decisive advantage. Nor will the issue be resolved in the near future. The Religious Right has been organizing around the homosexual issue ever since Anita Bryant's 1977 "Save Our Children" campaign. Attacking homosexuality was a major theme at the 1992 Republican National Convention. "In 1992 in Houston, I talked about the cultural war going on for the soul of America," Pat Buchanan reminded voters during the 1996 Republican primary campaign. "And that war is still going on! We cannot worship the false god of gay rights. To put that sort of relationship on the same level as marriage is a moral lie."[16] During the Republican primaries, Buchanan carried the standard against gay and lesbian rights. His demonization of homosexuality and attacks on same-sex marriage alarmed conservative voters about the homosexual threat and garnered support for his candidacy. Although in the end he did not win a large enough proportion to be a serious contender for the nomination, none of the other Republican candidates apart from Richard Lugar offered even token opposition to Buchanan's fervent gay bashing.

The larger context of Buchanan's political and cultural war is *American homo*—the interlocking structures of homoeroticism and homophobia—the hegemony of heterosexuality as a cultural system. Currently, heterosexuality as a sex/gender paradigm organizes intellectual categories, as well as Americans' everyday experience of sexuality, gender, and reproduction. "Heterosexuality" as a hegemonic social formation is an ensemble of putatively stable social forms, institutions, and practices. Together, they structurally contain and neutralize oppositional movements and communities, such as feminism; the lesbian and gay movement; the campaign for reproductive rights; and the rights of transgendered, bisexual, and erotic minorities.[17] Whereas any hegemonic social order is constantly renegotiated and is never conclusively established, "the heterosexual dictatorship" (to use a phrase of Christopher Isherwood's) has long succeeded in minimizing homosexuality's impact through religious teachings, social stigmatization, psychiatric and other medical therapies, and, in the most recent decades, direct political activity aimed at disenfranchising lesbians and gay men.

The lesbian and gay movement is transforming American social values and behavior. It has successfully organized its own sexual communities, which have allowed homosexuality and unconventional gender behavior of all forms to flourish. Although these developments have taken place unevenly and have constantly provoked conflict, the lesbian and gay movement has put homosexuality on America's political and cultural agenda.

Any sense of collective selfhood will always be contested, unstable, and full of unresolved differences. The social role designating a person as homosexual emerged in European-American cultures during the nineteenth century or even earlier. Even though homosexuality has existed in many societies and historical periods, the person who identifies as "homosexual" is a relatively recent creation. As with all such creations, this one will change and presumably disappear at some point. However transitory the historical character of the lesbian and gay identities, it is impossible to overestimate the significance of gay and lesbian identity politics in the late twentieth century.

BECOMING MYSELF:
DISCOVERING "THE SOCIAL"

I was dyslexic and unable to read until I was ten years old. That year, I read my first book and reading became an important source of pleasure for me. Coincidentally, that was the same year I first experienced vivid homoerotic fantasies.

In my late teens, after my first sexual experiences, I tracked down everything I could read on homosexuality. I constantly sought information about homosexuality and worked hard to develop intellectual justifications for my own sexual orientation. In my freshman year at college, we read Plato's *Symposium*. On my own I read Baldwin's *Giovanni's Room*, Gide's *Corydon* and *If It Die*, Cocteau's *The White Book*, a life of Rimbaud, Jean Genet's *Our Lady of the Flowers*, Sartre's *Saint Genet*, Petronius's *Satyricon*—anything that offered a view of homosexuality as important, good, and normal.

I had my first homosexual experience at sixteen during the summer of 1959. After that, I thirsted for wild adventure. Growing up on Staten Island, realizing my queerness in its sleepy working-class communities, I viewed Greenwich Village as Shangri-la. I cut classes to go cruise in the Village. During the summers while I was in college, I'd pretend that I was working all night at my job as a security guard and cruise Washington Square Park for the strangers who introduced me to gay life. One-night stands, first names only, kissing and jerking off in the dark corners of parks and promenades, lonely train rides in from Brooklyn at two in the morning. These night classes provided me with a "sentimental education," but it was my experience of the 1960s that gave me a political education.

The 1960s arrived on my college campus in the fall of 1963, when I was a senior. The freshman class seemed to have brought with it marijuana for everyone, along with peyote and other drugs. The previous summer, I had hitchhiked to Mexico through Louisiana and Texas in the footsteps of Jack Kerouac and William Burroughs, bringing back bottles of amphetamines and sexually explicit books such as Genet's *Thief's Journal*.

That fall, I returned to college fired up with a new cause—I had been converted to Herbert Marcuse's and Norman O. Brown's bold vision of sexual revolution.[18] My friends eagerly listened to my accounts of Brown's and Marcuse's theories. My friend Tom even made a little jingle to promote Brown's vision of the redemptive power of polymorphous perversity—"Polymorphous perversity / That's why we came to the university." I drew hope from Brown's vision of polymorphous perversity and Marcuse's identification of the homosexual as a revolutionary figure who refused to endorse repressive patriarchal reproduction. These ideas reassured me that, as a queer, I was not destined for a socially meaningless life. Few of my friends knew that I was queer because I was still in the closet. Although we discussed other people's sex lives all the time, most people had no idea about my sexuality. I also lied about it.

The fall of 1963 brought political turmoil—the assassination of John F. Kennedy and the wild political fears and fantasies that were disseminated across America. That summer, hitching from New Orleans to Laredo, Texas, I had seen the pervasive hatred of Kennedy and of blacks. Outside Baton Rouge, I rode with an old guy who drank mint-flavored gin as he drove, stopping in every bar on the way to the Mexican border. In these bars, angry white men watched a televised civil rights march in Washington. I heard them mutter, "Look at all them coons," and threaten to kill President Kennedy.

Mexico City was my Paris. I went to boxing matches, bullfights, and cafés that promised a bohemian atmosphere. I read William Burroughs, Jean Genet, Ernest Hemingway, and Henry Miller. Although I cruised constantly for sexual adventures, I never found my Verlaine or my Genet.

My first great love was someone with whom I could lie in bed after sex, smoking a cigarette and talking about ideas and philosophy. It was a tortured relationship so familiar in that period—he claimed that he was straight, I knew that I was queer. We remained sexually involved off and on for six years, even as he drifted toward heterosexuality. We both moved to New York, where I enrolled in graduate school at Columbia. Over the next four years, I had a series of closeted homosexual affairs, usually with other graduate students but eventually with an artist in Andy Warhol's circle. On the hot days of 1967's Summer of Love, I roamed the East Village holding hands with a man, spent long nights at Max's Kansas City, went to freak bars, smoked marijuana and hashish, and listened, often stoned and practically in a trance, to the Rolling Stones, and for a while to the Beatles' *Sgt. Pepper's Lonely Hearts Club Band.* Life seemed to promise a utopian moment: "free" stores (in which things were given away at no charge), free rock concerts, and free universities were sprouting up all over. The counterculture with its bohemian flavor was much more my milieu than the antiwar movement, where I was put off by the macho style of many of the movement's men.

Amid the chaos, cultural turmoil, bad drug experiences, riots, and demonstrations, I (like the rest of my generation) read like crazy: Herbert Marcuse, Paul Goodman, Leroi Jones, Norman O. Brown, Allen Ginsberg, Lionel Trilling, Norman Mailer, C. Wright Mills, James Baldwin, Rosa Luxemburg, Jean-Paul Sartre, Randolph Bourne, Christopher Lasch, Harold Cruse, Susan Sontag, Claude Lévi-Strauss, and Eldridge Cleaver.

Somehow we suddenly knew something in our guts that we hadn't known before, or at least hadn't known as assuredly or profoundly: "Human beings make their own history," as Marx wrote in 1852. Throughout the late 1960s and early 1970s, we realized that whatever had seemed "natural" in the 1950s, such as war, race relations, gender roles, sexuality, and capitalism, had in fact been shaped by social processes. The utopian promise of the 1960s was that we could and would change society. Years later, we learned the lesson embodied in the second half of Marx's famous formulation: "... but [they make their own history] not of their own free will; not under circumstances they themselves have chosen, but under the given and inherited circumstances with which they are directly confronted. The tradition of the dead generations weighs like a nightmare on the minds of the living."[19]

Nonetheless, the years between 1968 and 1971 were a utopian moment in American culture. Black power, feminism, and socialism were on the agenda. When the account of the Stonewall riots appeared in the *Village Voice* in June 1969, my life changed all at once. I had long known that I was queer—that is, a *homosexual*—but I had *never* applied the word *gay* to myself. (*Gay* was the word used by homosexuals themselves.) Although I did not immediately join the gay liberation movement that emerged from the riots, within months I had consciously begun the process of coming out.

I moved to Philadelphia in the fall of 1970, and I arrived there as an openly gay man. Soon I heard about the Philadelphia chapter of Gay Activists Alliance (GAA). I joined and, not too long afterward, became its president. But I knew nothing about gay life; I had just begun going to gay bars and did not really have a gay social life. In addition, although I had immersed myself in the radical political theory of the New Left, I was a closet activist and had not participated very much in the antiwar movement. I was suddenly a "leader," but I was pretty ignorant about political organizing. I imagined a political vision by adapting theories and political strategies from the black liberation and women's liberation movements. My comrades and I in Philadelphia's GAA also took guidance from the ideas and strategies of several groups, including the original GAA chapter in New York; activists in New York and Philadelphia who had been involved in the Gay Liberation Front (the organization that had preceded GAA); and the older members of the Homophile Action League, Philadelphia's pre-Stonewall homosexual civil rights organization, particularly Barbara Gittings and Kay Tobin.

Like many people in other 1960s movements, we thought only of the future. We had little interest in the gay and lesbian culture that already existed, except for relying on it to find sexual partners. Instead, we set out to create a liberated gay culture. Those of us in GAA constituted a new generation. We were often more contemptuous than we had any right to be of the older lesbians and gay men who participated in the "old" world of gay bars, butch/femme roles, and drag balls. At the same time, we dismissed a little too glibly those who, as "homophiles," had sought to prove that homosexuals were not sick and were, in fact, just like other Americans, aside from having sex with members of their own gender.

TRYING TO MAKE HISTORY

A whole generation of men and women made an exhilarating discovery: so many of the stultifying norms, oppressive institutions, and social customs in 1950s America were not *natural* or permanent, but rather were *social*. It was a profound revelation. Racial injustice was not a natural law. Poverty could be eliminated. Young men did not necessarily have to fight wars that older men had started. Young men and women were able to break with what seemed to be eternal customs and mores: they could fuck whomever they wanted, smoke marijuana, and challenge authority.

There are very few moments in history when a whole generation is gripped by such a complex idea. When a moment like this occurs, it can have cathartic effects. The French Revolution was such an event, as were the unsuccessful European revolutions of 1848 and, after World War II, the independence movements in Africa and Asia.[20]

So much of what one thinks of as "the 1960s"—its politics, sexual revolutions, drug experiences, and even ultimately the disillusionment of those involved—makes no sense unless one remembers the wildly exhilarating discovery that human beings could change the world. Of course, the militants of social change eventually discovered for themselves that history was hard to make—that "the social" could indeed prove intractable. The backlash against the 1960s—with a retreat to New Age fads, religion, therapy, and recovery—grew out of this disappointment.

In the wake of the disillusionment and frustrations about the social struggles of the 1960s, the significance *and* the awareness of the social almost disappeared. Because social change was difficult, painful, and demanding, requiring patience and persistence, we began to deny that it was possible. It seemed easier to try to change ourselves—to go to workshops on "the games people play"; to experience the primal scream; to learn massage, Zen meditation, or tai chi; to run or go to the gym; to stop smoking, drinking, eating, and fucking; to search for that oceanic feeling, that spiritual connection to nature or the goddess. The emotional turmoil of social change, as well as our youth, led us to seek refuge in religion or spiritual disciplines. There was a Zen to the art of motorcycle maintenance, but was there also a Zen of revolution—a *wisdom* that would enable us, potentially, to cope with the emotional trials of making history?

We lost sight of the social and its corollary—that men and women can make their history. Instead, we began to think increasingly in terms of psychological explanations or cultural interpretations. We reduced the social to a person's needs, experiences, and childhood traumas, or to texts in which we searched for cultural codes. By a process of reduction and substitution, we impoverished the idea of the social—we now consider only economic processes and institutions to be social. All those other processes that shape our society (such as class formation, social stratification, or acculturation) have disappeared from our everyday intellectual frameworks. Many of these processes became "renaturalized" in the 1980s; people began to view gender differences, intelligence, ethnic characteristics, and sexuality as innate processes, not social ones. Without a sociological imagination, we lost our ability to navigate social change.

THE IDENTITY TRAP

Discovering that human beings actually created so much that originally seemed natural, and that was therefore social, sparked an epiphany for the radicals of the 1960s. That realization was also pivotal in the movement to emancipate lesbians, gay men, and bisexuals from the stigma, oppression, and violence that have made homosexuality socially unacceptable. Lesbian and gay liberation would be impossible without the cognitive flash that human action decisively shapes social life, often in unanticipated ways.

A social world that nourished homosexual life was created through the confluence of long-term historical processes, various individual and collective actions, and numerous unintended consequences of those actions. The founding impulse of the gay and lesbian movements was initially personal—claiming the right to love—but this impulse, primarily a desire for personal authenticity, resonated widely within American society. Soon, others who shared homosexual desires openly expressed them and generalized the impulse. In this way, the pursuit of authenticity provided a sufficient basis for the creation of a community.[21] The irony is that this process of achieving authenticity, of finding solidarity and community, is also potentially a trap that results in a fixed sense of identity.

Ideally, the "authentic" human being can make moral or political judgments in his or her own name and not in an imitative, socially acceptable manner.[22] In the late 1960s and early 1970s, the "authentic homosexual"—politicized by the feminist, lesbian, or gay movements and by the process of coming out—took responsibility for satisfying his or her real sexual needs. Coming out—the public disclosure of one's homosexuality—was and still is a cathartic moment. In this moment, a transformation of one's identity takes place. One rejects self-hatred and affirms the previously stigmatized self. The dialectic of self-definition requires a confrontation between individual autonomy and established moral codes. For gay men and women, this ethic of authenticity became a project of collective action when it galvanized a loose network of social circles, habituees of dimly lit meeting places, and the customers of marginal businesses into communities. The Stonewall riots were the founding myth of a liberated gay and lesbian community.

Throughout the late 1950s and the 1960s, the impulse toward authenticity often led to some sort of collective action. Both the militants of the black civil rights movement and the bohemians of the beat generation managed to combine, in very different ways, acts of individual self-determination with the solidarity of a community.

Community implies a self-conscious social group made up of individuals who have some shared interests, characteristics, or values—and who express or recognize themselves as members of such a community. It is a group of significant others. In addition, the community confers on its members a form of recognition—a shared recognition of identity. Membership in a community often implies a harmonious reciprocity with other members.

The irony of a politics built on the ethic of authenticity, however, was the concomitant creation of a community that, itself, articulated new moral codes and norms of behavior. These new ethical codes, reified and often resulting from a new communal solidarity, periodically posed all-too-familiar dilemmas for those lesbians and gay men who found themselves excluded, at that particular moment of history, by the new social norms of conduct. The new norms and ethical codes defined as "deviant" those who experienced the new communal values as "inauthentic" or as not matching their own values. Those "deviants" at one time or another included drag queens, pornographers, practitioners of casual sex, believers in monogamy, advocates of S/M, lesbians who practiced butch/femme, fairies, and boy lovers—depending on the constellation of norms dominant at any given moment. In addition, lesbians and gay men each developed norms that seemed to reflect the socialization and experience of the two genders—which further complicated the mix of values and norms. Many of the groups who felt alienated from community norms were also implicated in the growing tensions between women and men, because many practices— such as S/M, butch/femme, and transvestism—seemed to play off of gender roles and behavior.

These new "liberated" communities of *authentic* lesbians or gay men were presumed to be unified organic wholes predicated on the harmonious fusion of identical lesbians or gay men.[23] But, in fact, lesbians and gay men as a joint community or as separate, gender-specific communities were not "unified organic entities," because, of course, not all homosexuals are identical.

Instead, lesbians and gay men pursued homosexual lives with multiple commitments to other arenas of life (jobs, political parties, religious affiliations) or other communities (different races, gender identities, class experiences, and erotic preferences) that other members of the lesbian or gay communities did not necessarily share. Class, race, gender, and other differences divided the communities. Some homosexuals adopted a form of "populist essentialism"—the belief that coming out could reveal an essential and authentic self, thus enabling lesbians and gay men to minimize the significance of accidents of birth and history. A community of "authentic" and exclusive homosexual selves requires a kind of closure that insulates community members from ties and loyalties to people outside the community. Without that closure, members of the community cannot escape the complex web of affiliations with families and other groups; the loyalties of ethnicity, religion, and social class will reassert themselves and disrupt the sense of community. As homosexuals, however, we join gay and lesbian communities only as adults, after powerful socialization experiences have made a deep impression, binding us to many other communities. Therefore, closure is not really possible—or even desirable—without a radical physical isolation. The final result is that our relation to community, created by a politics of authenticity, was often one of inauthenticity.[24]

CIVIL SOCIETY AND THE MAINSTREAM

The most difficult arena within which to define integration into the mainstream is lesbian and gay participation in civil society—that broad, amorphous terrain of social life that, to some degree, can be distinguished from the market and the state. It is the world of voluntary associations, nonprofit community organizations, and community media in which social norms, roles, practices, relationships, cultural patterns, and networks of friendship, kinship, and collective identity are critical factors. Gay and lesbian communities have flourished in precisely this terrain of American society. What almost everyone calls "the community" consists precisely in these networks of associations, face-to-face relationships, and group-oriented businesses.

The dynamic of self and community that motivates the emancipation of "the inauthentic self" from the normative repression of mainstream society encourages collective action as a remedy for certain problems. But as soon as this new, politicized community and its members enter into relations with other social groups, the community is compelled to redefine its relationship to society at large.

The meaning and desirability of mainstreaming are topics of perennial debate in communities that have historically been excluded from conventional social and institutional life—"lure and loathing" is how Gerald Early has described this simultaneous attraction to and repulsion from mainstream life.[25] Like so many political terms, "mainstreaming" is open to radically different interpretations. To some, it is clearly a good thing—a token of acceptance, a chance to fit in, a place at the table—while to others, it is deeply problematic, a compromise, a form of co-optation, or the loss of something distinctive. In addition to the normative interpretations, it also has a variety of empirical definitions: institutionalizing the patterns of life in lesbian and gay communities, incorporating gay and lesbian rights into American politics, including homosexuals in the negotiation of governmental policy (as has been the case with AIDS), creating a niche market for gay and lesbian consumers, increasing representations of homosexuals in commercial mass media, and developing lesbian and gay studies in universities. All of these things have already happened, to one degree or another.

The essays in this book explore ambivalences about inclusion from a number of angles—cultural, economic, academic, and political. Currently, the relation of gay men and lesbians to what is called "the mainstream" is a major theme of debate among activists and intellectuals. But the rigid opposition between sweeping celebrations or condemnations of mainstreaming poses an obstacle to critical theorizing.

To an extent, some "mainstreaming" is inevitable if a movement succeeds in challenging social norms, institutional inequalities, and prejudices. The struggle of any social group—whether it seeks to overturn stigmas, protect itself from violence, or create a new culture—is partly a quest for recognition as legitimate members of society. When such struggles are successful, members of that group will enter into mainstream life. When a character in a movie or television sitcom is homosexual only incidentally, when mainstream retailers (Barnes & Noble, American Express, or AT&T) routinely market to lesbians and gay men, and when political candidates address gay voters, such efforts partially incorporate gay men and lesbians into mainstream life as accepted figures, consumers, or citizens. This process of selection and tacit negotiation helps to blend some aspects of gay culture into the dominant culture. Over time, in the course of a group's struggle for recognition, this process is constantly repeated. The group must continue to challenge mainstream society, to assert itself, to define its identity, and to offer its interpretations of the language used to describe the group members. During this process of assimilation, the group's identity undergoes redefinition continually, but remains ambivalent—partly inside society, partly outside. Although being incorporated into the mainstream often resembles recognition, it is also ambiguous and confusing.

While the culture wars flare on the perimeters of the lesbian and gay communities, debates rage within the communities. Many homosexuals, especially activists and intellectuals, are deeply divided about fundamental values, such as the need to "belong" (assimilation), the importance of same-sex marriage, the necessity of being out to the general public, the acceptability of publicly visible sexual expression, and appropriate political tactics to guarantee gay and lesbian rights. Most intellectual and political debates revolve around whether the source of homosexuality's stigma is the political power of established institutions (religious institutions, psychiatry, the media); deep cultural structures (heteronormativity, the open secrecy of the closet); or ignorance, homophobia, and prejudice (the benighted). The last few years have generated a vigorous and wide-ranging debate, both among homosexuals and within U.S. society, about the fundamental philosophical orientation toward homosexual issues.

In *A Place at the Table*, Bruce Bawer argues for the inclusion of gay men and lesbians as valued, "normal" members of American society. He blames a minority of flamboyant, highly visible, and provocative gay activists for inciting the hatred and bigotry directed toward homosexuals.[26] The sexually explicit, carnivalesque demonstrations of homosexuality at gay pride parades, the marketing that caters to consumer expectations of gay men and lesbians, the stridency of debates marked by "political correctness," and the defense of the freedom to engage in unregulated sexual activities, whatever they are, all contribute, in Bawer's view, to the heterosexual's suspicion and fear of homosexuals. For Bawer, sexual desire is no more important to lesbians and gay men than to heterosexuals. In his opinion, coming out is neither a necessary nor an important act for the gay individual. Nor does Bawer recognize "coming out" as a useful building block for the community of lesbians and gay men. For Bawer, the political centerpiece of gay and lesbian lives is marriage, which represents a way to blend into the mainstream.

The irony is that, in this book, Bawer discusses his own coming out, which was clearly an important and necessary step for him in developing self-respect. This act would have been much more difficult, if not impossible, without the precedent or presence of the community of which he so vehemently disapproves. Even such a vigorous defender of assimilation needs the distinctive community (and niche in the book marketplace) that continues to exist partly outside the mainstream.

Urvashi Vaid, among others, represents an opposing perspective. "A mainstream civil rights strategy cannot deliver genuine freedom or full equality," she argues, "for one fundamental reason: the goal of winning mainstream tolerance, or 'toleration,' as Representative Newt Gingrich calls it, differs from the goal of winning liberation or changing social institutions in lasting, long-term ways."[27] Mainstreaming, Vaid believes, can only deliver "virtual equality"—a simulacrum of equality that lacks the real benefits. If the lesbian and gay movement has indeed entered the mainstream, Vaid believes that it has done so at the expense of true "equality."

Queer politics and queer theory, its intellectual counterpart, have challenged the way lesbian and gay politics has been conducted and thought about for the last twenty years.[28] Since Stonewall, homosexuals have drawn on the model of politics used by waves of urban blacks and immigrants to shape their communities' political strategies. Queer theorists have challenged this "ethnic model"—or identity politics, as it has come to be known—as reductive (overly simplifying the homo-

sexual identity), assimilationist (integrating homosexuals into a putatively liberal, pluralistic society), and exclusionary (failing to embrace
explicitly those who are bisexual, transgendered, S/M practitioners,
sexual minorities, and members of other "queer" sexualities). Queer
politics sought to displace the "liberal" lesbian and gay political
agenda, which stresses civil rights, the right to marry, the right to serve
in the military, tolerance, and the election of "sympathetic" or homosexual officials. The strategy in queer politics has also been to emphasize the relation between power and knowledge of homosexuality,
to critique the "homosexual identity," and, as Michael Warner has
pointed out, to resist "regimes of the normal."[29]

Each of these perspectives privileges one aspect of the status of lesbians and gay men in American society. Bawer gives priority to the
sense of *belonging*, whereas Vaid stresses objective *equality*, and queer
theory focuses on the impact of heterocentric cultural *norms*. As Warner
notes, "Queer politics has not just replaced older modes of lesbian and
gay identity; it has come to exist alongside those older modes."[30] Ironically, both Bruce Bawer and queer theorists oversimplify how lesbians
and gay men participate in society at large. They ignore the relationships gay people have to the economy, state, and civil society—that
terrain of social life that exists somewhat informally outside of either
economic or political institutions.

Debating the relation of gay and lesbian communities to the mainstream substitutes for a more elaborate social theory. Bawer fails to see
the potentially disastrous effects of normalization and discounts what
is gained when homosexuals collectively resist normalization. Vaid
judges mainstreaming by an external and idealized standard of "objective" equality, as opposed to "virtual" equality, as though political action could achieve some form of permanent equality for homosexuals
in American political life without the need for constant struggle. Queer
theory presumes that we can overthrow all heterocentric norms and
create a society without establishing new processes of normalization.
All three positions fail to articulate our relation as homosexuals to "society." We need a social theory—one that seeks to explain the existence
and development of homosexuality, both historically and socially.[31]

There are two ways in which lesbians and gay men are integrated into the mainstream. Probably the most common is that they individually work or live with the straight majority. They interact with heterosexuals who accept homosexuality to some degree. Bawer considers this individual means of integration the only legitimate means. This form of assimilation has only one degree of separation from the closet—public knowledge of the integrated person's homosexuality. It puts enormous pressure on the lesbian or gay man who lives primarily in the straight world to manage degrees of disclosure and concealment.

Lesbians and gay men can also be integrated into the dominant culture as part of a group. They may be included as representatives (or representations) in mainstream institutions—for instance, gay or lesbian characters on a television sitcom—or they can be employed as liaisons or intermediaries to the gay and lesbian community. Some degree of integration can also occur if mainstream economic or governmental institutions decide to operate within "the community" and to offer goods and services previously provided by gay and lesbian small businesses, voluntary organizations, or nonprofit agencies—for example, Barnes & Nobles rather than the gay bookstore, or Banana Republic rather than the lesbian- or gay-owned boutique. Both Vaid and queer theory are uneasy that these forms of integration may have an insidious effect if they encourage homosexuals to accept only limited rights or restrictions on their cultural expression.

The development of new norms, practices, and attitudes toward homosexuality takes place through public debate, negotiations with existing institutions, and the creation of new norms, practices, and values in civil society. Many such changes require mainstream economic and political institutions to modify their behavior.

The gay and lesbian movement cannot step outside of civil life and create a new society from scratch. Nor should gay men and lesbians slip quietly into the suburbs and pretend to be exemplars of the all-American family. The gay and lesbian community must strive to achieve a freer, more democratic, and more honest society through a permanent process of radical reform.

POLYMORPHOUS PERVERSITY

The gulf between the civil society and sexual desire never closes. "Desire emerges in multiple forms," writes gay theorist Guy Hocquenghem. "Just like heterosexual desire, homosexual desire is an arbitrarily frozen frame in an unbroken and polyvocal flux."[32] Social processes continuously regulate sexuality and desire and are a crucial element of sexual liberation, but the creative, chaotic impetus of "polymorphous perversity" is equally powerful.

Early in his career, in *Three Essays on Sexuality*, Freud identified polymorphous perversity as undifferentiated sexual desire. Over the course of individual sexual development (culminating in the oedipal complex), "civilizing processes" shape this sexual desire into procreative genital sexuality or into "perversions" such as homosexuality. In these essays, Freud proposes that the positive achievements of "civilized society" are "to a great extent obtained through the suppression of what are known as the *perverse* elements of sexual excitation."[33] Later, in *Civilization and Its Discontents*, Freud argued more forcefully that perverse sexual desire is fundamentally incompatible with "civilized" social life.[34]

It is impossible to understand lesbian and gay life without understanding the profound role that perverse sexual activity, in addition to the utopian fantasies stirred by sexual desire itself, has had on our identities and social lives. Leo Bersani and Jonathan Dollimore have both recently explored "the perverse dynamic" in sexual life—particularly in a homosexual life.[35] Through sexual perversity, gay men and lesbians have access to the "shock, disturbance, even loss, which is proper to ecstasy, to bliss," because the pleasures of sexual perversity encourage lesbians and gay men to escape from the normalized gender roles that compulsory heterosexuality dictates.[36] Perversity makes us sexual outlaws.[37] The "shattering" effects of sexual activity allow an individual to escape from stifling and socially sanctioned forms of generalized social hostility.[38] It unsettles the individual self, thus dismembering the community. With its potential for disrupting socialized identities and rendering them precarious, perverse sexuality stimulates personal and social creativity.

In *Homos*, his most recent book, Bersani criticizes queer theory for rejecting identity as a political category. To do away with "homosexual" identity and replace it with a "queer" identity, Bersani argues, contributes to the potential erasure of homosexuality's erotic significance. Moreover, it is just as much a process of normalization—or, in Foucault's terminology, a disciplinary project—to create a queer identity as it is to fashion a gay or lesbian identity.[39] More significantly, Bersani also warns that discrediting gay identity undercuts the ability to resist the Religious Right's war on homosexuality: "We have erased ourselves in the process of denaturalizing the epistemic and political regimes that constructed us."[40]

Bersani's primary concern is that "critiques of homosexual identity have generally been *desexualizing* discourses," the net effect of which is to downplay or obscure the political significance of the sexual.[41] For Bersani, "the perverse dynamic" (as Dollimore termed it) nurtures the "anticommunitarian impulses in homosexual desire," because perverse desire creates only momentary solidarities, temporary communities made up of ever shifting memberships and repeatedly shattering identities.

Bersani is deeply suspicious of the communitarian impulse in gay and lesbian life. He is suspicious, precisely, of the normalizing (or, to use his word, "redemptive") effects of community norms and moral codes. He believes that a sense of community stifles the shattering and liberatory impulses of the perverse. Rather than opening up homosexuals to the perverse as sublime, community sublimates or "civilizes" the perverse. Throughout *Homos*, Bersani defends the perverse dynamic for generating a flow of experiences that disrupt routine, communal patterns.

The social acceptance or normalizing of homosexuality is, in Bersani's analysis, inevitably a process of degaying and desexualizing. Bersani criticized Tony Kushner's play *Angels in America* for reassuring heterosexual America that homosexuals are morally sincere and culturally significant—and part of American history and society.[42] Kushner responded to Bersani's criticism by reaffirming the importance of community, but only as a point of leverage—a necessary place to stand.

Kushner nevertheless concludes with a flight of utopian fantasy that appears to synthesize queer theory and Bersani's thinking:

> A politics that seeks to dismantle normalizing categories of gender; that seeks to retrieve a history from violently enforced forgetting; a politics that seeks enfranchisement not only for new kinds of citizens, but for Sexuality itself, that seeks to introduce fucking and sucking, licking and smelling, kink, sleaze, clits and assholes and games people play with them, into the previously chaste Temple of Democracy; and even more daring still, a politics that seeks a synthesis between desire and transformation, that seeks some union between the deepest recesses and cavities of the human heart and body and soul, and the sacrifices and responsibilities building communities and movement, building progress and power entails: This politics . . . had better be capable of extravagance, had better not be tame.[43]

Kushner's blend of communitarianism and perversity derives its energy from the historical tension between the fervid and perverse homoeroticism that courses through American culture and the equally deep American tradition of homophobia.

THE AMBIVALENCE OF IDENTITY

The debate about participating in the mainstream is in part about the meaning of adopting an identity or the possibility of repudiating it. Homosexual, lesbian, gay, queer, dyke, black gay, gay black, Latino/a, African American, Ms.—each word, each name implies a relationship to the social majority or to "mainstream" society. For anyone to invest emotionally and politically in a social identity, he or she must believe that adopting this "identity" is, in fact, a viable strategy for both satisfying emotional needs and negotiating social pressures.

Loyalties to more than one identity intensify ambivalence. In terms of race, James Baldwin, Hanif Kureishi, Audre Lorde, and the authors of *This Bridge Called My Back* have explored this problem of multiple allegiances. Overlapping identities, formed by the intersection of someone's various personal and community discourses, generate a "culture clash" of vocabularies, slang, behavioral norms, codes of dress, cultural forms, styles of humor, and political interpretations. This uneasy blend thwarts unequivocal loyalty to any single community.

Even when an adopted "identity" offers a solution to an individual's long-standing social and emotional struggles, identity politics cannot resolve that individual's conflicting loyalties to other groups. One way to resolve competing loyalties is the questionable and rather simplistic belief in the presumed existence of enduring and distinct homosexual identities. Identity politics, in fact, is characterized by a fundamental *ambivalence*—the community that is politicized through identity politics can neither embrace the dominant society and its identity standards (that's assimilation!) nor maintain its political mobilization by rejecting dominant society completely (that's separatism!).[44]

It is only when lesbians, gay men, and other homosexual minorities act to establish their own relatively autonomous communities—their own social institutions—that they achieve some sort of liberation from the oppressive norms and beliefs of the majority society. Insofar as the stigma attached to homosexuality encourages a reaction from those who practice it, lesbian and gay identities created in the course of political activities exist as "inverted" images of hegemonic representations of "the heterosexual." As long as gay men and lesbians remain "pariahs," however, they operate within a social realm that protects the homosexual experience from the distortions that accompany assimilation.[45] The politics of "Queer Nation" represented such a perspective and, as such, it kept alive a certain utopian hope. But queer nationalism, like other forms of pariah politics or nationalisms, inevitably establishes new norms and ethical codes that create new deviants—the pariahs of pariahs. Thus, the struggle continues on the terrain that exists between the gay and lesbian communities and mainstream society. Many of us are divided between these two worlds. We work in the straight world and play in the queer world. Both sides alienate those who do not fit in—some people feel inauthentic in either world.

Identity politics is permeated by ambivalence. We *are* members of the dominant society and yet we *are not really* members. This contradiction is our fate. We face a constant challenge to develop a political strategy that nourishes and protects the many ways of being homosexual. It may be easy to recognize what is inauthentic in this twilight zone of ambivalence and contradiction, but slowly it dawns on us that there may be no "authentic" solution at all.

Part One **Sexual Revolution**

Contemporary lesbian and gay studies, particularly in the form of queer theory, has focused on how culture can and cannot represent homosexuality. But queer theory and cultural studies cannot grasp the basic causes of social change in history. It cannot explain, for example, the emergence of the modern homosexual identity in western Europe or North America. Nor can it account, with any degree of historical pertinence, for the dating of its emergence or the spatial patterns of its diffusion. Lyotard has argued that we are living in a period in which the grand narratives of modernity can no longer make sense of people's experience.[1] Although the credibility and, perhaps even more significantly, the legitimacy of historical explanations have fallen into question, we cannot understand many of the contemporary political or social issues concerning homosexuality without attempting a theoretical and historical account.

Virtually all the essays in this book can be understood as explorations of "sexual revolution"—that long process of change in the U.S. sex/gender system.[2] This revolution—like the first industrial revolution—has been an immense and contradictory process stretching out over the life span of two generations. In studying the sexual revolution, one must take into account the point made by Perry Anderson: "There is no plumb line between necessity and contingency in historical explanation, dividing separate types of enquiry—'long-run' versus 'short-run' or 'abstract' versus 'concrete'—from each other."[3]

Since World War II, the political mobilization of youth, women, and homosexuals has transformed the social relations of gender and sexuality in America. The sex/gender system encodes biological capacities into the social and cultural patterns that shape our lives as gendered and sexual human beings.[4] The term *sexual revolution* encompasses these changes in the sex/gender system and evokes a long war, including progressive changes as well as undesirable ones, enlightened reforms as well as conservative reactions. The term encompasses a whole series or cluster of interrelated gender and sexual phenomena such as abortion, sexual harassment, lesbian and gay rights, homophobic violence, modified gender roles, the feminization of love, machismo, and so on. It also refers to the struggle of movements and individuals to change sex and gender roles.[5] As Jeffrey Weeks has noted:

> Over the past generation, many of the old organizing patterns and controls have been challenged, and often undermined, and sexuality has come closer than ever before to the center of public debate. This has produced a crisis over sexuality: a crisis in the relations of sex, especially between men and women, but also perhaps more fundamentally, a crisis around the meaning of sexuality in our society. In the resulting confusion there has been an unprecedented mobilization of political forces around sexual issues.[6]

The essays in part 1 explore the social and economic conditions under which homosexuals have fashioned an identity and built a community. The sexual revolution is the broad historical context for these developments—whether they are economic patterns of behavior or the imagining of a homosexual social world. In chapter 1, "Sexual Revolution and the Politics of Gay Identity," I sketch the historical sociology of the postwar American sex/gender system and the emergence of homosexual identity.

The social disruptions of World War II and postwar adjustments caused important shifts in sex/gender relations within American society. This essay identifies three historical moments: Kinsey's discovery of the gap between sexual norms and behavior; the period in which Keynesian economic policies shaped sharply contrasting policies toward women, sexuality, and reproduction; and the sexual revolution and emergence of the women's and gay movements.

The next essay focuses on the economic conditions that existed before the Stonewall riots and the emergence of the gay liberation movement. Chapter 2, "The Political Economy of the Closet," explores how the stigma toward homosexuality reinforced the closet and made it essential to control information about one's identity. Together, these conditions had a particular impact on the economics of homosexuality before Stonewall. Needing to conceal their homosexuality imposed extraordinary economic burdens on gay men and lesbians. It also made homosexuals vulnerable to various forms of extortion and protection rackets. The post-Stonewall process of coming out was the only political strategy that could modify the "economic" oppression of lesbians and gay men.

Imagining a social life allowed homosexuals to envision a more "normal" life—one free from the distorted psychological stereotypes that characterized the homophobic discourses of the 1950s and early 1960s. Chapter 3, "Homosexuality and the Sociological Imagination," studies the dozen or so popular sociological books on homosexuality published between 1951 and 1968. The sociological emphasis of those books about homosexuality was relatively new and signified the postwar discovery of the existence of the gay and lesbian *communities*. Since there are no readership statistics or surveys that allow us to gauge this literature's significance to homosexuals in the 1950s or 1960s, I have drawn on my own experience. I try to understand the relationship a reader might have had to that body of literature and reconstruct my own reaction to the idea of a gay identity and community. Finally, I evaluate the psychological and political significance of "the discovery of the social" by tracing its significance for myself as a young homosexual.

One element of the "sociological imagination" so necessary even to theorize about homosexuality is the recognition that large-scale, impersonal, historical processes—such as economic forces and social structure—shape the context in which we act and represent ourselves. To some degree, Marx's famous comment that human beings "make their own history, but not in circumstances of their own choosing" exemplifies this perspective. Both the political project of "making history" of homosexuals and the intellectual project of "making knowledge" of homosexuality inevitably occur in circumstances over which we have little control. We can only negotiate the *longue durée* by conjointly exercising our capacities to act and to think historically.

1 SEXUAL REVOLUTION AND THE POLITICS OF GAY IDENTITY

This dispersion and reconstitution of the *self.*
That's the whole story.

BAUDELAIRE

The lesbian and gay movements have achieved a recognized presence in American life.[1] There are open communities of lesbians and gay men in many cities. Community organizations and businesses cater specifically to the needs of the homosexual population. Until recently, there was a lesbian and gay caucus in the Democratic Party, and there are lesbian and gay political clubs in most cities. Openly gay men and lesbians have been elected to city councils, state legislatures, and the United States Congress. These remarkable developments have occurred because the lesbian and gay movements have stressed a politics of identity closely modeled on the politics of ethnic and racial minorities.

This chapter is a slightly revised version of an essay originally published in *Socialist Review*, no. 82/83, vol. 15, nos. 4/5 (July–October 1985).

The homosexual politics of identity successfully married interest-group politics to a radical reinterpretation of the social definitions of gender and sexuality. The original sense of identity was based on people's shared sexual preferences and on similar encounters with homophobia. The fundamental ambivalence of homosexuals, which originates in being raised as heterosexuals, makes the discursive process of identity formation central to gay and lesbian politics. The "ethnic model" of homosexual identity emerged when lesbians and gay men had accumulated enough political and economic resources to contend with other interest groups.

In the 1980s, lesbian and gay male communities entered a new period in relation to the homosexual identity developed in the 1970s. Both lesbians and gay men have created a network of institutions that reaches outside their shared sexual preferences; in addition, they have adopted norms of conduct that guide their members, and they have a small degree of power in American society. Within this context, other forms of sexual expression (e.g., bisexuality, S/M, butch/femme role-playing, and transgendered identities) have provoked intense and highly politicized debates. Since the early 1980s, the AIDS crisis in the gay male community has provoked a full-scale reassessment of sexual behavior and its relationship to gay identity.

These developments have brought into question the belief in a fixed homosexual identity with permanent sexual and political significance.[2] Questioning this belief poses problems of great theoretical and political urgency. Should the lesbian and gay movements abandon the politics of identity? Why are sexual identities political? What historical conditions underlie the emergence of the gay and lesbian movements? Before we can address the political and strategic question of whether or not homosexuals should abandon a politics of identity, we must address the theoretical and historical issues of why and how sexual identities are politicized.

TRANSFORMATIONS OF THE SEX/GENDER SYSTEM

Since World War II, various groups dissatisfied with the social relations of sex and gender have become political subjects and have mobilized to redefine the social relations and norms that regulate gender and sexuality. It is not possible to understand this history without referring to the ensemble of discourses, practices, and institutions that structure and regulate the social relations of gender and the varieties of sexual behavior. This ensemble of discourses, practices, and institutions—which Gayle Rubin calls the sex/gender system—maps biological capacities onto the symbolic and social patterns that constitute our lives as gendered and sexual human beings.[3]

The sex/gender system operates through different types of social structures. Among the most important are *forms of domination*, which privilege certain groups of people and restrict the rights of others. For example, men exercise power over women and children in the patriarchal nuclear family, stigmatized sexual activities are allowed to take place in urban back regions, and women and minorities earn less than white men in a segmented labor market. Another set of structures is *normative regulations:* these include the sexual double standard, which establishes different standards of sexual behavior for men (casual or extrarelationship sex is okay) and women (who are denigrated if they engage in casual or frequent sexual activities); the heterosexual presumption, which enforces the assumption that everyone is heterosexual, thus putting the socially awkward burden on homosexuals to identify themselves; and the male breadwinner ethic, which promotes the male as the sole provider of a family's economic support. A third group of structures is *symbolic codes*, which are ideological formulations such as the idea of romantic love, the Christian conception of marriage, biological reproduction as an evolutionary responsibility, and the belief in children's sexual innocence.[4]

Sexual identities result from historical struggles between groups (for example, prostitutes' conflict with the state) and from social relations in the sex/gender system. As forms of subjectivity and agency, sexual identities are continually in the process of forming. They are not uniquely determined by the economic, political, normative, or symbolic aspects of the sex/gender system—the outcomes and meanings of this process are reconstituted at each moment of history. Historically, the politicized struggles of sexual identities have modified the conditions under which the identities initially formed. The sex/gender system is not an isolated system of institutions and practices. Rather, it interacts with the economy, the state, and other social ensembles, such as those devoted to racial formation, class structure, or generational differences.[5]

Beginning in 1940, the massive mobilization of civilians and armed services during World War II transformed the American sex/gender system. This transformation is immense and contradictory (very much as the Industrial Revolution was). The process of changing the sex/gender system should not be understood as necessarily coherent or "progressive," but as involving antagonistic movements and ideologies that contend for their own visions of possible sexual and gender arrangements. This dynamic process of historical change—with its moments of rupture and periods of stability—is what I mean by "sexual revolution."

The postwar sexual revolution underwent, I believe, three politically and analytically distinct "moments" (which are *not* strictly chronological). The first occurred when Alfred Kinsey and his colleagues discovered a gap between sexual norms and sexual behavior. On the basis of this discovery, Kinsey critiqued sexual norms.

The second moment emerged during the highly contradictory period of postwar prosperity, which Keynesian economic policies created. This period involved marked reactionary tendencies toward gender roles (the attempt to keep women in the home) and extreme pronatalism (the baby boom). The consumption ethos of the times, however, tended to undermine the repressive measures toward women and sexual minorities. In this period, a number of intellectuals critiqued sexual repression and its power to enforce norms of gender and sexuality. The works of these intellectuals helped to develop the sexual revolution's political identities.

In the third moment, the gay liberation movement emerged in the wake of the women's movement. As the male-dominated family declined and as women reacted to the sexism they discovered in the student movement and the New Left, they mobilized politically. Inspired by the women's movement, and building on a gay urban subculture that existed since World War II, gay people forged a collective sexual culture and thus, to some extent, reinterpreted the symbolism of sexuality and gender.

Before we can examine these developments in the post–World War II period, we must abandon the assumption that the social regulation of sexuality operates only through repression.[6] Transforming the sex/gender system means not only eliminating repressive strictures on sexual behavior but also continually and affirmatively establishing new forms of gender and sexuality. These transformations affect economic and political relations, attitudes, and laws, and in turn influence the symbolic and cultural meanings of gender and sexuality.

Historical and anthropological research has shown that homosexual *persons* (i.e., people who occupy a social position or role as homosexuals) do not exist in many societies, whereas homosexual *behavior* occurs in virtually every society.[7] Therefore, we must distinguish between homosexual *behavior* and homosexual *identity*. One term refers to one's sexual activity per se (whether casual or regular); the other word defines homosexuality as a social role, with its emotional and sexual components. Such a distinction is consciously rooted in historical and cross-cultural comparisons between homosexuality in advanced industrial societies and homosexuality in other cultures or eras. For instance, in ancient Greece, homosexual relationships between older men and younger men were commonly accepted as pedagogic. Within the context of an erotic relation, the older man taught the younger one military, intellectual, and political skills. The older men, however, were also often husbands and fathers. Neither sexual relationship excluded the other. Thus, although ancient Greek society recognized male homosexual activity as a valid form of sexuality, the men involved in these relationships rarely defined themselves as primarily "homosexual."[8]

Another institutionalized form of homosexuality existed in many American Indian societies. Girls and boys in these societies could refuse initiation into their adult gender roles and instead adopt the social role of the other gender. For example, men who dressed and acted in accordance with the adult female role were known as "two-spirit" or *berdache* (originally the French term for these Indians). The *berdache* often married Indian men. The partners in these marriages did not define themselves as "homosexuals," nor did their societies recognize them as such, but their marital sex life consisted of homosexual sexual relations.[9]

This theoretical distinction between behavior and identity is crucial to the histories of homosexuality, and, frequently, to the histories of the gay and lesbian emancipation movements.[10]

KINSEY AND THE LIBERAL IMAGINATION

The mobilization for World War II profoundly rocked the social relations of gender and sexuality in the United States. Young men and women left the haven of their families and lived for four years among other people, far from parental guidance.

Recognition of a sexual revolution dawned slowly after the war. Alfred Kinsey's two pathbreaking volumes on human sexuality, *Sexual Behavior in the Human Male*, which was published in 1948, and *Sexual Behavior in the Human Female*, which was published in 1953, probably influenced modern conceptions of sexuality more than any work since Freud's. Kinsey's work mapped in detail a submerged continent known only from the exposed mountaintops of archipelagoes. The report sparked moral outrage and a great deal of hypocrisy, but made most Americans acutely aware of the gap between daily sexual activities and public attitudes toward that sexual behavior.

In his review of the first volume, the cultural critic Lionel Trilling saw the Kinsey report as a symptomatic failure of the liberal imagination: "The *Report* has the intention of habituating its readers to sexuality in all its manifestations: it wants to establish as it were, a democratic pluralism of sexuality. . . . That this generosity of mind is much to be admired goes without saying. . . . [But] it goes with a nearly conscious aversion from making intellectual distinctions, almost as if out of the belief that an intellectual distinction must inevitably lead to a social discrimination or exclusion."[11]

Although many of Kinsey's analyses and assumptions can be criticized, both volumes offer sophisticated and often subtle discussions of many aspects of sexual life. Nevertheless, many intellectuals and readers objected to Kinsey's project for its empirical, materialistic, and ostensibly value-free investigation into human sexuality. Although Kinsey never espoused tolerance explicitly as a moral position, that ethic was fundamental to his work; in both volumes, he stressed acceptance of people as they are and repeatedly noted people's limited ability to modify their sexual behavior.[12]

Struck by the extraordinary extent of individual variation in sexual behavior, Kinsey argued that any attempt to establish uniform standards of sexual behavior was both impracticable and unjust. He supplemented this theme of individual variation by stressing what Paul Robinson has called our "common deviance."[13] Kinsey believed that this widespread deviation from accepted sexual standards showed that attempts to regulate sexual behavior were doomed to failure and that "the only proper sexual policy was no policy at all."[14]

As texts, Kinsey's studies united a positivistic-empirical investigation of sexual behavior and an amoral attitude of tolerance. Kinsey achieved this synthesis through his radical materialism, which led him to measure sexual experience by tabulating the number of orgasms experienced during a sexual encounter. Kinsey demoted heterosexual intercourse to only one of six possible "sexual outlets" or orgasms, which included masturbation, nocturnal emission, heterosexual petting, homosexual relations, and intercourse with animals. Kinsey's tolerance was less a moral idea than a statistical concept reflecting inclusiveness. From this perspective, the sole distinction between heterosexuals and homosexuals is that the former are attracted to people of the other gender, whereas the latter are attracted to those of the same gender. Wherever Kinsey discusses the religious and moral attitudes that regulate sexual behavior, he valorizes the behavior and characterizes the norms as naive, mystifying, and ideological.

One of the major shortcomings of Kinsey's volumes is the absence of any historical perspective. Although Kinsey actually collected statistical material for a decade (from 1938 to 1947), his analysis collapses any possible diachronic dimension. The historical aspect survives only in his analysis of sexual behavior by age, but even then, Kinsey views age as a stage of the life cycle, rather than acknowledging generational differences. Kinsey's blindness toward history obscures the political climate within which his studies were published. Although the Kinsey reports emerged at the beginning of a second "sexual revolution" (an earlier one occurred in the late nineteenth century and early twentieth century, between 1890 and 1919), Kinsey's data reflected the sexual behavior of the generations that came to adulthood between 1920 and 1940, a period that evidenced little sexual change.

Kinsey's data did show traces of an earlier sexual revolution, but he did not publish these data in either of the two reports.[15] An earlier survey of sexual behavior had already revealed that twice as many women born between 1890 and 1899 (and therefore reaching maturity between 1910 and 1920) had premarital intercourse as did women born before 1890.[16] Although the Kinsey reports did not capture the post–World War II sexual revolution (partly because they studied the interwar generations and partly because they assumed that sexuality as a physiological activity did not have a history), they did come to symbolize that revolution in the popular consciousness and in the history of ideas. For American liberals, the Kinsey reports unified heterogeneous intellectual and political elements. They offered an interpretation of sexual acts that was empirically grounded, embedded in a critique of accepted sexual norms, and politically united by an ethic of tolerance. The Kinsey reports served as the basis of the liberal theory of sexual liberation, in which all types of sexual activity were equally valid.

Kinsey's findings on homosexuality were among the most controversial and widely publicized. His volume on male sexuality concluded that 37 percent of the U.S. male population had had at least one homosexual experience to orgasm between adolescence and old age. The data also seemed to suggest that many adults were neither permanently nor exclusively homosexual or heterosexual but evidenced a fluid continuum of sexual behavior. Kinsey measured this fluidity along the Kinsey scale of heterosexual to homosexual behavior and fantasy, ranging from 0 (exclusively heterosexual) through 6 (exclusively homosexual). Although Kinsey's findings clearly encouraged him to reject homosexuality as a pathological syndrome, the range and fluidity of many Americans' sexual behavior also led him to reject the idea of a sexual identity; he believed that there were no homosexual persons, only homosexual acts.[17]

Kinsey's emphasis on acts and the number of orgasms ignored the political and historical meaning of his analysis. If his synchronic analysis of sexual outlets obscured the emergence of sexual revolution, his ontology of acts failed to recognize potential political actors—such as youth, women, and homosexuals—who would make the postwar sexual revolution. Although Kinsey's paradigm had an enormous emancipatory impact on American society (its other major contribution was to recognize female sexuality), its positivistic methodology and its conception of tolerance overlooked the significance of gay cultural developments in the early 1950s.

Homosexuals themselves were divided over what their emerging sense of "group consciousness" meant. The Mattachine Society, founded in Los Angeles in 1951, marked the beginning of a continuous history of homosexual emancipation movements in the United States.[18] Many of the Mattachine Society's founders had extensive political experience in the Communist Party or on the Left before they began organizing homosexuals. The parallel experiences of Communist Party members and homosexuals in the late 1940s and early 1950s led the early Mattachine leaders to model their new organization on the Communist Party, emphasizing secrecy, centralized leadership, and a hierarchy of "cells."[19]

Marxist analysis also helped the early Mattachine leaders develop a political analysis of homosexual oppression that emphasized its "socially determined pattern." From their early group discussions, these Mattachine members concluded that homosexuals were an oppressed cultural minority. They believed that rigid definitions of gender behavior led men and women to accept unquestioningly social roles that equated "male, masculine, man *only* with husband and Father" and that equated "female, feminine, women *only* with wife and Mother." These early homosexual emancipationists saw homosexual women and men as victims of a "language and culture that did not admit the existence of a Homosexual Minority." For those activists, homosexuals constituted a social minority imprisoned within a dominant culture. Largely, they were a minority unaware of themselves as a distinct group.[20]

Although this analysis seemed consistent with the experience of many gay women and men at the time, as well as with subsequent history, other homosexuals in the Mattachine Society argued that the cultural and social characteristics of gay life resulted from ostracism and oppression itself. Against the "cultural minority" thesis, these critics often adopted Kinsey's argument that homosexuals and heterosexuals differed only in their sexual preferences.

Each line of argument conceptualized the homosexual self differently, and each implied alternative political strategies. The cultural minority thesis argued that homosexuals had developed differently because they had been excluded from dominant heterosexual culture. The "secondary socialization" of homosexuals into a distinct subculture helped them to develop appropriate new values, relationships, and cultural forms because homosexual life "did not fit the patterns of heterosexual love, marriage, children, etc. upon which the dominant culture rests."[21] The proponents of the cultural minority thesis recognized that homosexuals also internalized the dominant culture's view of themselves as aberrant and were often forced by social stigma to lead lives of secrecy, hypocrisy, and emotional stress. These proponents therefore emphasized the need for a critique of this internalized self-oppression and the development of "an ethical homosexual culture."

The alternative "assimilationist" position sought to achieve societal acceptance of homosexuals by emphasizing the similarities between homosexuals and heterosexuals. Proponents felt that the "secondary socialization" of homosexuals resulted from a life given over to hiding, isolation, and internalized self-hatred. For this reason, homosexuals should adopt a "pattern of behavior that is acceptable to society in general and compatible with [the] recognized institutions . . . of home, church and state," rather than creating an "ethical homosexual culture," which would only accentuate the perceived differences between homosexuals and heterosexuals and provoke continued hostility. The "cultural minority" analysis was hotly debated in the early years of the Mattachine Society, but after many battles, marked also by anticommunism, the assimilationist thesis prevailed and served as the ideological basis for the homosexual rights movement during the 1950s and 1960s.

Thus, throughout the 1950s and 1960s, Kinsey's paradigm permeated the political discourses of sexual emancipation. We find its marks on homosexual politics,[22] on popular conceptions of female sexuality, on the sociological analysis of the premarital sexual activities of young men and women,[23] and on the "philosophy" of *Playboy* magazine.[24] The Kinsey paradigm validated sexual activity (lots of orgasms) and criticized the normative regulation of sexual behavior. But this approach offered no theory of sexual coding (i.e., the symbolic and cultural significance of sexual acts). Not only did it therefore ignore the mundane importance of "romantic love," but it also played down the social construction of sexuality and the role of subcultures and secondary socialization in an individual's sexual development. In a corresponding fashion, the assimilationist position of the Mattachine Society overlooked the possible significance of sexual culture. This made it not only difficult to conceive of homosexuals as political subjects but also impossible to imagine the gay subculture as a community that had resources to mobilize and that could organize politically.

The Kinsey reports' lack of historical perspective on sexuality also made it difficult to interpret the radical transformation of the sex/gender system that, in the wake of World War II, began to modify the everyday significance of family life, gender roles, and sexual behavior. Both the cultural minority thesis and the assimilation argument also suffered from their lack of historical perspective. Although the cultural minority thesis could easily have accommodated an account of the historical development of a homosexual minority, it did not find the ideological space to do so. The assimilationist perspective implied a history of sexual oppression (because no difference "really" existed between homosexuals and heterosexuals, history alone could explain the peculiar reasons and means heterosexuals had for repressing homosexuality), but such a history was not articulated. Both kinds of history would have been useful, but neither developed during the late 1950s and early 1960s.

Both the liberal imagination and the homophile movement (as the homosexual emancipation movement of that time called itself in order to downplay the "sexual") conceptualized sexual emancipation as a critique of ideological and unrealistic sexual norms in favor of people's actual sexual behavior. Neither perspective emphasized the family as a form of dominance or criticized sexual repression for its impact on the culture and institutions of American society. A critique of sexual repression in American society eventually emerged from a leftist analysis of the economic role of sexual repression.

THE SEXUAL CONTRADICTIONS OF KEYNESIANISM

Throughout World War II, most economists, politicians, and the general public had no doubt that the most important postwar economic and political problem would be that of providing full employment. Many people feared a return to the grim economic realities of the 1930s. Policymakers subordinated other postwar economic and social policies to the goal of full employment.[25] The labor movement also pushed hard for full-employment legislation.

A series of important pieces of labor legislation (the Wagner Act of 1935, the Social Security Act of 1935, and the postwar Taft-Hartley and McCarran Acts) helped to alter the relations between labor demand and labor supply. These acts culminated in the Employment Act, the centerpiece of postwar capital-labor relations, which established full employment as a priority of the federal government's economic policy.[26] In the two decades leading up to the Employment Act, restrictive immigration legislation in the 1920s and the declining U.S. birthrate during the 1920s and 1930s contributed to the tight labor markets of the 1940s and 1950s that helped spur on the postwar baby boom.[27]

The watered-down version of the Employment Act that eventually passed in 1946 only established the principle of the federal government's maintaining "maximum employment, production and purchasing power." Even so, additional legislation bolstered the act's rather vague guidelines, creating unemployment compensation, minimum-wage legislation, and old-age and survivor insurance. If the 1946 Employment Act provided the Keynesian rationale for full employment as a governmental policy in the postwar period, the military budget supplied the bulk of federal spending that sustained high levels of aggregate demand throughout the 1950s and 1960s.[28]

Through these long-term modifications in the labor relations and macroeconomic policy, the Keynesian welfare state had a considerable impact on the dynamics of autonomy and dependence between family members. Other aspects of the immediate postwar economic situation also destabilized relations within the family. Reestablishing a peacetime economy led to a temporary drop in women's participation in the labor force. By January 1946, four million fewer women worked than at the 1944 wartime employment peak; most lost their jobs. At the same time, total civilian employment increased from 52.8 million to 57.8 million as soldiers left the armed services.[29]

From 1945 to 1955, there was a concerted effort to reestablish "traditional values." Not only had the war disrupted men's dominance in the family but the depression had also severely undermined the "male breadwinner role."[30] Social upheavals, the unprecedented migration and breakup of families, and women's entry into the labor force during the war years were counteracted in the postwar period by a barrage of publicity. For instance, many sociologists during the late 1940s and early 1950s argued that if women continued to work, children would be neglected and the home would be endangered. They argued for restoring the paternalistic family.[31] Postwar ideological campaigns that portrayed women's place as being in the home, postwar federal economic policies, and private industry's personnel policies were all intended to revitalize the male-led nuclear family and reestablish the pre-depression relations of autonomy and dependence in the family.

During the depression, the high level of male unemployment and the economic difficulties that most households experienced had begun to alter the relations of autonomy and dependence within the family. Many married women and children entered the labor market in order to compensate for the decline of the male breadwinner's earnings.[32] Children frequently took on adult responsibilities at an early age. Girls were drawn into the domestic management of the household, whereas boys were forced to take on breadwinning responsibilities. Following on this, the war experience offered unprecedented personal autonomy and economic independence to the generation reared in the 1930s. Because of this, many men and women found it difficult to return to more traditional gender roles when the war ended. Many married women reentered the labor force soon after the demobilization was complete. By 1952, some 10.4 million wives held jobs—2 million more than at the height of World War II. Substantial numbers of these women were the middle-aged wives who had first found it respectable to be employed outside the home during the war.

The baby boom represented a significant development in heterosexual behavior during the postwar period. Marital fertility rates had been declining since 1800, and the baby boom reversed that trend. The change occurred because, compared with their predecessors, a high proportion of women born in the 1920s and 1930s married at a young age and began families soon afterward.[33] The extended postwar prosperity may have encouraged marriage and childbearing; it implicitly promised a better economic future than the one most people experienced during the 1930s.[34] The postwar period also saw unprecedented attention paid to sexual pleasure in marriage; the National Fertility Studies of 1965 and 1970 revealed a great number of unwanted pregnancies in the 1950s.[35] Postwar ideological and attitudinal shifts toward home, family, and children also resulted from suburbanization. This process established new communities on the fringes of large cities. Husbands began making long commutes. Community life became centered around the activities of children and mothers.

These demographic trends merged with certain political developments that surfaced immediately after the war. For example, the pronatalism and the attempted restoration of the patriarchal family also coincided with the postwar moral panic about "the homosexual menace" and "the sexual offender." Throughout the postwar period, many states and cities launched campaigns to control sexual psychopaths and "deviants." The McCarthy witch-hunts focused on homosexuals in the government as "security risks" and as morally and politically suspect.[36]

The Keynesian prosperity of the 1950s and 1960s created a double bind for the postwar family. The exploding cost of rearing children and family members' rising consumer expectations eventually rendered the family wage (based on the man's earnings) insufficient. The family needed a supplemental income to attain the new postwar standard of living. Although a woman's earnings were usually below even her own subsistence level, they were nevertheless high enough to affect the family's standard of living.[37] This Keynesian double bind is the foundation of what Daniel Bell has called "the cultural contradictions of capitalism"—the tension between work, accumulation, and production as ends in themselves and work as a means to consumption and hedonistic gratification.[38]

As married women increasingly entered the labor force, gender roles within the family began to change.[39] Thus, women's labor-force participation continued to undermine the male-dominated family in the postwar sex/gender system. In the late 1950s, normative family regulations—"the breadwinner ethic" and "a woman's place is in the home" —had less and less relevance to most people's behavior. Young men and women began living outside family households, fueling a host of cultural revolts and urban subcultures. Wage and job discrimination against women and single men, reinforced by the gender-segregated labor market, perpetuated some of the economic imbalances in power and resources between men and women in families.

From 1950 through 1964, men frequently opposed the norms of gender and sex. Even with the economic support provided by government spending and other Keynesian full-employment policies, many men resisted the burden of being the primary breadwinner, as Barbara Ehrenreich has shown in *The Hearts of Men*. Failure to sustain the breadwinner role implied immaturity and was considered symptomatic of latent homosexuality or a mother fixation.[40] Minor revolts ranged from the "Gray Flannel dissidents" (rebels in business suits) and the Beat generation to the readers of *Playboy* magazine. The male rebellions of the 1950s took place within the context of the attempted revival of male-dominated sex/gender arrangements.

Men often directed resentment at the women and children for whom men had to commit themselves to boring and unsatisfactory jobs, whereas women who were still full-time housewives often displaced resentment onto their fellow prisoners in the home—their children.[41]

Family responsibilities began to bear more heavily on many male workers when wives went to work in order to maintain the family standard of living.

Many blue-collar workers were dissatisfied with the meaninglessness of their work and with feeling powerlessness to affect the course of production. Increasingly, the problems of labor and workers' discontentment received public attention.[42] As the 1950s wore on, postwar affluence did not allay these frustrations and anxieties.

By 1960, three books had appeared that would become extremely influential in the coming decade: Herbert Marcuse's *Eros and Civilization* (1955), Norman O. Brown's *Life against Death* (1959), and Paul Goodman's *Growing up Absurd* (1960). Although substantial differences exist among these authors, all three critiqued what Marcuse called "the performance principle" in the name of erotic and sensual gratification. All three examined the consequences of the social repression of "instinctual" erotic needs. Although each work explored different aspects, they all questioned the organization of work (particularly Goodman and Marcuse) and the role of family in the repression of sexual desire. In recognition of American society's display of economic abundance, Marcuse claimed that there was "surplus repression," that is, more repression than necessary for society to function. Marcuse and Goodman also identified possible sources of political and historical change; in other words, they identified political subjects as agents of social change.

In terms of sexuality, Marcuse saw "perversions" as the champions of the pleasure principle; they upheld sexuality as an end in itself. He claimed that "they thus place themselves outside the domination of the performance principle and challenge its very foundation."[43] He cited "narcissism" and "homosexuality" as revolutionary sexualities because they were not procreative. Both Marcuse and Brown championed "polymorphous perversity," a sexuality not narrowly focused on any specific object or activity.

Paul Goodman's argument rested on a more orthodox Reichian foundation—it focused on "repression" rather than Brown's and Marcuse's polymorphous perversity. In an essay published right after the war, Goodman had argued that "the repression of infantile and adolescent sexuality is the direct cause of submissiveness of the people to present political rule of whatever kind."[44] Thus, in *Growing up Absurd* he identified youth as the political subject who must rebel against meaningless work and sensual repression.

In some form or another, all three writers managed to depict the tangled web of sexuality and economics that characterized the 1950s. All assumed that economic abundance was a necessary condition for eliminating any "surplus repression." All criticized the repressive expectations of work life and family life, the linking of procreation and work, and the denial of pleasure in work and sexuality.

In identifying the homosexual as a champion of pleasure and eros, Marcuse named one of the moral bogeymen of the 1950s as a figure of liberation. In contrast, both Brown and Marcuse resisted equating sex with Kinsey's notion of outlets—that is, orgasm. They both criticized "the tyranny of the orgasm" as a form of repressed sexuality. Instead, they argued for the primeval innocence of polymorphous perversity. In addition, Goodman argued that youth was the group most likely to break the stranglehold of repression. Indeed, it was this postwar generation that really began the sexual revolution in all its aspects.

The radical critique of sexual repression may have encouraged politically conscious youth to challenge the norms of sexual and gender behavior effectively. The affluence and consumption ethic of "permissive" Keynesianism probably had a larger impact on the sexual revolution, though, by undermining the disciplinary effect of the breadwinner ethic and hence the paternalistic family's cohesiveness. The radical critique did offer an effective basis for sexual politics—more so than the Kinsey critique, which restricted itself merely to a critique of sexual norms. Neither a critique of norms nor a critique of repression could help change the symbolic significance of sex, however. Changing that required a third "moment"—the creation of a collective sexual culture.

THE SEX/GENDER CODE

Although the Kinsey reports helped homosexuals recognize that a large number of Americans had had homosexual experience, simply recognizing the gap between sexual norms and behavior did not provide an adequate ideological basis for mobilizing the homosexual population. The quantitative empiricism of the Kinsey perspective precluded a clear conception of the homosexual identity. The behavioral continuum of the Kinsey scale created uncertainty about the existence of a sense of group identity in response to social stigma. The contemporary sense of "homosexual identity" did not first appear in the post–World War II period; it had become increasingly defined at least since the end of the nineteenth century.

In the United States, physicians first posed homosexuality as a theoretical problem in medical discourse.[45] Nineteenth-century physicians were puzzled by a broad range of deviant gender behavior. For instance, they observed women dressing in male clothes, living and passing as men, and having sexual relations with women; women who could whistle admirably; men who never smoked, never married, and were entirely averse to outdoor pursuits; and women who drank, smoked, and were very independent in their ways.[46] Physicians applied the term "sexual inversion" to a whole spectrum of gender-role variations, only one of which involved sexual desire for someone of the same gender. Inverts were men and women who did not conform to accepted norms of gender behavior. But the theory of sexual inversion could not explain the traditional "feminine" partners of female inverts or the "masculine" partners of male inverts. Thus, physicians increasingly began to distinguish homosexual desire (or sexual perversion in nineteenth-century terms) from gender-role nonconformity (or inversion).

Once homosexual desire became analytically distinct from gender behavior, physicians attempted to explain homosexuality by arguing that homosexuals were in fact hermaphrodites—incorporating the biological traits of both genders. Although medical research in this period often claimed to find evidence of hermaphroditism (such as a lesbian with a large clitoris or a male homosexual with feminine bodily characteristics), concepts of somatic hermaphroditism gave way to psychic hermaphroditism. According to this theory, a person might have the anatomical characteristics of his or her own gender but the soul of the other gender.

It was important to nineteenth-century homosexual intellectuals to clarify these issues. Karl Ulrichs, a German writer who first envisioned a homosexual emancipation movement in the 1860s, suggested that the male homosexual had a "woman's spirit in a man's body."[47] In the early twentieth century, homosexual activists Magnus Hirschfield and Edward Carpenter proposed a version of this idea, characterizing homosexuals as an "intermediate sex" that incorporated psychological qualities of both males and females.[48]

In all these theories, homosexuality is explained in relation to the biological or behavioral definition of gender. This remained the case until the late 1960s. The psychoanalytic tradition, and especially the work of Irving Bieber, continued to rely on the assumption that there is a necessary relationship between the development of masculinity and femininity and heterosexuality or homosexuality.[49]

Whether physicians or homosexuals themselves have formulated these theories of homosexuality, a deeply held, widely disseminated cultural "code" underlies all such attempts. Historically, this code has shaped our interpretation of the sex/gender system. In a pathbreaking formulation, Barbara Ponse has called this master code "the principle of consistency."[50]

The principle of consistency links *genetic assignment* (i.e., whether a person has XX or XY chromosomes) to *anatomy* (there are, in fact, syndromes in which this link does not occur) to a *gender identity* (which is usually based on the gender assignment at birth).[51] *Gender identity* is the privately held awareness of oneself as male or female. The principle of consistency then projects the *gender role* as a function of gender identity. Gender role is learned behavior, and although it is usually related to one's genetic assignment and gender identity, they do not necessarily determine gender role. In other words, to be born female does not guarantee femininity. According to the theory, gender roles imply *sexual object choice*. The principle of consistency assumes that one's gender role determines which gender one will find sexually attractive. The theory sees these elements as inseparable and natural. The principle of consistency explains why if one element is reversed, or "inverted," the other elements must be consistently inverted as well. A woman who wears men's clothes (or indeed chooses to pass as a man) must be a man either biologically or psychologically ("a man's spirit in a woman's body"), as well as a lesbian.

In recent years, the emergence of lesbian and gay identities has led to some modifications in the principle of consistency. Ponse herself includes *sexual identity* (whether a person is homosexual, heterosexual, or bisexual) as an element. One can elaborate this further by adding *sexual role*, which allows for active/passive, top/bottom, butch/femme.[52] These amendments, however, imply a weakening of the principle; rigidly categorizing sex/gender behavior as male or female, heterosexual or homosexual, no longer has the force of earlier interpretations.

If the principle of consistency ideologically binds the ensemble of practices, discourses, and institutions in the sex/gender system, then the homosexual can only emerge as a subject, particularly as a political subject, with a reinterpretation of sexuality and gender's meanings. Otherwise, as long as people use a discourse of consistency when considering homosexuality, most aspects of homosexual life will be interpreted as *anomalous* and *unnatural*.

CULTURAL POLITICS IN THE CITY OF NIGHT

How powerful is the principle of consistency as an underlying code in American culture? The principle shapes everyday social interactions in the form of the *heterosexual assumption*—the way most people presume everyone is heterosexual. Although the assumption has been weakened in certain cities with large homosexual populations and in certain occupational or cultural milieus, it still governs most social interactions. In the years before the gay movement was reborn in 1969, the social stigma attached to homosexuality reinforced this heterosexual assumption. Together, the heterosexual assumption and the stigma of homosexuality forced most lesbians and gay men to keep their homosexual feelings or activities secret. The stigma and the heterosexual assumption established the *political horizon* for all homosexual acts—they became both physical and symbolic.

In the period after World War II, most homosexuals were in the closet. Most of them sought to "pass" as heterosexual in public settings such as the workplace or even within their families. Nevertheless, a vigorous underground culture emerged in cities such as New York, Chicago, San Francisco, Los Angeles, and Philadelphia. As women and men sought sexual partners, they created this urban, homosexual subculture. Unlike with ethnic or racial subcultures, families did not pass on and share the homosexual subculture. Most people had been reared in heterosexual families with the expectation that they would be heterosexual in adult life. Homosexuals often adopted those heterosexual expectations and social values for many years. But outside of lucky accidents (which often help people crystallize their sexual desires), most homosexual women and men had to go outside their social circles to find partners who shared their sexual desires. How was this possible when there were no public or explicit avowals of homosexuality? When there were no publicly acknowledged social spaces where lesbians or gay men could meet each other? When the heterosexual assumption and the stigma of homosexuality enforced silence, invisibility, and hostility?

Lesbians and gay men devised special tactics in order to identify sexual partners without much explicit discussion. In a study of oppositional social practices in everyday life, Michel de Certeau has emphasized that "tactics" are ways of using imposed cultural systems to achieve one's own desires. They introduce alternative or heterogeneous meanings into the dominant cultural system. Like wit, tactics require one to seize opportunities or time.[53] Communication with a desired partner of unknown sexual preference requires great "tact." One must use the language of innuendo, well-placed pauses, carefully worded jokes, or ambiguous expression. For example, in John Rechy's 1963 novel *City of Night*, the narrator is propositioned on his first night at a New York City YMCA by another resident:

> "They dont call this Y the French Embassy for nothing," the merchant marine laughs. He has sized me up slyly: broke and green in the big city—and he said: "You wouldnt believe if youd been at Mary's last night—thats a place in the Village and everything goes." He watches me evenly for some reaction, determining, Im sure, how far he can go how quickly. "So I spot this cute kid there—" Hes still studying me

carefully, and when I dont say anything, he continues with more as-
surance: "So I spot him and I want him—yeah sure Im queer—whatya
expect?" he challenges. He pauses longer this time, watching me still
calculatingly. He goes on: "And the kid's looking for maybe a pad to
flop in and breakfast—hes not queer himself. I dont like em queer: If I
did Id go with a woman—why fuck around with substitutes? . . . So
this kid goes with me—Im feeling Good, just off the ship flush—I lay
50 bucks on him."[54]

Rechy's account captures the ambiguities: "a place in the Village and
everything goes" and the well-placed pauses and innuendoes, such as
"So I spot this cute kid. . . ." The merchant marine doesn't say anything
about the kid's gender; somehow it's understood, but not yet explicit.
After the pause, he makes it clear when he continues, "So I spot *him*
and I *want* him. . . ." After another pause, he adds, "Yeah, sure Im
queer—whatya expect?"

The tactical uses of language were central to the lesbian and gay
experience of the 1940s, 1950s, and 1960s. Making sexual contacts, however, often required "tactical" elaborations on a large scale. Sacha Lewis
quotes from an account of such maneuvering:

When I was in high school I didn't even know the word *lesbian*, much
less how to be one. I just knew I wanted to be with women. I wanted
to go steady, date and have a woman to share intimate sexual feelings
with. So I looked very carefully at how the boys in school got girls to
date, go steady, neck and the rest. What I saw was that boys had short
hair. What I saw was that boys wore shirts and pants. And what I
saw at the time was that the most desirable boys were into leather
jackets and chains and these huge silver rings that were kind of like
brass knuckles—a real 40s thing. "Okay," I said, "that must be how
you get girls." So that's what I did. . . . I must have looked pretty
funny, but it [was a] very serious thing with me at the time because it
worked. There were other girls who were gay and I guess I was so
obvious that they had an easy time following me.[55]

This woman's solution to the problem of satisfying her homosexual
desires was to reinterpret the principle of consistency. She wanted to
attract women, so she modeled herself on males. Thus, she created a

code that communicated a desire to establish sexual relations with women. By adopting a male role behavior, she became "obvious" to other women with homosexual preferences. Butch/femme roles were common (though certainly not universal) in the lesbian culture of the 1950s.[56]

Because butch and femme roles appeared to be imitations of heterosexual roles, they were later denigrated in the early days of lesbian feminism. Butch/femme roles, however, actually *reinterpreted* male/female roles. Because women adopted both roles, they were *in fact* different from traditional heterosexual roles. Butch/femme dynamics became what William Simon and John Gagnon have called a sexual script.[57] Butch and femme lesbians elaborated a mutual interpretative scheme that orchestrated their desires and integrated their biological capacities for arousal, climax, and resolution into sexually significant events. Joan Nestle saw her butch/femme relationships as "complex erotic statements." Butch lesbians were "tabooed women who were willing to identify their passion for other women by wearing clothes that symbolized the taking of responsibility. Part of this responsibility was sexual expertise. In the 1950s, this courage to feel comfortable with arousing another woman became a political act."[58]

Butch and femme lesbian roles involved neither a repudiation of gender roles nor an exaltation of them. For example, whereas the lesbian butch may have adopted masculine behavior for its initiatory or managerial qualities, her primary preoccupation in sex was to forgo the macho behavior of pleasing herself first, instead pleasing the femme. Both roles allowed women to play with and to extend the range of possible behavior within a firm sense of female gender identity.[59]

There was similar playfulness among gay men on the gender inversion theme, which in gay slang was called "camping it up." When "camping," men adopted feminine mannerisms, emphasizing through humor the apparent incongruity of a man's having sex with another man. Camp rested on the assumption that gender behavior is a *role*, something that can be adopted, changed, or dropped. It was a style of humor that allowed homosexuals to react to their situation with wry laughter rather than despair.[60]

Camp as an aesthetic philosophy received public recognition in Susan Sontag's famous essay "Notes on Camp," published in the *Partisan Review* in 1964. Sontag acknowledged its roots in the homosexual community: "The peculiar relation between Camp taste and homosexuality has to be explained. While it's not true that Camp taste *is* homosexual taste, there is no doubt a peculiar affinity and overlap. But homosexuals, by and large, constitute the vanguard—and most articulate audience—of Camp."[61] Sontag ignored that camp grew out of the gay culture's process of recoding the sexual significance of gender and the principle of consistency. Although the camp sensibility, like butch/femme, cannot be attributed to all gay men and lesbians, it offered a counterhegemonic challenge to the sex/gender system.[62] Both butch/femme role-playing and the camp sensibility reinterpreted sexual preference and sexual behavior as they related to gender. With wit and role-playing, homosexuals thereby drove a wedge between gender and sexuality. Homosexuals' everyday sexual practices, their butch/femme role-playing, and their camp sensibility significantly modified the dominant culture's notions of gender and sex for lesbians and gay men. In the 1950s, camp was the ideology of the homosexual subculture, which treated gender roles *as* performances with a sense of bitter irony. Gay cultural expressions such as camp became a fundamental challenge to the prevalent notions that gender, sexual preference, and sexual identity were *natural*.

In a predominantly hostile world, homosexuals limited their vulnerability by keeping their social and sexual transactions as invisible as possible. Many homosexuals joined highly closeted social circles in hopes of meeting other homosexuals in a relatively safe social setting. The homosexual stigma kept gay social spaces in "back regions" hidden from public view. These spaces were therefore vulnerable to illegal intrusions, such as criminal activity (many cities had Mafia-controlled gay bars) and police brutality and corruption (gay sexual activity often "hides" in red-light districts).[63] Nevertheless, homosexuals (more often male, because public space has been traditionally dominated by men) established physical and social spaces within urban areas—bars, hotel lobbies, YMCAs, bathhouses, street corners, men's rooms, and gyms.

They appropriated space from the dominant culture (gay bars often evolved from bohemian or artists' bars) by introducing anomalous and coded practices, which often remained invisible to heterosexuals passing through (e.g., certain men's rooms become sites of sexual activity).[64]

Throughout the 1950s and early 1960s, urban police departments all over the United States attempted to close gay bars and other homosexual meeting places. Although these drives severely disrupted the lives of homosexuals, they provoked political responses over and over again.[65] These developments in gay life since the end of World War II—the increasingly elaborate cultural expressions; the proliferation of gay spaces; and the numerous, if minor, political mobilizations—created a sense of social identity.

THE SEARCH FOR A GAY IDENTITY

The debate between the assimilationist perspective and the cultural minority thesis resurfaced in the mid-1960s.[66] Mary McIntosh, a lesbian sociologist long active in the British Left, made an important contribution to this debate both in the United States and in Britain in 1968. She wrote her pioneering article "The Homosexual Role" as a direct response to the narrowly civil libertarian approach of the homophile movement.[67] Her article helped to revive the debate that had taken place during the 1950s in the Mattachine Society between the assimilation approach and the cultural minority thesis.[68] McIntosh argued that the homosexual role did not simply involve "sexual behavior" but a whole pattern of feelings, expectations, and strategies that emerged in response to the stigmatizing of homosexuals as pathological outcasts. McIntosh amplified her analysis of the distinction between sexual behavior and role or identity (as later theorists have called it) by documenting the development of the homosexual role in England.

Only one year later, hustlers, drag queens, and gay-bar patrons fought against police when they raided the Stonewall Inn in New York City. Several days of demonstrations followed. Established leaders from the homosexual Mattachine Society of New York and the lesbian organization Daughters of Bilitis responded cautiously. Mattachine leaders still held that defining the homosexual as a unique minority defeats the very cause for which the homosexual strives—*to be an integral part of society.* A new group—the Gay Liberation Front (GLF)—formed, modeling itself on New Left organizations. Many of its members had participated in the antiwar movement and the counterculture. Instead of allying themselves with the preexisting movement, GLF leaders broke with "old-line" homosexuals.

After the 1969 Stonewall riots, a homosexual emancipation movement emerged. This movement, called "gay liberation," resulted from a clash of two cultures and two generations—the homosexual subculture of the 1950s and 1960s and the New Left counterculture of 1960s youth. Ideologically, the camp sensibility of the 1950s and early 1960s had served as a strategy of containment; it had balanced its scorn for the principle of consistency with a bitter consciousness of oppression in a framework that offered no vision of historical change. The gay liberationists, who rarely had much appreciation for traditional gay life, proposed a radical cultural revolution. Instead of protecting the right to privacy, gay liberation radicals insisted on coming out—the public disclosure of one's homosexuality—which then became the centerpiece of gay political strategy. For the gay movement, coming out was what Gramsci called a "catharsis." This occurs, he said, when a "structure ceases to be an external force which causes man, assimilates him to itself and makes him passive and is transformed into a means of freedom, an instrument to create a new ethnopolitical form and a source of new initiatives."[69] To come "out of the closet" (originally a phrase of gay slang) was to do the very thing most feared in the gay culture of the 1950s and early 1960s.

Dennis Altman made the most sophisticated theoretical elaboration of the new gay politics in his 1971 book *Homosexual: Oppression and Liberation.*[70] The process of "coming out" is at the center of his analysis. This frequently difficult and painful process is both personal and political. The process could involve years of coming to terms with the specific cultural or religious beliefs that stigmatize homosexual behavior. The gay liberation movement gave a political meaning to coming out by extending the psychological-personal process into public life; the movement encouraged lesbians and gay men to acknowledge their homosexuality publicly. Coming out thus became praxis. Altman interpreted this extended process of coming out as a search for identity. This identity, in his view, already existed and did not need to be self-consciously or politically constructed.[71] Altman linked his analysis of the gay search for identity to Herbert Marcuse's and Norman O. Brown's ideas about the political potential of homosexuality and polymorphous perversity; Altman proposed that sexual liberation involved "a resurrection of our original impulse to take enjoyment from the total body" and that with liberation, homosexuality and heterosexuality would cease to be viewed as separate sexualities.[72]

Like Marcuse and Brown, Altman analyzed how society has repressed polymorphous perversity by removing the erotic from all areas of life and denying people's inherent bisexuality by polarizing gender roles. He went on to argue, "How far sexual freedom can be conceived without coming to grips with the basic features of our society is a key ideological concern of both the women's and gay movements. Yet there is a sense in which we should be suspicious of attempts to deny the centrality of sexuality in any discussion of liberation."[73]

In his synthesis, Altman attempted to bridge the old-line gay culture of the 1950s and 1960s and the countercultural gay movement of the late 1960s and early 1970s.[74] The coming-out strategy, he argued, would politicize the gay identity of the 1950s and 1960s. Altman situated both the "old" gay culture and the "new" gay identity within the framework of Marcuse's and Brown's utopian sexual theory. In his concluding chapter "The End of the Homosexual?" Altman posited gay liberation as "part of a much wider movement that is challenging the basic cultural norms of our advanced industrial, capitalist, and bureaucratic individual consciousness and new identities and life styles." He concluded: "One hopes that the answer lies in the creation of a new human for whom such distinctions no longer are necessary for the establishment of identity. The creation of this new human demands the acceptance of new definition of man- and womanhood such as are being urged by gay and women's liberation."[75]

Although many gay activists shared Altman's utopian sexual hopes, they chose a political strategy of encouraging people to come out and supporting that decision. The focus on coming out created a new type of gay politics. The public announcement of one's homosexuality became a sign of self-acceptance. As vast numbers of homosexuals felt encouraged to emerge from their closets, the movement grew until it achieved a political impact that the homophile movement never attained.

Coming out had two important effects. First, it allowed people to create a formal network serving a range of previously unsatisfied needs. The network included religious, educational, political, recreational, and professional organizations; newspapers and periodicals; social service institutions (e.g., counseling services); and mutual aid societies. Second, as people came out and mobilized, and as they formed community institutions, homosexuals gained an increasingly well-defined public identity.

Lesbians and gay men had to be visible before they could establish communities. Many homosexuals moved away from families and jobs or careers in which they could not be openly gay, and migrated to cities with visible lesbian and gay communities. Visible homosexuals created gay neighborhoods that resembled the urban neighborhoods of immigrant groups in the late nineteenth and early twentieth centuries. With their new visibility, homosexuals created political groups that influenced elections and gay-owned or gay-patronized businesses that thrived.

Among gay intellectuals in the mid-1970s, particularly those who had been active in the antiwar movement and the New Left, there was a movement to reclaim the historical and cultural experience of homosexuals in a way modeled on black intellectuals' recovery of black culture and history. In addition, gay historians soon discovered that many early participants of homosexual emancipation came from the political Left. Many lesbians and gay men had only a vague awareness that a homophile movement had existed before the 1969 Stonewall riots, and most were completely surprised to discover that homosexual emancipation movements had antedated World War II.

Probably the most important book to explore the homosexual experience in the United States was *Gay American History* by Jonathan Ned Katz. Published in 1976, this documentary history of homosexuality included material from 1528 through the mid-1970s. Influenced by the gay movement's moment of catharsis in the early 1970s, Katz wrote of homosexuals: "We were a people perceived out of time and out of place—socially unsituated, without a history. . . . That time is over. The people of the shadows have seen the light; Gay People are coming out—and moving on—to organized action against an oppressive society."[76]

Katz's pioneering work unintentionally undermined the definition of homosexual identity that the movement had assumed. The section "Native Americans / Gay Americans" showed homosexual behavior embedded in societies in which men and women could change gender roles. Whereas switching gender roles implied that a person was homosexual, the sexual partner who had not changed gender roles was not stigmatized or labeled. Katz also categorized as homosexual some passionate male-male or female-female relations that may have had no homoerotic component at all—for instance, a passionate correspondence between Alexander Hamilton and John Laurens. The long history of coding homosexual feelings as "friendship" makes Katz's decision to include such material plausible but not necessarily valid. Katz's research also unearthed an important new category of deviants—women who passed as men to improve their wages or to travel. Undoubtedly, some of these were lesbians but many were not. In *Gay American History*, Katz intended to offer the history of homosexuals, but he also "rediscovered" the history of gender nonconformity and homosexual behavior. Katz adopted a contradictory approach, on the one hand presenting a history of homosexuals as a distinct and fixed minority and on the other espousing the radical historicism that all homosexuality is situational.

Finally, a group of activists and historians associated with a British journal called *Gay Left* (which existed from 1975 through 1979) articulated a history of the homosexual identity.[77] Among this group, Jeffrey Weeks explored the implications of Mary McIntosh's 1968 essay "The

Homosexual Role" in a series of essays and in *Coming Out*, his history of homosexual politics in Britain. The *Gay Left* approach combined symbolic interactionist sociology (emphasizing socially created meanings in everyday life) with Marxist analysis.[78] Weeks, Kenneth Plummer, and other *Gay Left* historians identified the specific social and economic conditions that permitted a homosexual subculture and its psychological-political outgrowth—the modern lesbian and gay male identity—to develop. They saw sexual identity as resulting from a historical process, not a natural one. In "Capitalism and Gay Identity," a theoretical essay, and in *Sexual Politics, Sexual Communities*, a history of the pre-Stonewall gay movement, John D'Emilio also contributed to this analytical tradition.[79]

This search for a theory of gay identity originated among gay Left intellectuals. Starting from an "ethnic model" of history that at first assumed an already existing identity or social group, they eventually discovered that homosexuals were historically constructed subjects. For these leftists, as well as for many other lesbian and gay activists, the theory of a lesbian or gay identity is believed to be both a description of reality *and* a normative basis for politics.

The lesbian and gay movements certify—politically and socially—the existence of the homosexual identity. The lesbian and gay contribution to transforming the sex/gender system was to split sexual object preference from gender and to legitimize the social construction of sexual identity by challenging the heterosexual assumption. These developments seriously weakened the cultural grip of the principle of consistency.

IDENTITY, TRANSGRESSION, AND THE POLITICS OF DIFFERENCE

Lesbian and gay identities emerged from the political mobilization of a subculture that has started to recode the sexual significance of gender and sexual preference. The existence of large, visible, lesbian and gay communities has helped to institutionalize homosexual identities. To extend the principle of consistency to include "sexual identity," and thereby homosexuality, is to create an uneasy alliance. This incorporation, however, has undermined the idea of a "natural" relationship between gender identity, family formation, and reproduction, which the principle of consistency signifies.

The cumulative modifications in the postwar American sex/gender system—the increasing independence of adolescents from parental control, the growing equality of women, and the political emergence of homosexuals—have threatened the beliefs and privileges of many Americans who, for religious or other reasons, are committed to traditional family patterns. In particular, the political mobilization of women and homosexuals during the 1970s threatened the economic and social status of the lower middle class and white Christian working class.

The New Right has tapped into the resentments that this postwar transformation has generated. Thus, this political group is the most recent political subject to emerge from the turmoil of the sexual revolution.[80] In reaction, the New Right is attempting to restore the principle of consistency as natural law. Conservative critics of gay rights have argued that "the case for homosexuality is a vulgarization of a philosophical anarchism which denies the existence of nature." In their minds, advocating gay rights also denies that human bodies are better designed for heterosexual than homosexual intercourse, which should be overwhelmingly obvious.[81] The principal of consistency as symbolic order or master code works only as long as society takes it for granted. The political mobilization of the New Right can only succeed in defending a particular sex/gender subculture. It cannot restore the heterosexual and paternalistic family form to its earlier position of unchallenged dominance.

The sex/gender arrangements that prevailed in America in 1940 have changed radically. World War II, the contradictory postwar demands for family discipline and mass consumption, and the grassroots political mobilizations by youth, women, and the New Right have all modified the sex/gender system.[82] Like the gay movement, each of these mobilizations has created a particular form of political subjectivity. Each form of political identity is, in turn, vulnerable to recodings due to shifts in age, social context, and political developments.

In the early stages of creating a collective subjectivity, politically mobilized homosexuals (or women, for example) adopted norms and codes of conduct that served as "recipes for an appropriate attitude regarding the self."[83] These norms, often articulated in opposition to homophobia, provided a platform for politics and social criticism. They also responded to the personal distress and humiliation that homosexuals had suffered. Thus, the personal became the political. Although the initial political mobilization drew on these feelings of oppression, the lesbian and gay communities made tremendous political progress because so many individuals in the movement accepted their own homosexuality. The mobilization of homosexuals as collective subjects emphasized their *shared* experiences of oppression, and was therefore a militant affirmation of commonality.

Every form of political subjectivity, however, is only a relay that transports us from one point to another. Affirming shared experience within any group soon exposes limits and differences. Everyone's identity exists as the nexus in a web of opposing or merely different group affiliations and personal commitments. In gay politics, affirming shared experience resulted in the consolidation of homosexual differences. In this drive for affirmation, however, irremovable differences have emerged among the members of homosexual communities. Political action eventually provokes internal conflict or splits movements along the most significant social fault lines of a historical period—such as class, religion, race, or generation. Even an individual's identity is never completely harmonious or unified internally. This is the transgressive experience through which we discover the limits of our membership, our real heterogeneity. Thus, the politics of identity must also be a politics of difference. The politics of identity is a totalizing drive that attempts to universalize its norms and conduct; the politics of difference affirms limited and heterogeneous subjects.[84] As intense and controversial sexual differences have emerged within the lesbian and gay male communities, new forms of sexual politics are developing throughout American society.

2 THE POLITICAL ECONOMY OF THE CLOSET

Toward an Economic History of
Gay and Lesbian Life before Stonewall

The market process has often played an important role—a positive as well as negative one—in the development of gay and lesbian communities.[1] It has helped to expand the goods and services available to gay men and lesbians, particularly for those products and services uniquely desired by homosexuals. But it has also reified and limited the needs satisfied by those goods. Bars are one example of an economic institution that has had immense historical significance in gay and lesbian life. There is a body of scholarship and opinion about the development of lesbian and

This chapter is a slightly revised version of an essay originally published in Amy Gluckman and Betsy Reed, eds., *Homo/Economics: Capitalism, Community and Lesbian and Gay Life in the United States* (New York: Routledge, 1997).

gay communities, but apart from practical matters, little attention has been devoted to understanding the "homo economy." Large corporations and mainstream businesses are increasingly catering to a lesbian and gay market, making it harder for small gay- or lesbian-owned businesses to stay afloat. Now more than ever, it is therefore imperative to explore the interdependencies, as well as the tensions, between the growth of lesbian and gay markets and our goals as communities.

We have only the barest sense of the economic history of the lesbian and gay communities. It is marked, as are the economic lives of many oppressed populations, by the economic domination of outsiders. Because so many homosexuals have lived in secrecy, lesbian and gay businesses have often existed on the margins of illegality. We do know that the homo economy has always catered more to men because they have had more employment opportunities and greater income and mobility.

I believe that there are four broad periods or phases (with considerable overlap) in the post–World War II economic history of homosexual communities. We are, however, currently moving into a new phase—hypercommodification—as mainstream corporations target the homo market niche.[2] The first phase is the Closet Economy. The primary economic institutions were bars, supplemented by adult bookstores, bathhouses, and mail-order services—most of which operated on the margins of legality. The second period, initiated by Stonewall, might be called the Liberation Economy. Its dominant economic institutions were the proliferating retail businesses; bars, bookstores, bathhouses, and consumer services emerged from the confines of semilegality. Political and other voluntary organizations also provided previously unavailable public services. The third phase of the homo economy was the Territorial Economy of the late 1970s, marked by the spread of gentrification and community development. This process was cut short by the emergence of AIDS and development of the AIDS Economy; in this fourth period, aside from educational and other nonprofit organizations, the largest institutions of the homo economy provide AIDS services.

In this essay, I want to sketch out some economic aspects of gay and lesbian community life—in particular, the period before visible gay and lesbian communities emerged in American cities, or roughly between 1945 and 1969. For the most part, the economic history of lesbian and gay collective life is unknown territory. All economic research on gay and lesbian life suffers from the virtual nonexistence of empirical information. No systematic or periodic social surveys have ever been undertaken, nor have statistics of gay and lesbian life been routinely collected, because homosexuals, historically stigmatized, have been invisible to "the gaze" of the random sampling methodology of American social science. In part, this invisibility results from the fear many lesbians and gay men have of being identified as homosexuals.

Nevertheless, economic research about lesbians and gay men has slowly accumulated. Since the mid-1970s, social surveys and market researching have begun to provide some economic information about homosexuals.[3] Economists, lawyers, and other social scientists have also begun to study the effects of economic discrimination, especially in the workplace.[4] Only recently has research on employment discrimination and the growth of a gay market for consumer goods begun to appear.[5] A number of writers have also explored the impact of economic change on the emergence of gay and lesbian identities.[6]

According to historians of gay and lesbian life, homosexual communities have existed in some U.S. cities at least since the end of World War II.[7] An economic history is therefore conceivable, because homosexual communal life cannot have existed without economic resources or without lesbians and gay men engaging in economic decision making. The economic history of homosexual communities has to be pieced together on the basis of fragments and anecdotes embedded in personal narratives, historical works, or older sociological research.[8] Like an archaeologist or paleontologist, the homo economic historian has to work from the slenderest of facts to imagine and identify larger economic forces. Almost all homo economic research today is at a stage that requires ingenuity, speculation, and, of course—to paraphrase Gwen Verdon in *Damn Yankees*—"a little thisa, a little data." I will try to delineate gay and lesbian economic history by bringing together some of these historical fragments and by drawing on the theory of institutional development in the work of economic historians and theorists.[9]

THE ECONOMIC CONSEQUENCES OF THE CLOSET

Before Stonewall, two decisive factors shaped gay and lesbian socio-economic life. The first was the social stigma attached to homosexuality, which was so severe that millions of homosexual men and women feared even engaging in sexual relations with people who attracted them sexually and appealed to them emotionally. In 1963, in his book on stigmas, Erving Goffman explored the structural consequences of being homosexual. He identified two kinds of stigmas that had radically different effects on those stigmatized. One sort of stigma was visible—for example, race. People often respond to visible stigmas by feeling tense. Therefore, those with visible stigmas have frequently had to manage others' tension.[10] As history demonstrates, social tension provoked by racial difference has frequently sparked violence toward African Americans.

The other sort of stigma that Goffman identified was not visible or obvious. Such a stigma poses an altogether different challenge to those who could be stigmatized by some "discrediting" piece of information. Out of fear of a ruined reputation, people who could be stigmatized in this way were vulnerable to intimidation and threats of blackmail. Members of this group often tried to manage information about themselves closely.

Homosexuality was not usually a visible, stigmatizing trait. Of course, this was not exclusively true. Frequently, drag queens and butch lesbians were visible representatives of the stigmatized population. As with racial minorities or other visible stigmatized groups, they constantly encountered tense social situations that often resulted in violence. As open homosexuals *and* as targeted victims, drag queens and butch lesbians marked the outer perimeter of tolerance by which society was able to contain homosexuality. During the late 1940s and 1950s at least, the homosexual closet was constructed by the dialectic between the management of information and the threat of violence posed by visibility.

In addition to homosexuality's stigma, the second factor shaping gay and lesbian life before Stonewall was homosexuality's illegality throughout the United States. As with liquor during Prohibition or drugs today, criminalization shaped the provision of goods and services and the related social institutions of the homo economy. The unlawfulness made it all the more necessary for homosexuals to control information about themselves. Together, these two factors—the social stigma and the criminalization of homosexuality—contributed to the construction of what we now call "the closet."

The economic repercussions of social stigma have varied considerably, of course, in different historical periods, communities, and geographical regions. Characteristics such as age, gender, physical traits or abilities, class, and race also come into play. In this essay, I will explore broadly the economic consequences that the twin challenges of managing information and the threat of violence posed for the homosexual community.

Organizing a social world around the strict segregation of information generates a number of outcomes. First, managing secrets shapes individuals' lives,[11] bifurcating public and private, and generating a trade-off between space and time. Second, many people with strong homosexual desires tended to migrate to large cities, whose anonymity offered more room for stigmatized activities and identities.[12] Third, whatever social life there is takes place in the shadow of protection rackets. Fourth, cultural codes became necessary.[13] All these dimensions of lesbian and gay life have had economic consequences.

THE HIGH COST OF A DOUBLE LIFE

Until 1969, the severe stigma caused homosexual activity to be profoundly "asocial"—that is, it had few social institutions and existed outside mainstream society.[14] In the vast majority of cases, male homosexuals engaged in sexual relationships with other isolated men in private or anonymous social spaces (such as restrooms), whereas lesbians often formed isolated couples or small social circles. Nonetheless, homosexuals were able to find one another and establish shared social patterns and institutions.[15]

Before Stonewall, the overwhelming power of the stigma fostered homosexual social institutions premised on the segregation of information between the gay and straight worlds. It was possible to participate in institutionalized homosexual social life while continuing to remain in the closet. This meant living a double life, being divided between two worlds. At work, with their families, and in public, lesbians and gay men appeared "straight." In another world, they might have sex with someone of the same gender, dress or act like the opposite gender, know other people only by a first name, or even an alias, and have no idea where others lived or worked. They lied to their families and heterosexual friends—often to their sexual partners. These deceptions, along with the strict bifurcation in their lives, created enormous emotional stress for lesbians and gay men.

The closet had a tremendous impact on gay men's and lesbians' work lives, in particular. Lesbians and gay men did not take their lovers to the company Christmas party, nor did they discuss their vacations with coworkers or the boss. To the degree that this sort of rapport in the workplace helps grease the wheels and leads to employment and promotion opportunities, gay men and lesbians lost out.[16] If they were not married, they often failed to win certain promotions. Many homosexuals responded to these barriers by scaling back their career expectations and, thus, their earning potential.

Maintaining this strict separation between the straight and gay worlds implied strict separations in terms of time and space. Lesbians and gay men completely sequestered their social-sexual life from their work, hid "friends" (one of the traditional ways to refer to partners) and lovers from family and employers, and frequented gay or lesbian gathering places such as bars or bathhouses that were often quite a distance from their homes and workplaces.

This dramatic segmentation of private life from public life made everyday "transaction costs"—essentially the price of concealing one's homosexuality—quite high for homosexuals. In contrast, heterosexuals had no such costs. Closeted homosexuals spent more of their individual income and resources than heterosexuals on routine adult activities. Such costs may have included the extra costs of transportation, liquor, multiple sets of clothing, and even the expense of maintaining separate households instead of living with a lover. Concealment made it harder to have stable sexual/emotional relationships, manage an ambitious career, or create political and social organizations.

Whereas the closet generated substantial transaction costs in this period, so did being out and known (particularly if one was a butch lesbian, drag queen, or even an effeminate gay man). Managing a public identity as a homosexual also created considerable stress. Nevertheless, in strictly economic terms, the benefits of a closeted life that was sexually active or emotionally expressive exceeded the costs imposed by concealment. By remaining in the closet, homosexuals were able to maintain career and employment opportunities. Being publicly gay often meant forfeiting jobs and economic security. Only when political developments made it easier to come out could those transaction costs cease to be an obstacle to leading a socially and psychologically rich gay or lesbian life.

Lesbians and gay men could reduce some of these concealment costs by living in or migrating to large cities. The socially and ethnically diverse populations allowed homosexuals to blend in and be anonymous. The population density and scale of large cities also allowed for spatial separation of homosexual activities from residences and workplaces.

THE PROTECTION BUSINESS: BARS, BATHS, AND BOOKSTORES

The most significant factor in the development of early lesbian or gay social institutions was that homosexual behavior was illegal. As long as those laws were enforced, they imposed not only severe psychological and social burdens on bisexuals, gay men, and lesbians but also economic ones. In the 1950s and 1960s, police raids of bars, tearooms, and parks led to arrests, legal fees, and public humiliation, as well as the loss of jobs, blackmail, and physical harm—all of which added to the economic burden of being homosexual.[17]

From 1945 through 1969, the bar was at the center of gay or lesbian communal life, and therefore economic life. Baths and certain same-sex venues, however, also provided institutional contexts for socializing, engaging in sex, and establishing intimate relationships.[18] Although bars were often raided, they afforded some protection against entrapment, physical assaults, and blackmail. Because gay and lesbian bars catered to people who were stigmatized or who engaged in "criminal acts," bar owners in most American cities were forced to pay the police or organized crime for "protection." Any businesses that catered to gay men and lesbians implicitly promised customers freedom from harassment; for this reason, bars had to pay for protection.[19] Bar owners sought to recover this cost by charging higher prices for drinks.

Gay men's greater social and economic freedom during this period, as well as men's ready access to public space, led to a far greater number of gay male institutions and venues. Men tended to transform certain "public" spaces into sexual cruising venues: gyms, "Y"s, public parks, and restrooms. For women, same-sex social situations enabled lesbian socializing, primarily in all-female rooming houses, shops, girls' schools, colleges. Thus, an institutionalized social world emerged earlier for male homosexuals than for lesbians. Most likely, the social and economic costs of gay male cruising (time, riskiness, and inconvenience) also prompted men to seek and patronize "protected" environments such as bars.

The bifurcation of homosexual life, along with the need for "protection," often meant that gay and lesbian bars, bathhouses, or other businesses sought to be as inconspicuous as possible—their outside appearances were often muted, their signs cryptic or insignificant. Bouncers often "screened" customers in order to minimize the intrusions of hostile outsiders or undercover police. Bars, adult bookstores, and bathhouses maintained a certain degree of anonymity. Therefore, they were located in neighborhoods that were segregated from everyday businesses and residential activities—industrial areas, red-light districts, waterfront bars catering to sailors, or isolated roads in rural areas.[20]

Although the bars may have been economic institutions, they provided few jobs or little income to homosexuals. Businesses catering to lesbian and gay men were essentially "black-market" operations. They operated under the guise of being some other legitimate business: a neighborhood bar, a men's health club, a women's residence, a book-store. Lesbians or gay men rarely owned gay and lesbian bars. Selling alcohol to an illegal population would have made homosexual owners vulnerable to both legal and illegal pressures. The pattern of bar own-ership did, however, vary from one region or city to the next. In the East, bars tended to be owned and controlled by organized crime—the Mafia, whereas in cities such as San Francisco, gay men and lesbians owned perhaps 25 to 30 percent of the gay bars in the mid-1960s.[21] Thus, most of the profits and income generated by gay and lesbian customers went to straight owners and was not reinvested in activities catering to other lesbian and gay needs or to develop communal insti-tutions. Despite their importance as homosexually oriented business activities, bars did little to create economic surplus in the gay and les-bian community.[22]

Probably the most powerful obstacle to the development of com-munal economic or political institutions has been the potential cost to individual gay men and lesbians of publicly disclosing homosexual identity. The ubiquity of "extortion" in gay and lesbian economic life—ranging from crude efforts at blackmail to the refined "protection" pro-vided when a gay bar paid off police and organized crime—was sup-plemented by the emergence of strong lesbian and gay social norms against revealing names and identities of fellow homosexuals. Extortion depended on homosexuals' desire to keep their identities secret. Black-mail or extortion threatened to reveal those identities unless homosex-uals were willing to pay the price. Thus, their collusion in maintaining the secrecy of their fellow lesbian and gay men's names and identities reinforced the extortionate economy.[23] Nevertheless, the effectiveness of the norm frequently broke down under the pressure of arrests, raids, and health officials' tracking down former partners after discovering a sexually transmitted disease.[24]

THE PRODUCTION OF DESIRE:
CODES AND COMMODIFICATION

Many early commentators on "the homosexual community," which emerged slowly in the 1950s and 1960s, wondered whether or not lesbians and gay men actually had anything that could be called "gay culture." Even observers as sympathetic as Gagnon and Simon adopted a thesis of "cultural impoverishment" based on the belief that "community members often have only their sexual commitment in common."[25]

Indeed, the stigma and the closet's discipline meant that very few public representations of homosexuality circulated within mainstream culture. In 1926, for instance, the British government banned Radclyffe Hall's novel *The Well of Loneliness* on the grounds of obscenity, although it was a serious literary exploration of lesbianism as a social problem and although it contained no sexually explicit passages. Thus, in many works, homosexual themes were often heavily coded and expressed through euphemism and double entendre.

Certain artworks and erotic commodities, however, were produced and circulated even before the well-developed communities existed. Men in Europe and North America purchased and circulated erotically suggestive and sexually explicit drawings and photographs ever since the nineteenth century. Such early forms of pornography not only satisfied the need for sexual fantasy but they also stimulated, defined, and multiplied those fantasies.

The businesses formed to market "cultural commodities" to homosexuals tended to operate in the same margin of illegality as bars and bathhouses. For instance, such businesses sold erotic photographs or drawings in the early twentieth century, nude magazines after World War II (sexually explicit commercial pornography developed in the 1970s), cheap pornographic fiction, and sex toys (vibrators).

The cultural impoverishment thesis not only underestimated the value and significance of limited sexual representations, but it also overlooked the coded cultural representations that circulated in mainstream culture: Walt Whitman's Calamus poems, Frank Marcus's *The Killing of Sister George*, Tennessee Williams's *Cat on a Hot Tin Roof*, Emily Dickinson's poems, Colette's Claudine novels, and Judy Garland's singing.[26] Members of homosexual audiences, in the midst of personal struggles to interpret their own desires, were frequently able to identify homosexual leitmotifs in mainstream culture. Such works helped readers and viewers to recognize their erotic desires and perhaps come to identify as homosexual. The cultural impoverishment thesis was plausible only as long as it was not possible to market these cultural goods openly to lesbians and gay men.

Eventually, the creation of gay and lesbian social institutions and businesses provided an economic framework for the production and distribution of cultural goods. This new homosexual market was first identified in the *Mattachine Review, One,* and the *Ladder,* publications of the early homophile organizations. Consequently, a series of mail-order businesses developed that catered to gay men and lesbians. One of capitalism's most ambiguous characteristics is its liberatory ability to stimulate and shape desire, in addition to crassly exploiting it.[27] Analogously, the supply of any gay- and lesbian-oriented commodities, services, and cultural works contributed to the discursive process of identity formation, thereby creating the basis for political action, at the same time rigidly defining it.

THE ECONOMIC ORIGINS OF THE GAY GHETTO

Gay ghettos in large American cities (for example, Greenwich Village in New York City and North Beach in San Francisco) developed over fifty years. As a complex of social and economic institutions, the gay ghetto reached its maturity in the Territorial Economy of the late 1970s. It owed its economic foundations to the spatial dynamics of gay and lesbian social institutions in the period before Stonewall—the location of homosexually oriented businesses in industrial, shipping, red-light, or immigrant neighborhoods somewhat distant from middle-class residential areas. The ghetto, whether in its origins in Jewish history or in more modern forms such as racially segregated communities, is a spatial and socioeconomic form of containment—in other words, it tends to function as a collective closet.

A number of factors came together to establish the spatial concentration later called "the gay ghetto." The massive social dislocations occasioned by World War II created the demographic basis for the economic and social development of gay and lesbian communities. Young men enlisted or were drafted into the armed services, and young women moved to the cities to work in war plants. As these young men and women left their hometowns, they established new social relations outside the purview of their families and local communities. The young men moved into military housing, and the young women often set up households with other young women. These social conditions set the stage for these young men and women to explore their sexuality and emotional capabilities. These wartime developments only reinforced other long-term postwar trends, such as the increasing number of individuals living alone and households of unrelated adults. These developments created the residential base for homosexual communities.[28]

In the emerging gay and lesbian communities of the 1950s and 1960s, a cluster of bars, baths, adult bookstores, and cruising areas developed in certain districts or neighborhoods. Homosexuals also began to settle in certain bohemian neighborhoods in cities such as New York and San Francisco, because they offered higher degrees of tolerance as well as proximity to gay or lesbian gathering places. This process of spatial concentration reduced some of the everyday transaction costs imposed by the closet. The coming together of residential and social institutions permitted a slightly greater degree of openness—thus, certain lesbian and gay cultural traits became more visible within those neighborhoods.[29]

In capitalist societies, markets can only develop when adequate information exists about the number and location of customers, potential goods and services that can be sold, and the profits that can be made. Customers who conceal important information about their needs, identities, and whereabouts pose significant obstacles to the organization of a market. Thus, homosexual communities only developed into full-fledged gay ghettos as their economies changed from "black-market" or "protected" operations to conventional markets. The proliferation of political organizations, nonprofit service organizations, gay churches, community newspapers, and other publications and cultural institutions after Stonewall enabled the lesbian and gay communities to make this economic transition. In the process, gay men and lesbians gained greater economic control of community institutions and businesses from outsiders.[30]

IDENTITY POLITICS AND PUBLIC GOODS

The emergence of a gay and lesbian political movement in the wake of the Stonewall riots decisively transformed the organization of the homo economy. The centerpiece of the new movement's political strategy was to encourage lesbians and gay men to come out. At the time, and even now, the movement put most of its efforts toward seeking legal and social protection for those who were openly homosexual. Such a strategy challenged the black-market character of the homo economy. The extortionist dimensions of bars, bathhouses, and police harassment were greatly mitigated and have slowly declined as an important element in many of the largest urban gay and lesbian communities. The weakening of the closet's extortion economy fostered greater social solidarity within the lesbian and gay communities. Political mobilization also had a substantial impact on the "transaction costs" in the lives of many lesbians and gay men.

Thus, the gay and lesbian movement dramatically changed the framework within which lesbian and gay economic decisions were made. In terms of economic analysis, the movement allowed for the provision of public goods—that is, intangible goods and services that more than a single individual could enjoy at the same time. For example, governments supply such public goods as national defense, police services, and public parks. The gay and lesbian movement sought to provide "protection" for openly identified homosexuals—thus it became easier (and cheaper without the old exorbitant transaction costs) to start businesses and organizations (for example, nonprofit counseling services) that catered to gay and lesbian communities.

Organizing to create protection for all lesbians and gay men reinforced a sense of community. It became more comfortable to purchase goods and services specifically addressing homosexual needs—clothing and jewelry, books and magazines, dildos and other sex toys, enter-

tainment and travel. Thus, another consequence of the political movement was to reorganize the homo economy into a full-fledged gay
ghetto—which has never ceased to incite tensions between community
and market. The irony of that transformation is that the ghetto is another sort of closet.

Although the organization of gay and lesbian economic life has
changed radically, the economic history of the closet is not simply ar-
cane knowledge. Even today, the closet continues to play an important
role in the political limitations that lesbians and gay men encounter in
contemporary life. The enemies of homosexual emancipation want to
push lesbians and gay men back into the closet; "Don't ask, don't tell"
is symptomatic. It is the contemporary formulation of containment, the
attempt to reimpose an economic burden. The visible existence of gay
and lesbian communities is an important bulwark against the tide of
reaction. The economic vitality of contemporary lesbian and gay communities erodes conservatives' ability to revive the closet. The specter
of the closet haunts lesbian and gay politics—and lurks in every social
and political action that seeks to isolate and contain lesbian and gay
communities.

3 HOMOSEXUALITY AND THE SOCIOLOGICAL IMAGINATION

Hegemonic Discourses, the Circulation of Ideas, and the Process of Reading in the 1950s and 1960s

> The sociological imagination enables its possessor to understand the larger historical scene in terms of its meaning for the inner life and the external career of a variety of individuals. . . . By such means the personal uneasiness of individuals is focused upon explicit troubles and the indifference of publics is transformed into involvement with public issues.
>
> C. WRIGHT MILLS,
> *The Sociological Imagination*

In the fall of 1960, I drove to my first day of college with a young man with whom I was in love. Although I had already had a couple of homosexual affairs in high school, I had not yet identified myself as a homosexual. I was worried that I was queer, but I thought (perhaps hoped is more accurate), "Who knows? Maybe I'm bisexual." I had as yet no knowledge of the gay world. I knew that there were cruising spots and bars, but I was not very brave and had not had any casual sexual encounters. My homosexual feelings were about love; homosexual sex seemed like only a pleasant, but also anxiety-producing, by-

This chapter was originally delivered as a lecture at the University of California, Davis, in January 1992. A shorter version of this chapter was published in Martin Duberman, ed., *A Queer World: Transforming the Categories* (New York: New York University Press, 1997).

product of these profound feelings for other males. How did I eventually figure out that I was homosexual, find a way out of my closet, and enter the social world of other homosexuals?

It took almost ten years before I entered and joined the gay world fully. Before this happened, I embarked on a rather prolix process of learning to identify myself as homosexual. I started this process by reading, by searching through the available discourse for the knowledge I needed. Eventually, by adopting positive representations and rejecting homophobic ones, I identified myself as a homosexual. There were no maps to guide an earnest young homosexual through the quagmire of discourses dominated by medical and psychiatric theories. Only now, some thirty years later, do I begin to see the patterns that the discourses formed as I try to understand the role that the popular sociological books on homosexuality played.

During the early 1960s, I read my way through the literature on homosexuality. Meanwhile, notions that homosexuals had a social world of their own, even a community, circulated through the hodgepodge of discourses regulating interpretations of homosexuality, whether popular, psychological, legal, or literary. This "discovery" of the homosexual subculture was increasingly accompanied by the idea that homosexuality was a benign variation of sexual behavior. Thus, three very different sources influenced my socialization into "the homosexual role" (as sociologist Mary McIntosh called it): the hegemonic discourses on homosexuality, new ideas about of homosexual identity and community, and my own rather idiosyncratic reading.

One of the most important developments for lesbians and gay men in the 1950s and 1960s was the increasing appearance of public representations that revealed the social dimension of gay life. For homosexual women and men living relatively isolated lives, discovering that the gay world had an enduring pattern of symbolic interaction and social interrelations was no inconsequential event. Lesbians or gay men had to find a way out of their individual isolation into such a social world, even if they only did so through their intellects or imaginations at first.

For this reason, discourses such as those in popular sociology books and articles had all the more significance. These were homosexualizing discourses; they provided new categories and interpretations of social knowledge about gay life, as well as new categories of self-interpretation and presentation of an individual's identity.

Many of us arrived in the gay social sphere on a road paved with only imperfectly "homosexualizing" discourses. Nevertheless, our adopted representations of the gay social world, as an imagined community or a social imaginary, provided the basis for individual "homosexualization" and for social action. The existence of a homosexual social world implied that lesbians and gay men could lead a life (even if it was a secret to the straight people in their lives) that included friends, durable relationships, and a social and cultural life.

It is almost impossible to know what effect the popular sociology literature had on homosexuals themselves—there were no surveys and no one collected readership statistics or sales figures to tell us who or how many people read these books. Because I was a young man coming to terms with my homosexuality at that time, I will use myself as a piece of evidence in gauging the significance of this small body of publications.

During the 1950s, the sway of conformity in American society demonstrated the power of the social. The ideology of conformism constructed everyday social life in postwar America. The emerging homosexual identity depended on this experience of conformism, which both denied homosexuality and yet, at the same time, created the conditions that made it possible.

"The imagined social world" is one of the "*a priori*" of social life, according to Georg Simmel—it is a representation of *ourselves and others* in which we identify certain others as potential "coinhabitant[s] of the same specific world."[1] For Simmel, "the social *a priori*" not only conveys some practical sense of the social consequences of interactional processes but also some intuitive sense of a possible "perfect society." Although this perfect society may never be realized, it nevertheless suggests the potential benefits of social life.[2] The development of an "imagined social world" endowed homosexuals with a socially realized present and the basis for reconstructing a past.

THE DISCOVERY OF THE SOCIAL

In the year of Stonewall, the psychiatric discourse on homosexuality was hegemonic. Three years later, Allen Young noted how few books about homosexuality were available in the average bookstore or public library. Of those few, virtually all had been written by "six shrinks" whom Young placed "in the ranks of the worst of war criminals." The texts by the members of this rogues' gallery included: Edmund Bergler, *Homosexuality: Disease or a Way of Life?* (1957); Irving Bieber, *Homosexuality* (1962); Albert Ellis, *Homosexuality: Its Causes and Cure* (1964); Charles Socarides, *The Overt Homosexual* (1968); Lionel Ovesey, *Homosexuality and Pseudo-homosexuality* (1969); and Lawrence Hatterer, *Changing Homosexuality in the Male* (1970). In contrast, "The only pro-gay book of the 1950s, Donald Cory's *The Homosexual in America*, was published by a tiny publishing house and was generally unavailable."[3] Young starkly juxtaposed the powerful but repressive and antihomosexual psychoanalytic literature to the more affirmative, though still somewhat ambivalent, literature of popular sociology about the homosexual community.

The small but growing literature about the homosexual social world represented an important contribution to the public representations of homosexuality. As Pierre Bourdieu notes, it is the capacity "to make explicit, to publish, and to make public" what has existed socially but has not been acknowledged publicly, that makes it possible to forge a collective identity and make social groups. "Knowledge of the social world," he writes, "and more precisely, the categories that make it possible, are the stakes, par excellence, of political struggle."[4]

The emergence of a discourse in popular sociology about homosexuality initiated a process that potentially disrupted the hegemony of the psychiatric discourse of individual pathology. In two ways, these writers refashioned homosexuality as a social phenomenon, rather than a purely psychological or individual one. First, they defined homosexuality as a *social problem*, ambiguously framing it either as an issue of homosexuals' social adjustment or as a matter of eliminating prejudice against homosexuals. Second, these writers publicly recognized the existence of a homosexual social world. From the immediate postwar period through the 1960s, homosexuality emerged as a social issue in several bodies of discourse.[5]

Immediately after World War II, homosexuality emerged in Americans' public consciousness with surprising vigor. The controversy in 1948, after Alfred Kinsey reported widespread incidence of homosexual experience, firmly established homosexuality as a public issue.[6] In the early 1950s, Senator McCarthy reinforced this with his highly publicized witch-hunt to fire homosexuals, as well as communists, from government employment. These two events alone probably made homosexuality an issue in American public life more than any other source.

Not only did Kinsey publish his report at the end of the 1940s, but many fictional works about homosexuality appeared at that time as well. Most such fiction was published in only the last two years of that decade—1948 and 1949.[7] Homosexuality's threat to the postwar social order, as well as the plight of homosexuals, was extensively examined in novels, plays, and popular magazines.[8] In his comparative study of the writers from the two world wars, John Aldridge argued that post–World War II writers (such as John Horne Burns, Gore Vidal, Paul Bowles, Norman Mailer, Truman Capote, and Merle Miller) had to compensate for Hemingway's and Fitzgerald's exhaustion of the modernist tradition by developing "new subject matter which [had] not been fully exploited in the past and which, therefore, still [had] emotive power. They . . . made two important discoveries in this area—homosexuality and racial conflict."[9]

Images of the gay social world also began to surface in the mass media. Three of the more notable examples were: the famous gay bar scene in the popular 1962 Hollywood movie *Advise and Consent*, which was the first representation of gay life in movies since the Production Code was adopted in the 1930s; the 1964 *Life* magazine article called "Homosexuality in America"; and the 1969 *Esquire* article titled "The New Homosexual."[10]

Nevertheless, throughout the 1950s and early 1960s, the literary and popular sociology discourses on homosexuality were overshadowed by psychoanalysis, which remained the hegemonic discourse.[11] The Kinsey reports, for example, had almost no impact on psychoanalytic discussions. In fact, the psychoanalytic profession's writing on male homosexuality throughout the 1950s and early 1960s took on an ever more moralistic tone and tended increasingly to reflect conventional social values.[12]

The political hysteria of McCarthyism exacerbated the postwar demand for a return to an idealized version of prewar American life.[13] The political turmoil and anxieties of the late 1940s and early 1950s provoked reactions on a number of fronts, including Hollywood film noir, which depicted postwar anxieties about how returning war veterans could fit into American life;[14] the theater of Arthur Miller and Tennessee Williams;[15] and the outpouring of publications by intellectuals on the psychological pressures of conformism and the problem of alienation.[16]

Critical writing on the psychological and sociological consequences of conformism served as an important bridge to the discovery of the gay social world. Postwar conformism emphasized the norm and stigmatized the deviant—for instance, the homosexual. In this period, an academic literature on the sociology of deviance also emerged. Initially, deviance was interpreted as resulting from psychological maladjustment.

One man forcefully and articulately opposed this understanding of deviance, however. Psychoanalyst Robert Lindner was best known as the author of a book-length case history called *Rebel without a Cause: The Story of a Criminal Psychopath* (the movie of the same name shares little more than the title itself). In a series of essays first published in 1956 as *Must You Conform?* Lindner explored the issues of rebellious youth, political dissent, educational theory, and homosexuality.[17]

Lindner saw homosexuality as a "solution to the conflict between the urgency of the sexual instincts and repressive efforts brought to bear upon sexual expression by the reigning sex morality." He concluded then, "The condition is . . . a reaction of non-conformity, a rebellion of the personality that seeks to find—and discovers—a way in which to obtain expression for the confined erotic drives. . . . It seems that the issue of sexual conformity is raised more acutely and at an earlier period than it is with heterosexuals."[18]

Although Lindner promoted rebellion against conformity and criticized prejudice against homosexuals, he also claimed, "The proposal that homosexuality is directly related to sex-conformance pressure offers the hope that it can be eradicated." He believed that "homosexuality is the source of immense quantities of unhappiness and frustration of individuals and a chronically irritating generator of intrahuman hostility."[19] "To me," Lindner concluded, "it seems rather obvious that, while the refusal or (in some cases, perhaps) the inability to conform to fundamentally antibiological enforced morality traditionally and increasingly enforced in Western society is commendable, the character of this revolt must be designated negative."[20]

Toward the end of this same essay, Lindner published a long exchange of letters between himself and an unnamed Indonesian homosexual militant about the Homosexual World Organization and homosexual emancipation movements in Europe. "The meaning of this correspondence . . . is clear. It is all there: a history of hostility, contempt, and oppression, the appearance of an idealistic leadership, the formation of secret societies and an underground movement, the recruitment of allies and, at last, solidification and the attempt of expression. It means, in short, that another minority is discovering itself and beginning to struggle for its rights."[21]

Lindner devoted his life to combating one of the dominant myths of the 1950s and early 1960s—that nonconformity and mental illness are synonymous. Clearly, however, he was unable to disentangle himself from the psychoanalytic interpretation of homosexuality long enough to endorse unequivocally the homosexual revolt against the socially constructed ethos of conformity. Nor could he support the emergence of the homosexual social world. However admirable a homosexual movement might be, he sees it as a form of rebellion, as evidence that "culture, the maker of man . . . now threatens to unman him. . . . At this point culture, now designated Society, abandons humanity."[22]

Lindner is an interesting transitional figure between the postwar politics of adjustment and the sexual revolutionary credo of Norman Mailer, Herbert Marcuse, Norman O. Brown, and Paul Goodman, but Lindner never really freed himself from the conflation of psychoanalytic theory and conventional sexual norms.[23] Lindner viewed society as a repressive order that distorted and restrained instinctual biological energies. These energies, Lindner believed, formed the basis for rebellion against stale social conventions.[24] This discourse owes a great deal to the radical psychoanalyst Wilhelm Reich. In accordance with Reich's thinking on homosexuality, Lindner implied that heterosexuality and standard forms of gender behavior were biological norms. Lindner's work offers an interesting attempt to apply theories about the role of social processes and repression to homosexuality. Lindner and other radicals, however, were unable to acknowledge the positive role of social activity and institutionalized social life in the gay community.[25]

The ambivalence underlying the critique of conformism provided no useful way for most homosexuals to grapple with their identities. Given this ambivalence, it seemed impossible either to acknowledge their homosexuality actively, thereby suffering the rejection of a conformist society, or to view themselves as unhappy and frustrated rebels who should give up such a hopelessly negative form of revolt.[26]

In discussing homosexuality, neither the critical discourse on conformity and alienation nor mainstream journalism and the mass media could escape the powerful psychological and cultural norms that dominated American social life in this period. In addition, acknowledging homosexuality as a social problem did not immediately provide the symbolic capital necessary to banish the stigmatizing norms of mainstream American culture. Only exploring the existing social life of homosexuals could provide public categories of social knowledge about this everyday reality.

A POPULAR SOCIOLOGY OF HOMOSEXUALITY

During the 1950s and 1960s, popular sociology books frequently made the best-seller list. *The Lonely Crowd* (1950) by David Reisman, *The Organization Man* by William Whyte (1956), C. Wright Mills's *The Power Elite* (1956), Robert Lindner's *Must You Conform?* (1956), Vance Packard's *The Hidden Persuaders* (1957), Paul Goodman's *Growing up Absurd* (1960)—these books, which were all profoundly critical of the status quo and conformism, had tremendous influence on the American politics and culture of the period. They all grew out of a deep sense of frustration and were motivated by the possibility of social change. All of them recognized the growing desire for social reform in American life. Homosexuality was ripe for popular sociology. From 1951 through 1968, the year before the Stonewall riots, almost a dozen books were published that portrayed the social world of the homosexual.[27] Addressed to the general public, these popular sociology books explored homosexuality as a *social* problem—"perhaps *the most serious undiscussed problem* in the United States today," in the words of Martin Hoffman, author of *The Gay World*.[28]

It's not at all clear whether academic sociology had any influence whatsoever on these books of popular sociology.[29] Several authors—for example, Donald Webster Cory and Martin Hoffman—may have been aware of the interactionist tradition in American sociology, which influenced the sociology of deviance during 1960s.[30] Whether they were aware of it or not, their books would easily have fit into that tradition.

The interactionist tradition in sociology seeks to explain human action as a result of the meanings that interacting people attach to actions and things. For example, symbolic interactionists (one of the most influential schools in this tradition) interpreted deviance "not [as] a quality of the act a person commits but rather [as] the consequence of the application by others of rules and sanctions to an 'offender.' "[31] The interactionist tradition (going back to Georg Simmel, pragmatism, and George Herbert Mead) emphasizes sociation and interaction as the constitutive acts of the social.[32] This contrasts sharply with the concept of society that other authors expressed. For instance, Robert Lindner believed that all postwar forms of social life repressed "healthy" instinctual energies, and Jess Stern seemed to view social life as an ideal moral order threatened by deviant or decadent behavior.

Throughout this period, psychological works, which often treated homosexuality as an individualized pathological form of sexual behavior, remained the most influential nonfiction genre that addressed homosexuality for a general audience.[33] The new popular sociology approach marked a growing awareness that homosexual communities existed in American cities. Among the popular sociology authors, both Donald Cory and Martin Hoffman knew that the existence and development of a gay social world implied something new and important about homosexuality.

Although two of the popular sociology books explored lesbian life, this discourse was preoccupied primarily with male homosexuality. The emphasis on male homosexuality reflected a widespread preoccupation in U.S. society with its implications for masculinity. An obsession with effeminacy and its significance in gay male life pervades all the books that address male homosexuality. These authors commonly viewed homosexual desires as a threat to a man's masculinity. Cory emphatically downplays the cultural presence of flamboyant effeminacy. The queen, he states "is a rarity even in gay circles."[34] He does go on, however, to create a loving portrait of drag balls.[35] Stern, on the other hand, constantly uses words such as "mincing," "swishing," and "sashaying" as if they were objective terms of description. Hoffman doesn't even refer to effeminacy as an issue. It is certain, though, that effeminacy, camp humor, and drag were prominent aspects of gay life in the 1950s and early 1960s. We also know that fear of effeminacy prohibited many men from acknowledging their homosexuality and entering the gay social world.

The first work to reveal the social world of homosexuals came, naturally enough, from within the homosexual community itself. Donald Webster Cory, the pseudonymous alter ego of Edward Sagarin (who later, ironically, became an extremely homophobic critic of gay liberation), published the first exploration of homosexual society in 1951. Between 1951 and 1964, Cory and his occasional collaborator John P. LeRoy published the four most thorough and sophisticated books about homosexual life to predate Stonewall. Cory's books covered the full range of gay life—relationships, the social origins of homophobia, the role of gay bars, the significance of the gay contribution to culture, and a critique of the psychological theory of homosexuality. Cory's books probably never reached a very large public because they were all published by small presses, although at least one, *The Lesbian in America*, was reprinted as a mass-market paperback by MacFadden Books in 1965.[36]

It would be interesting to know what concrete social situation existed in 1951 that enabled Donald Webster Cory to write and publish *The Homosexual in America*—the first work of American popular sociology on homosexuality. The pseudonym Donald Webster Cory was an inverted play on "Corydon," the title and main interlocutor of André Gide's dialogues in defense of homosexuality. Cory's book, an ambitious defense of the homosexual way of life, derives its strength from his fundamental belief that homosexual patterns of behavior are socially constructed. Moreover, Cory quite self-consciously views the existence of a gay social world as the necessary foundation of homosexuals' happiness.[37] In his concluding chapter, he directly addresses his fellow homosexuals. "Do not fear the group life of the gay world," is one of his most ardent pleas. "In the gay life," he urges us, "you can be yourself and form friendships with those who know what you are and who acccpt you and love you. . . . The group life is not a thing of shame, a den of iniquity. It is a circle of protection, a necessary part of a minority society."[38]

But even such a profoundly sociological approach could not escape the hegemony of psychiatric discourse. In *The Homosexual in America*, Cory engages in a dialogue with mainstream American society and confronts its homophobia (a word not yet at his disposal). Although he addresses his fellow gay men (and to a much lesser extent lesbians), he devotes considerable energy to challenging the discourse of psychiatry. Over and over again, Cory takes on notions about homosexuals that derive from psychiatry—the causes of homosexuality, whether it is possible to cure homosexuals, whether sublimation allows people to avoid a homosexual way of life—and offers many strong and cogent criticisms of the psychiatric arguments.

If Cory displays any ambivalence, it is in the way he dismisses certain aspects of gay life that he finds negative. His discussion of effeminacy overlooks the cultural centrality of camp, and he dismisses as a stereotype the importance of queens in the gay life of the 1940s and 1950s. He glosses over the significance of alcoholism. There is no discussion at all of potentially embarrassing topics, such as sexually transmitted diseases or public sex in restrooms. The major tragedy of gay life is, in Cory's view, the need for concealment. He interprets many of

the psychological characteristics and social patterns of gay life as resulting from the stigma and the need for secrecy.

In the middle of this twenty-year publishing arc, Jess Stern produced
The Sixth Man (on male homosexuality) and *The Grapevine* (on lesbians).
They were published by Doubleday, one of the largest American publishing houses at that time. They also both appeared in mass-market
paperback form. A former reporter for the *New York Daily News* and an
editor of *Newsweek*, Jess Stern claimed that his study of male homosexuals, *The Sixth Man*, "is as unbiased a report . . . as a disinterested reporter could make it."[39] Despite his stated intention to adopt a neutral
journalistic approach, however, Stern's books displayed ambivalence,
hypocrisy, and contempt toward homosexuals.

With a false liberalism, he set out to report on "the everyday aspects
of the homosexual's world—his social adjustment to himself, his job,
his friends, and his family—but even more importantly, perhaps, the
non-homosexual's problem with him."[40] Homosexuality, in Stern's
view, was a tragedy for homosexuals and society. The homosexual
world, he wrote, was "a glittering make-believe world—at times tragic,
sometimes ludicrous, even comical." The dire aspect of gay life was so
apparent to him that he announced, "I had yet to meet a truly happy
homosexual."[41] This very idea of tragedy encapsulated the moralistic
liberal's patronizing expression of sympathy and contempt.

Stern set his exploration of the new gay social world within the
grand narrative of "the Decline of the West."[42] Virtually every chapter
recounted the negative impact of homosexuality on American life. Stern
devoted several chapters to the role of homosexuals in the fashion industry. These were the most vicious chapters in the book. He believed
that homosexuals had an overwhelmingly bad influence on the fashion
industry; in his view, they promoted fashion models who were beautiful but too thin and flat-chested, all because homosexuals hated
women and wanted them to look like boys.[43] Other chapters examined
the impact of homosexuals on the entertainment, white-collar, and fit-
ness industries, as well as the marriages of closeted gay men to unsus-
pecting women. Everywhere, from his perspective, the presence of homosexuals undermined the norms of gender roles and sexual decency
because homosexuals were secretive and vindictive.

Stern was not always able to shape his material to reflect his gloomy, conspiratorial vision, however. Occasionally, he encountered a gay person who was not ambivalent about being a homosexual, but he attempted to use such examples to demonstrate homosexuals' antisocial ethos. At one point, he interviewed a "typical American college boy" whom he found it difficult to believe was gay: "His face looked out alertly, a slight smile playing on sensitive lips. His hair a crewcut, his eyes clear. . . ." His conversation with the college boy, Frank, could almost be a dialogue between a young gay militant of the 1990s with a tough-minded liberal from the 1950s.

> "I'm quite happy being a homosexual. I don't want to be anything else."
> He seemed amused. "You remind me of my father," he said.
> I pointed out that I had understood he actually was not a confirmed homosexual, and could go either way. "You certainly don't look the part," I said.
> "You mean," he said almost mockingly, "I have a chance."
> He seemed to be enjoying himself. "If instead of trying to help us, people would just leave us alone, there would be no problem. . . ."
> "If everybody felt like you," I said, "it might be the end of the human race."
> "And what would be so horrible about that?" he asked with an engaging grin. "After all, if everything we read is true, we're on the verge of destruction any day, anyway."
> "Don't you feel there's a certain morality involved?"
> "I don't see how I'm being immoral by being with somebody who wants to be with me. There's no force or coercion, and I am not picking on small children."
> . . . "Don't you ever wonder whether you're kidding yourself?"
> His eyes went blank. "I don't understand."
> "Actually, haven't you chosen a way of life which is wrong, for purely selfish reasons, and are now trying to justify it philosophically?"
> He smiled almost pityingly. "Why should I have to justify it at all?"[44]

This young college student prefigured a new generation of homosexual men who were more and more visible in the books and magazines of the 1960s.

One of the most important contributions to the new discourse that built on the discovery of the social was Hendrik Ruitenbeek's anthology *The Problem of Homosexuality in Modern Society*, which Dutton published as a widely available quality paperback original. It captured perfectly the period's ambivalent mix of psychoanalysis and sociology. Ruitenbeek's anthology republished a series of classic psychoanalytic essays by Sandor Ferenczi, Abram Kardiner, and Clara Thompson on the theory of homosexuality. It also included Freud's famous and very positive statement, "Letter to an American Mother" about her son's homosexuality, Simone de Beauvoir's chapter from *The Second Sex* called "The Lesbian," and Evelyn Hooker's pathbreaking article on the psychologically well-adjusted homosexual; this was one of the only times (perhaps the sole instance) that one of Hooker's articles was made available to a broad public. The anthology also included a number of articles giving sociological descriptions of the homosexual community, as well as several pieces on hustlers and George Devereux's classic study of institutionalized homosexuality among the Mohave Indians. Although Ruitenbeek's anthology had a more intellectual tone than any of the other popular sociology books, it was widely available in paperback.

Toward the end of the period immediately before the Stonewall riots, Martin Hoffman's *The Gay World* appeared. Appropriately enough, in light of the political developments taking place then, Martin Hoffman's *The Gay World* is primarily set in San Francisco in 1966.[45] In addition to being the only one of these books to use the term *gay* in the title, it was also published in a widely circulated mass-market paperback format that still shows up frequently in secondhand bookstores. Like the work of Robert Lindner and many of these popular sociology books (except for the work of Donald Cory), *The Gay World* is an amalgam of sociological observation and psychiatric expertise. It offers a fairly positive account of gay social life—tinged only with a concern for the difficult and sad state of affairs that homosexuals must experience.

Popular sociology represented the discovery by both homosexuals and nonhomosexuals of an image of the gay social world—an imagined community. Both kinds of people read these books and articles "to find themselves" through a process of either identification or counteridentification. They read these works to sort out their relation to the imagined homosexual world of American society in the 1950s and 1960s. In many of these works, particularly those by authors who were not openly homosexual, even those that represented themselves as sympathetic, homosexuals' lives were presented as tortured and unfulfilled, at the very least because of social oppression.

Reading such an ambivalent discourse generated "misrecognitions" for the individual undergoing a process of homosexual identity formation.[46] There were several different types of gay readers. Many, probably most, of the male homosexuals who were already familiar with the gay social world had found it by going to bars, by cruising parks and toilets, and through friends. The vast majority of homosexuals, however, were isolated and asocial members of the homosexual minority—they were in the closet. These closeted gay men used the popular sociology, literary, and psychoanalytic discourses to name themselves, describe themselves, judge themselves—and, by these means, to homosexualize themselves.

"MY OWN PRIVATE DISCOURSE": READING IN THE CLOSET

By the time I graduated from college in 1964, I was twenty-one years old. I had come to see myself as homosexual—"queer," as I often thought with a vacillating mixture of acceptance and self-contempt. I had still had no experience of the homosexual world itself, although I did have a number of homosexual affairs in college. I had put together my own representation of the homosexual world primarily from fictional works and books such as Hendrik Ruitenbeek's anthology.

During college, my main strategy of "consciousness raising" (or as we might say now, identity formation) was reading.[47] For a young college student who had little contact (or even initially, little idea of how to have contact) with other homosexual men or the gay community, this was an essential way of learning about homosexuality. As Roland Barthes observed, "Reading is steeped in Desire (or Disgust)."[48]

Later, during summer vacations, I supplemented my reading by cruising in Washington Square Park. Reading and cruising are not such dissimilar techniques. Both require one to "read" signs and to construct a discourse that opens one to a knowledge of homosexualities and a long process of reconstruction of one's sense of self.[49] Responding to or identifying with cultural themes and figures has helped people significantly to crystallize homosexual identities; for men, it has worked to take an interest in opera, female popular singers, or art, or even to have a strong disinterest in sports. Cultural media have often been extremely important to homosexuals' personal development. Reading also always involves the "double misreading of [the reader's] unconscious and of his ideology," according to Barthes. In this process of reading, as Barthes suggests, one rediscovers one's desires, fantasies, and even one's imagined place in society.[50]

"My own private discourse" began when I had my first homosexual affair during the summer after my sophomore year of high school. Richie and I decided that we weren't fags as long as we didn't kiss— although we fucked and sucked. Did I really believe that I wasn't a fag if we didn't kiss? I don't think so, but I thought my agreeing with that statement would reassure Richie.

I have no memory of what led me to James Baldwin's *Giovanni's Room*.[51] It was sometime later, after Richie and I had stopped seeing one another. It may have been an accident that I discovered it at the main library on Staten Island.[52] *Giovanni's Room* was the most explicit rendering of homosexual love I had ever encountered. My vivid memory of some scenes dates from my first reading. In *Giovanni's Room*, Baldwin recounted the main character David's first homosexual affair as an adolescent. This affair was a transfigurative experience of love, but David says it also opened up a "cavern . . . in my mind, black, full of rumor, suggestion. . . . I could have cried, cried for shame and terror, cried for not understanding how this could have happened to me."[53] After repeated flights from homosexual relationships, David becomes involved with a woman, Hella, only to fall in love once more with a man, Giovanni. Although Baldwin offered a positive portrait of homosexual love, it was doomed to fail, largely because the gay social world—haunted by the desperate search for sex—could not sustain it.

I began to look for other books that would help me understand myself. Soon I found *Advertisements for Myself* by Norman Mailer.[54] It contained two essays—"The White Negro" and "The Homosexual Villain"—that gave me license me to think more adventurously about my homosexuality.

"The Homosexual Villain" was a modest and candid piece that Mailer wrote for the homosexual rights magazine *One*. In the essay, Mailer examined the way he had characterized several villains in his novels as homosexuals. What particularly impressed me was his laudatory discussion of Donald Webster Cory's *The Homosexual in America*. "I can think of few books," Mailer wrote, "which cut so radically at my prejudices and altered my ideas so profoundly." Mailer realized that he had been closing himself off from understanding a very large part of life.[55] He also acknowledged that Cory's book had helped him to realize that his anxieties about "latent homosexuality" had disappeared when he accepted homosexuals: "Close friendships with homosexuals had become possible without sexual desire or even sexual nuance—at least no more sexual nuance than is present in all human relations."[56]

The other essay, "The White Negro," became my credo, my political manifesto. The essay was full of foolish, even repugnant things, but it also enunciated a philosophy of risk and psychological growth. It synthesized existentialism, the liberatory potential of jazz and black culture, sexual radicalism, and the violence of the psychopath. How often I would examine myself and strive to be one of those with the "knowledge that what is happening at each instant of the electric present is . . . good or bad for their cause, their love, their action, their need," and recognize that I was "moving through each moment of life forward into growth or backward into death."

"The White Negro" was a direct descendant of Robert Lindner's *Rebel without a Cause* (which Mailer quoted at length), for the white Negro was the hipster, the psychopath, the American existentialist.[57] Where Lindner had been unwilling to endorse homosexuality as rebellion against conformity, however, Mailer wholeheartedly included homosexuality as one form of sexual radicalism. Mailer's discussions in these two essays—of the sexual radicalism of black culture, and of homosexuality—contributed to my growing consciousness of homosexuality's social implications.

Norman Mailer's vision of the pivotal role of black culture and its sexual radicalism encouraged me to look to the black experience for lessons relevant to my situation as a homosexual. This was further reinforced when I discovered, through Leslie Fiedler's *Love and Death in the American Novel*, the homoerotic tradition in American literature that paired a white man with a man of color—for example, Ishmael and Queequeg, Huck Finn and Jim. Fiedler's book was rather homophobic (which I was quite aware of at the time); his Freudian analysis of American fiction emphasized the paucity of "mature" heterosexual relationships. I was grateful, nevertheless, that he had identified homoerotic themes in American fiction.

Exploring the homoerotic tradition in American literature provided a counterpoint to my other reading about black civil rights and black cultural politics, which allowed me to think through and politicize homosexual issues. Baldwin's homosexuality, and then the publication in 1962 of the essays that later made up *The Fire Next Time*, made him the perfect guide into my new homosexual "identity politics" (as it later came to be called). My awareness of the politics of identity was soon reinforced when "black power" emerged.

In those years, Baldwin explored the tragedy of difference, of divisions created by power and violence, of "definitions" of black and white, male and female, that we cannot transcend. In the novels and essays I read in this period, Baldwin seemed to explore the possibility of love and the difference that love might make in America's racial conflicts and in our sexual lives. He reached for "a region where there were no definitions of any kind, neither of color nor of male and female."[58]

Although Baldwin rejected any relationship to "the gay community,"[59] he did believe that homosexuality was a legitimate form of love. Baldwin was deeply ambivalent about homosexuality, yet for me his ambivalence was productive. He helped me situate my thinking about it in light of the most important social issues of the day. Coming to terms with homosexuality was part of my relationship to politics and society. Baldwin's vision of love, Mailer's sexual politics, and the homoerotic current of American literature encouraged me to enter into relationships with black men, which I pursued, off and on, for fifteen years.[60] Through my identification with Baldwin and my new sexual experiences, I began to think of myself as part of a minority—and the struggles of African Americans seemed linked to my own.

In addition to reading black writers, I explored the fiction of Jean Genet and John Rechy. On a more abstract level, I read *Corydon*, André Gide's defense of homosexuality; Jean-Paul Sartre's famous discussion of bad faith and authenticity in *Being and Nothingness*, in which he used the homosexual as an example; and the radical Freudian books of Herbert Marcuse and Norman O. Brown.

The "private" discourse of reading eventually opens up into social life.[61] Roland Barthes pointed out that "to read is to decode: letters, words, meanings, structures . . . but by accumulating decodings . . . the reader is caught up in a dialectical reversal: finally he does not decode, he *overcodes*."[62] Homosexual readers emancipate themselves by coding over the guilty knowledge they acquired by growing up in a homophobic society. By reading, they were able to discover practical knowledge of homosexuals who live communally and can transform this knowledge for their own use.

At some point as a homosexual reader, I began to accept my task as a historical actor. My intellectual development found no outlet until I moved to New York City after graduating in 1964 and began acquiring more sexual experience. During the Summer of Love in 1967, I first walked hand-in-hand with a man on the Lower East Side and publicly socialized with other gay people. I vividly remember reading the July 3, 1969, issue of the *Village Voice* with its account of the Stonewall riots. In the following months, I began to come out to my friends. When I moved to Philadelphia in 1970, I went as an openly gay man and was active in the gay movement there. I had finally entered the gay social world.

THE SOCIAL IN THE HEART OF THE INDIVIDUAL

We do not have empirical evidence revealing the effect that popular sociology discourse about homosexuality may have had on lesbians and gay men in the 1950s and 1960s. The appearance of that discourse, however, as well as the growing public discussion of homosexuality as a social problem, made a very significant contribution, I believe. When the social was discovered and elaborated in a number of discourses about homosexuality, it made explicit unrecognized factors governing the constitution of a homosexual social world. The public representation of a homosexual social world entered the network of homosexual discourses and altered psychiatry's dominant discourse on homosexuality.

When I realized how hard it is to evaluate the effects of recognizing the social dimension of homosexual life, I began to reflect on my own process of homosexualization. The popular sociology discourse emerged when I was struggling to come to terms with my homosexual desire. As a comparative exercise, I offer the history of my reading and sexuality against the backdrop of the discovery of the social. The social entered "my own private discourse" through many streams: Mailer's radical sexual politics, the homoerotic tradition in American literature, Ruitenbeek's social-psychoanalytical essays, and Baldwin's personal acceptance of homosexuality and his ultimate rejection of the gay social world.[63] By means of a personally constructed discourse, the social can be found in the very heart of the individual.[64]

The new political discourses of gay liberation dramatically reduced the gap between the privatized discourses of the closet and the public discourses of the social. The homosexual political movement that emerged in the wake of the Stonewall riots and feminism was thoroughly grounded in a social perspective. The gay liberation movement made one of its major priorities the dismantling of the psychiatric dominance of homosexual discourse.

Part Two Intellectuals and
Cultural Politics

Homosexual emancipation, like the Enlightenment, entails two interrelated projects: first, the political task of self-assertion in which homosexuals claim human dignity and rights; and second, an epistemo-
logical project that critically dismantles that strange syndrome of
incomprehension and knowledge called "homosexuality." These two
projects are intimately intertwined.[1] They are also in a state of tension—
homosexuals are pulled between erecting an "identity" and deconstructing a "behavior," between a historically and culturally specific
construction and an apparently universal, not to say natural, phenomenon.

Homosexual politics, as a project of self-assertion, nevertheless cannot take place without both self-knowledge and the production of
"worldly" knowledge. Homosexual activists are intellectuals, almost by

99

definition, and intellectuals who are homosexual have played an important role in this joint project—that is, constructing and deconstructing the interplay of power and knowledge that shapes homosexual possibilities.

The emergence of lesbian and gay studies as a recognized disciplinary field in the university is one of the most critical components of homosexual emancipation. Through its institutionalization in the university, the production of new knowledge—particularly of the complex interrelations of sexuality, gender, and varieties of transgendered experience—has received a major investment of intellectual skills, time, and resources. This moment represents a decisive shift in the political-intellectual life of homosexual communities. Until the mid-1980s, knowledge production and intellectual activity about lesbian and gay life largely took place outside the university, often as homosexuals organized and built communities.

The chapters in this part assess the significance of that shift. I wrote chapter 4, "Inside the Ivory Closet," in 1989, just a few years after a new wave of lesbian and gay studies had begun to surface. The essay represents a snapshot of the field at that time. An exercise in the sociology of knowledge, the essay sketches the development of lesbian and gay studies as an academic field since the early 1970s. I compare the new wave with one that had occurred almost fifteen years earlier. The two waves and the generations that contributed to the development of lesbian and gay studies have had very different career patterns and academic specialties. The first generation of gay and lesbian scholars often came from history and anthropology, whereas the later generation has emerged from literary, cultural, and film studies.

Many leaders of the new wave were unhappy with the essay. One argument particularly bothered them—that the new wave might lose touch with the lesbian and gay community. Although this dissatisfaction rarely showed up in print, there were many comments *sotto voce* at the Lesbian and Gay Studies Conference held in 1991 shortly after its publication. A *New York Times* reporter doing a piece on the emergence of lesbian and gay studies said to me in reference to the piece, "You're certainly an unpopular person here." A few years later, Lisa

Duggan discussed some of the controversy around the article in *GLQ,*
a lesbian and gay studies journal.[2]

Chapter 5, "From Community to University," is a revised version of
an essay that I wrote as a sequel to "Inside the Ivory Closet." I wanted
to expand the historical framework within which lesbian and gay studies are discussed. In "From Community to University," I compare in
detail the intellectual styles of different generations of scholars in lesbian and gay studies. This essay situates five influential paradigms in
the generational experiences of lesbian and gay intellectuals: the search
for authenticity (1969–1976), the social construction of identity (1976–
present), essential identity (1975–present), difference and race (1979–
present), and cultural studies (1985–present)—or as it is now called,
queer theory. Since I first published the essay, the intellectual dominance of the cultural studies paradigm has grown enormously. Although many "older" Stonewall scholars—the "old-guard humanistic
intellectual elite" as Steven Seidman called them[3]—have published important work in the last four or five years,[4] cultural studies scholarship
has literally poured from the presses and has been incredibly influential
for a new generation of graduate students.[5]

The third essay in the series also grew out of reaction to "Inside the
Ivory Closet." After I published what is now chapter 4, I found myself
in an awkward position. I was not an academic; what kind of relationship did I have to lesbian and gay studies? I did have a long history,
dating back to 1970, as an activist, editor, writer, publisher, and intellectual in the gay and lesbian community. Could I not speak legitimately as a community-based intellectual about "lesbian and gay studies"? How was my relationship to the community different from that
of academics? This issue took on a personal edge when a prominent
member of the post-Stonewall generation who teaches at an Ivy League
university dismissed my intellectual "credentials" while making a pass
at my lover. Which of us had the "authority" to speak about the intellectual status of lesbian and gay studies?

Chapter 6, "Intellectuals, Identity Politics, and the Contest for Cultural Authority," explores this tension between lesbian and gay academics and community-based intellectuals. Each kind of intellectual

produces different types of knowledge. The academic generates "disciplinary" knowledge within the formal fields of academic life. This type of knowledge is legitimated by its production within the university. The community intellectual produces "vernacular knowledge," which is more value-laden and more oriented toward communal solidarity. The contest between academics and community intellectuals for cultural authority is destructive—both disciplinary and vernacular knowledge are valuable and necessary—and each group suffers from a lack of critical dialogue with the other.

The last two essays in this part were both stimulated by books. Each essay approaches the role of intellectuals from an oblique angle. One discusses intellectuals, politics, and the university, whereas the other examines the inadequate conception of the social in queer theory. Chapter 7, "Pessimism of the Mind," starts from a review of Allan Bloom's *The Closing of the American Mind* and Russell Jacoby's *The Last Intellectuals*. This essay examines the role of the intellectual in post-1960s American society. Both Bloom and Jacoby criticize American intellectual life—Bloom for its domination by poststructuralism and the Left, and Jacoby because the intellectuals of his generation have gone into academia rather than playing a public role. Both Bloom and Jacoby overlook the vitality of intellectual life in social movements (the feminist and environmental movements) and minority communities (the lesbian and gay, Latino, or African American community). From the late 1960s through the 1970s and for most of the 1980s, community intellectuals—whether black, feminist, lesbian and gay, or environmentalist—served as public intellectuals, although they were rarely included in mainstream media.

Chapter 8, "Under the Sign of the Queer," discusses *Fear of a Queer Planet*, an anthology about queer politics and social theory that Michael Warner edited. In the essay, I examine whether queer theory and cultural studies can adequately serve as a basis for social theory about homosexuality. Warner offers a number of important arguments about the following matters: heteronormativity's impact on social theory, the implication of "the queer nature" of the world, and the shift from a rights-based confrontation with intolerance to a critique of normalization.

Queer theory, however, focuses too exclusively on the discursive aspects of knowledge or power and not enough on political and economic domination or the historical-social structures of repression. Ironically, our age demonstrates an awe-inspiring sophistication about cultural representations but is otherwise marked by a grave underestimation—perhaps even ignorance—of the social. Many political projects, improvement schemes, public policies, psychological therapies, and business plans betray a deeply flawed understanding of social and historical processes, sometimes to the point of self-destruction. In the lesbian and gay communities, there are many people who are naive about how social processes work—for example, queer theorists, media consultants, recovery participants, sincerely "politically correct" activists, and gay business owners.

Lesbian and gay studies reflects the twin goals of homosexual liberation—self-assertion and more reliable knowledge of homosexuality. In our society, lesbian and gay life has just recently surfaced from the shadow of long-term historical processes. We know so much about everyday gay and lesbian life mostly because of vernacular forms of knowledge. Yet, we also need the disciplined production of knowledge of social scientists, cultural scholars, and psychologists. Lesbian and gay studies absolutely depends on a substratum of vernacular knowledges. Dialogue between intellectuals and activists in the community, the university, and government agencies is the only guarantee we can have of access to self-knowledge.

4 INSIDE THE IVORY CLOSET

The Challenge Facing Lesbian and Gay Studies

Over the last four years, research centers, graduate seminars, under-graduate courses, and publishing programs in lesbian and gay studies have been established at a number of institutions across the country: Yale University, City University of New York (CUNY), City College of San Francisco (CCSF), Massachusetts Institute of Technology (MIT), University of California at Santa Cruz, and Duke University. Even though this development is a major step forward, it is an unsteady one. A gap is widening between the field's new historicists and the lesbian and gay communities, creating anew the same conflict between community responsibility and academic respectability that has divided eth-

This chapter is a slightly revised version of an essay originally published in *OUT/LOOK* 3, no. 2 (fall 1990).

nic and women's studies since their tumultuous beginnings. The growth of lesbian and gay studies forces an examination of whether it should, or can, exist without structural ties to lesbian and gay political struggles. Is it fair to insist on such relations between a community and its intellectuals?

Lesbian and gay studies brings together two waves or generations of scholars. One is a group of writers and scholars who experienced the euphoria of Stonewall and the women's movement in the early 1970s. Many of them are established professors who, as out academics, gained tenure only after brutal political battles and now teach at less prestigious institutions where they have less time to conduct research and to write because they have heavy teaching loads. Others are independent writers and scholars unaffiliated with any academic institution. Their books, essays, and articles broke fresh ground in the early days of lesbian and gay politics. Dennis Altman, John D'Emilio, Martin Duberman, Karla Jay, Jonathan Ned Katz, and Esther Newton are important figures in this early generation on both sides of the academic fence.

The second, younger group of scholars are ambitious young teachers and bright graduate students who trained at elite universities and who occupy jobs at more prestigious institutions. John Boswell, Lee Edelman, David Halperin, and Eve Kosofsky Sedgwick represent this post-Stonewall generation. In contrast to their predecessors, they emphasize sophisticated interpretation of texts rather than the social history or sociology of gay life.

These two generations take radically different approaches to their writing and research, and each finds itself in a correspondingly different relation to the lesbian and gay community. Influenced by work in social history and anthropology, the Stonewall-generation scholars relied on the community both for support and as a critical audience. Their work grew out of questions that had preoccupied lesbians and gay men in their struggles to forge strong, visible communities. The most original contributions on the history, culture, and sociology of gay life came largely from writers and intellectuals either situated outside the university or employed only occasionally as part-time or temporary lecturers. This group included Allan Bérubé, Jonathan Ned Katz, Audre Lorde, Kate Millett, Cherríe Moraga, and Vito Russo. These Stonewall scholars were in constant dialogue with the community.

Now, the apparently successful institutionalization of lesbian and gay studies in the university has created a new framework for gay scholarship that increasingly excludes those independent writers and scholars. The post-Stonewall generation has been able to take the development of lesbian and gay communities and many of their gains for granted. Turning away from social history and anthropology to the textual concerns of literary and cultural criticism, the younger generation uses a language that, for all its literary brilliance, is quite difficult. The links between the university and the communities were rendered less visible, reflected in the fact that this new wave of lesbian and gay scholars has not managed to incorporate women and people of color into their ranks and analyses. Together with the stylistic shift from the kind of research that the Stonewall generation produced to the new generation's more academic literary and cultural interpretations, these changes may create an unbridgeable gap between academics and the community.

GAY REVOLUTION IN THE UNIVERSITY?

The current round of new programs in lesbian and gay studies do not represent the first time that lesbian and gay scholars have tried to break out of the ivory closet. The early days of the gay movement were full of intellectual ferment. Almost immediately after Stonewall, a flood of books, periodicals, and other publications found an audience eager to explore the political and cultural implications of lesbian-feminism and gay liberation. The powerful lesbian-feminist manifesto "The Woman-Identified Woman" (written collectively by a group called Radicalesbians) was published in 1970. A year later, Dennis Altman published *Homosexual: Oppression and Liberation*, the first book after Stonewall on the politics of gay liberation. Between 1972 and 1978, Karla Jay and Allan Young published a series of anthologies (*Out of the Closets, After*

You're Out, Lavender Culture) that explored gay and lesbian history, psychological theories, the problems and possibilities of coming out, lesbian and gay culture before and after Stonewall, the gay movement's relation to the Left, the women's movement, the black civil rights movement, sex roles, and the images of gay men and lesbians in the media.

Scholars of the Stonewall generation made an effort to bring gay liberation and feminist perspectives to bear on their research and writing when they founded the Gay Academic Union (GAU) in March 1973. Professors, writers, students, and librarians banded together and, backed by three hundred like-minded people, sponsored the first GAU conference on November 23 and 24, 1973. New York hosted two other conferences before political divisions broke up the group: the annual conference moved out to Los Angeles, while GAU in New York maintained a shadowy existence for several years.

GAU grew out of a need to confront the virulent homophobia of academia. But from the very beginning, this early attempt to create a place for lesbian and gay studies also had to contend with the institutionalized gender imbalance of the university system. The organization was overwhelmingly male in membership, and the few women who attended meetings were constantly put in the awkward position of challenging the sexist comments and underlying chauvinism of their male colleagues. Divisions among the men occurred along lines of Left-versus-Right politics. Initially, GAU responded by publishing a political statement of purpose that listed opposition to all forms of discrimination against women within academia as the first priority and opposition to all forms of discrimination against gay people as the second. Nevertheless, all three GAU conferences in New York were marked by increasingly bitter confrontations between lesbians and gay men. By 1975, the radical gay men and most of the lesbians had left GAU.

The rapid growth of women's studies programs in the 1970s provided a safe space for courses with lesbian content and themes. For a while, lesbian studies thrived. The ideological basis for many of these courses was "cultural feminism," which emphasized the idea of a "female nature" and proposed the construction of a woman's culture reflecting that nature. The lesbian community seemed to fit this theoretical model as an example of a woman's culture unsullied by male domination.

Lesbian-feminism—defined by important pieces such as "The Woman-Identified Woman," the Radicalesbian manifesto, Jill Johnston's *Lesbian Nation*, and Adrienne Rich's essay "Compulsory Heterosexuality and Lesbian Existence"—presented lesbianism as an alternative model for female identity. Some of the major contributions to lesbian studies—such as Lillian Faderman's history of romantic friendship among women, *Surpassing the Love of Men*—were written in this tradition. Most significantly, women's studies programs often created a safe place for lesbians to come out and familiarize themselves with lesbian culture. In the 1980s, as these programs came under attack from conservatives and fell victim to budget cutbacks, the lesbian content of the courses was downplayed or eliminated.

OUTSIDE THE WALLS OF ACADEME

Battles for tenure and promotion hurt the Stonewall generation in its attempts to build an institutional framework for research on lesbian and gay life. The widespread homophobia of academic life discouraged many scholars from devoting themselves to research on homosexual themes. Emotionally drained by faculty politics, heavy teaching loads, and their colleagues' rejection of the legitimacy of research on homosexuality, many gay academics retreated into self-imposed exile. Most serious research on gay and lesbian life came from scholarly writers and intellectuals outside the university. Their work appeared in books, community newspapers, and magazines such as the *Body Politic, Sinister Wisdom, Gay Community News, Heresies,* and the *Advocate,* or in leftist journals such as *Radical America* and *Socialist Review.*

Although gay scholars gave up trying to form a national organization to advance lesbian and gay studies, some continued to work on their own research projects in isolation or outside the university. The new leftist idea of history from the bottom up, combined with the feminist motto "The Personal Is the Political," gave intellectual significance to what appeared individual and private. The widespread interest in black and women's social history inspired some activist-writers to look at gay history.

In 1971, gay activist Jonathan Ned Katz launched his research, starting only from the presumption that gay American history actually existed. In June 1972, he mounted a dramatization of some of his early discoveries in a documentary play *Coming Out*, modeled on Martin Duberman's successful off-Broadway play *In White America*. Eventually, Katz's research led to two huge collections of lesbian and gay historical documents: *Gay American History*, published in 1976, and *Gay/Lesbian Almanac*, published in 1983. Katz also served as the general editor of the Arno Press series called Homosexuality: Lesbians and Gay Men in Society, History, and Literature. He directed a massive reprinting of over one hundred books, both classic and obscure, from the nineteenth and twentieth centuries, that dealt with homosexuality. Also in the early 1970s, John D'Emilio and James Steakley—graduate students in history and German literature, respectively, as well as gay activists— explored homosexual emancipation movements in America during the 1940s and 1950s and in pre-Nazi Germany. First published in the Canadian gay journal the *Body Politic*, their work eventually appeared in book form. Lesbians and gay men interested in the past started community history projects such as the Lesbian Herstory Archives in New York and the San Francisco Lesbian and Gay History Project, where they collected historical materials and began to publish their results.

Throughout this period of apparent institutional dormancy—from the mid-1970s up to the late 1980s—some gay teachers, such as Jack Collins at City College of San Francisco, continued to teach lesbian or gay courses. In small liberal colleges, at big state schools, and in some elite universities, openly gay and lesbian teachers kept up the fight in their departments to teach courses dealing with homosexuality. In some instances, students took up the gauntlet and designed courses they taught themselves with the help of faculty sponsors.

During the following years, women's and gay caucuses formed in a number of academic professional associations, including the Modern Language Association (for teachers of language and literature), the

American Sociological Association, the American Psychological Association, the American Anthropological Association, and the American Historical Association. These groups became forums in which openly gay and closeted academics alike could meet and discuss research on homosexual themes, as well as addressing job and research biases within the professions. In this same period, the *Journal of Homosexuality* gradually transformed its focus. Founded in 1974 by psychologist Charles Silverstein (coauthor with Edmund White of *The Joy of Gay Sex*), and edited since 1977 by John DeCecco of San Francisco State University, it changed from a narrowly focused journal of psychology into a broad interdisciplinary journal of lesbian and gay studies.[1]

This outpouring of lesbian and gay social thought and history in the early 1970s initially assumed that the homosexual experience in different periods of history and in different cultures reveals a type of human personality called the homosexual. Scholars looked for their antecedents as a way of claiming ancestors, of validating themselves through the achievements of great and famous queers and dykes. They searched for evidence that homosexuality is transhistorical, natural, or essential. Arthur Evans wrote articles in this vein for the radical political newspaper *Fag Rag,* and then in his 1978 book *Witchcraft and the Gay Counterculture.*[2] In the book, Evans linked the persecution of gay people to the repression of pagan witches. This book became an important source for the fairy movement, which celebrates gay male spirituality.

Lesbian and gay historians also discovered that homosexual activity frequently took place in some societies without the presence of people defined as "homosexuals," and that intense homosocial or erotic relationships existed between people who did not otherwise appear to be homosexuals. One solution to these puzzles had already been ventured by the British sociologist Mary McIntosh, whose scholarly paper "The Homosexual Role" had been published in the American academic journal *Social Problems* in 1968—even before Stonewall. Challenging the belief that "homosexuals" and "heterosexuals" were different kinds of people, McIntosh argued that homosexuality should be seen as a social role rather than a natural condition. Furthermore, she claimed that the social role describes not simply a pattern of sexual behavior but other kinds of cultural activities as well.

A group of young British gay leftists worked out the historical and political implications of McIntosh's thinking in their journal *Gay Left* (1975 to 1979). This perspective on the emergence of the homosexual identity informed Jeffrey Weeks's *Coming Out: Homosexual Politics in Britain from the Nineteenth Century to the Present*, published in 1977. The Gay Left Collective writers elaborated on the making of the "modern homosexual" in a series of essays that they later collected in two anthologies: *Homosexuality: Power and Politics*, which they edited, and *The Making of the Modern Homosexual*, which Kenneth Plummer edited.[3]

Eventually, this approach to gay history was identified as the social-constructionist theory of homosexual identity. French historian Michel Foucault's 1978 work *History of Sexuality* offered a similar account of the historical creation of the homosexual identity, but his work also presented a full-scale philosophical critique of "essentialism"—the belief that sexual identity is natural or has always existed, unaffected by social context.

The development of a social-constructionist interpretation of homosexual history is one of the major intellectual achievements of the Stonewall generation of lesbian and gay scholars. This theoretical paradigm provides the criteria for historical and social research. Thus, the question that would send the social constructionist off to the archives would be, for instance, "Why doesn't every society organize homosexuality in the same way that the classical Greeks did?" rather than "Why did the Christian Church repress the natural impulse of homosexual love?"

Another intellectual development in the 1980s that made a major contribution to thinking about lesbian (and, by implication, gay male) identity was the publication of *This Bridge Called My Back*. Gloria Anzaldúa, Audre Lorde, Cherríe Moraga, and Barbara Smith, among others, contributed essays, poetry, and personal narratives to this anthology. Along with other books such as *Sister Outsider* (Lorde, 1984), *Home Girls* (edited by Smith, 1983), *Borderlands* (Anzaldúa, 1987), and *Loving in the War Years* (Moraga, 1983), *This Bridge Called My Back* proposed a new way of thinking about cultural identity and difference.

These women of color criticized the impulse, widely prevalent among cultural feminists, to emphasize the essential similarities of all women, rather than the differences of race, sexuality, and class among women. *This Bridge Called My Back* warned against an enforced women's identity and, by implication, all attempts to downplay or disregard differences of color, gender, and sexuality. These writers' exploration of the overlapping identities of gender, race, and sexuality also implies criticism of universalistic conceptions of the making of the homosexual identity. It dealt a double blow, however, to lesbian-feminist theory; not only did it subvert essentialist models of female identity, but it also challenged feminist thinking about lesbian sexuality. For example, in "What We're Rollin around in Bed with," a 1981 article in *Heresies*, Amber Hollibaugh and Cherríe Moraga looked at sexual roles, fantasy, and S/M as examples of sexual differences within the lesbian community. They saw simplistic notions of egalitarian relationships and the belief in politically correct sex as obstacles to freedom and an understanding of the true breadth of sexuality.

The political significance of different paradigms in lesbian and gay studies became apparent when lesbian and gay social constructionists clashed with cultural feminists over pornography and sexuality. Relying on gay and lesbian historical research that showed a wide range of sexual behavior and conceptions of identity among lesbians and gay men, social constructionists argued that shifting economic contexts, aesthetic standards, and social roles define sexual practices, sexual fantasy, and pornography. Cultural feminists, on the other hand, interpreted pornography as a transhistorical instrument of male domination and compulsory heterosexuality. These sex wars generated a body of groundbreaking writing that appeared in anthologies such as *Pleasure and Danger*, which Carole Vance edited, and *Powers of Desire*, which Ann Snitow, Christine Stansell, and Sharon Thompson edited.[4]

BIRTH PANGS OF A DISCIPLINE

Somewhere within this far-flung constellation of openly gay teachers, student-initiated courses, independent scholars, history projects, and journals, a post-Stonewall generation of lesbian and gay scholars emerged. Among the new generation are John Boswell, author of a widely read and reviewed book on Christian attitudes toward gay people in medieval Europe; Eve Kosofsky Sedgwick, who has explored male homosexuality and homosocial desire in literature; David Miller, author of an acclaimed book on police in the Victorian novel; David Halperin, who has pioneered a new interpretation of homosexuality in ancient Greece; and Lee Edelman, who has published a string of brilliant papers on gay literature, including a famous essay on the AIDS activist slogan "Silence = Death."[5]

Although the scholarship of this new generation builds on the large body of research in history and culture accumulated since the early 1970s, it also draws deeply on French cultural theory—on the work of authors such as Michel Foucault and Jacques Derrida who have written on sexuality, gender, and the social power of language and metaphor. This synthesis of social and cultural history with the sophisticated interpretative techniques of French critical theory ties the post-Stonewall generation to a new tendency in literary and cultural studies called "the new historicism." These new theoretical influences make the work of this new generation difficult and obscure to those outside the academy, and yet, at the same time, they have also secured the post-Stonewall generation's place in academia.

Now scholars from both the older and younger generations have banded together to create a new field of research and teaching, as well as the institutions to sustain it. In 1986, Martin Duberman and John Boswell initiated a new trend of faculty leadership by bringing together a group of scholars from both generations to start the Center for Lesbian and Gay Studies at Yale. The original group split, disagreeing about the participation of women, minorities, and independent scholars, but many other groups have established different academic programs that could eventually become the basis for officially recognized lesbian and gay studies. Boswell and a group of junior faculty and graduate students at Yale have held three annual conferences on lesbian and gay studies, with the fourth scheduled to take place this fall at Harvard.[6] Duberman, Esther Newton, and George Chauncey, all of whom had originally worked on the effort at Yale, have started the Committee for Lesbian and Gay Studies at CUNY. MIT and Columbia have special research seminars, the University of California at Santa Cruz sponsored a "Queer Theory" conference, and Duke planned a graduate seminar. At many of these institutions, regular departments of literature, sociology, and history also offer undergraduate and graduate courses on lesbian or gay themes.

So far, though, the only place with an officially established and funded department of gay and lesbian studies is CCSF. The guiding spirit and first chair of the department, Jack Collins, received his Ph.D. in comparative literature from Stanford and has taught a popular course in gay literature since 1972. The third largest single-campus community college in the United States, CCSF offers the lesbian and gay courses to undergraduates and those in its adult education programs.

The 1980 publication of John Boswell's *Christianity, Social Tolerance, and Homosexuality* by the University of Chicago Press marked the first mainstream success of the post-Stonewall generation of scholarship. Boswell's book was favorably reviewed throughout the national press and featured in mass-circulation magazines such as *Newsweek*. Since then, the University of Chicago Press has become a preeminent academic publisher of lesbian and gay studies, with an impressive list of authors and titles: John D'Emilio's *Sexual Politics, Sexual Communities*, David Greenberg's *The Construction of Homosexuality*,[7] *The Lesbian Issue* (a reprint of Chicago's women's studies journal *SIGNS*), and Esther Newton's *Mother Camp*. It will soon publish a new journal called *The Journal of the History of Sexuality*, which will deal extensively with lesbian and gay subject matter.[8] Last year, Columbia University Press initiated Between Men—Between Women, the first scholarly series devoted to lesbian and gay studies; it is under the leadership of Richard Mohr of the University of Illinois. Although there has been a recent boom in lesbian and gay publishing by small presses and commercial houses alike, university press publishing alone has conferred academic legitimacy on lesbian and gay studies.

Now, there is growing appreciation for the importance and originality of research in lesbian and gay studies. Because of the political changes within the university status system, research in lesbian and gay studies is (sometimes) even rewarded with a tenure-track job or a promotion. One consequence of this change is that the post-Stonewall scholars often have jobs at elite universities that offer them time and resources for research, whereas many of the earlier wave of academics and independent scholars must continue to work after hours. The institutional modifications required to establish lesbian and gay studies as an academic discipline will probably reinforce these generational differences in academic status.

This shift in academic legitimacy has another consequence, however. There are two possible ways to establish lesbian and gay studies as an academic discipline. One is to establish the field intellectually by setting up research-oriented programs, journals, and conferences (as at Yale and CUNY); the other approach is to design a lesbian and gay curriculum exclusively for undergraduates (as at CCSF). Both are ultimately necessary. The intellectual path offers greater prestige, whereas an undergraduate curriculum provides the economic base for any academic field in the humanities (in the form of greater revenues per student).

The problem is that most of the current efforts to start programs in lesbian and gay studies are primarily concerned with building up the field's intellectual status. This step may be necessary in order to gain legitimacy, and therefore funding and support within the academic community, but it encourages lesbian and gay scholars to respond more to academic and disciplinary standards than to the political and cultural concerns of the lesbian and gay communities outside the university. The intellectual work of scholars out of touch with those communities will shrink the audience and become increasingly irrelevant to the cultural and political needs of lesbians and gay men. Furthermore, the intellectual style of the post-Stonewall scholars only reinforces the potential for their academic isolation.

Neither the Stonewall generation nor the post-Stonewall generation has successfully incorporated women, people of color, or independent scholars into the institutional fabric of lesbian and gay studies. Although some white lesbian scholars and lesbian and gay minority scholars have found academic homes in programs of women's and ethnic studies, those departments do not necessarily support lesbian or gay research. Among women's studies faculties at some universities, there is hostility to lesbian and gay studies because of the field's domination by males, the anticipated competition for funds, and plain homophobia. For instance, at Yale, which has a number of out academics such as John Boswell, Ralph Hexter, and Wayne Kostenbaum, there is not one open lesbian on the faculty. Academics base their resistance to hiring some lesbian, minority lesbian and gay, and independent scholars on their lacking graduate training and degrees required for tenure-track academic teaching jobs.

These "asymmetries" were discussed in a highly charged plenary session at the 1989 Yale Lesbian and Gay Studies Conference. At that panel, Wayne Kostenbaum, a post-Stonewall scholar, gave a short, clever, and witty talk on the institutionalization of lesbian and gay studies, only to be faulted by a Latino student for a reading list that included few women and no people of color. Embarrassed, Kostenbaum acknowledged the truth of the challenge. He revealed some of the behind-the-scenes struggles associated with institutionalizing the field. Some senior colleagues in his department had not wanted him to teach a course on homosexuality in literature. They eventually relented, but insisted that he include "major" writers. The course covered a period when he thought there were few if any major writers who were women or people of color. Kostenbaum's dilemma exemplifies the need for teachers to be aware of and thoughtful about issues of race and gender.

These tensions within lesbian and gay studies pose major challenges to those within the field and make it vulnerable to its most powerful enemies: cultural conservatives. People such as William Bennett, former secretary of education; Allan Bloom, author of *The Closing of the American Mind;* not to speak of Jesse Helms and other conservative leaders, will see these programs—following in the footsteps of black and women's studies—as another sign of cultural decline; they already believe that homosexuality and its politics are harbingers of doom. This criticism is all the more reason for lesbian and gay studies to address its asymmetries. Otherwise, the field will ultimately become unrepresentative and narrow.

As an academic discipline, lesbian and gay studies must maintain a dialogue with the communities that created the political and social conditions for its existence. For a minority that does not experience the primary socialization of family and community, education in the community's traditions and contemporary problems is especially important. Teachers and scholars of lesbian and gay studies therefore have a responsibility to future generations of lesbians, gay men, and bisexuals. If the field can address those deep needs for understanding identity and sexuality, it may even contribute to more tolerant generations of heterosexuals.

5 FROM COMMUNITY TO UNIVERSITY

Generations, Paradigms, and Vernacular
Knowledge in Lesbian and Gay Studies

Homosexual emancipation is not possible without a politics of knowledge. The stigma that categorizes homosexuality behavior as morally, medically, or psychologically undesirable is bolstered by elaborate edifices of scientific theory, theological rationale, and normalizing behavioral modification. At the core of the stigmatizing process is the organization of knowledge. Since the late nineteenth century, homosexual emancipationists have battled deeply entrenched intellectual structures, which have perpetuated and disseminated the ignorance, silence, and hegemonic knowledge that sustained the social stigma against homo-

This chapter is an extensively revised version of an essay originally published in "Generations and Paradigms: Main Currents in Lesbian and Gay Studies," *Journal of Homosexuality* (winter 1992). A significant amount of new material has been added.

sexuality. Lesbians and gay men would never have been able to escape the serious effects of stigmatization if these cognitive structures remained in place, particularly those of the psychiatric and medical professions and those of religious institutions. Thus, from the very beginning of modern homosexual emancipation, knowledge became one of the primary targets of political mobilization.

One of the major political or cultural resources has been the knowledge that guides the conduct of everyday lesbian and gay life.[1] In the period before Stonewall, this stock of everyday knowledge about homosexuality, adaptive social patterns, and the predatory behavior of hostile outsiders (police, lawyers, blackmailers) was distributed unevenly because closeted homosexuals were isolated from each other, and because society's homophobic discourses circumscribe this knowledge, preventing it from spreading. The explicit intellectual articulation of theories and interpretations derived from this stock of vernacular knowledge has been a crucial dimension of lesbian and gay political organizing and has given rise to an effective critique of medical, psychiatric, and religious discourses.

The explicit rendering of vernacular knowledge has also played a political role within the community—it helps to socialize new entrants into gay life and facilitates the transmission of community traditions to new generations. Gay and lesbian activists have often been profoundly ignorant about the social life, history, and culture of homosexuality—as indeed has been true of many longtime participants in the gay subculture.

Collective action has reinforced the need for explicit knowledge of homosexuality and gay and lesbian culture and for critical perspectives on the knowledges implicated in the homosexual stigma. Newspapers, study groups, and all kinds of writing proliferated to create a public arena for the discussion of these issues. These media have found eager audiences among homosexuals outside and inside the militant gay liberation organizations.

There have been earlier times and places in which writers and activists have mobilized, creating intellectual resources to combat homophobic frameworks of knowledge. Literature and knowledge about homosexuals served as powerful tools of self-knowledge and acceptance for earlier generations of gay men and lesbians. To realize the absolute significance of cultural and intellectual contributions to the emergence of the modern homosexual, one has only to think of the historical role that *The Well of Loneliness*—despite all its flaws—has played for generations of lesbians, or that Walt Whitman's "Calamus" poems had for male homosexuals such as Oscar Wilde, J. A. Symonds, and Edward Carpenter in late-nineteenth-century Britain.[2]

Gay men and lesbians, like all competent social actors, are also amateur "social theorists" who, as a matter of routine, offer interpretations of their conduct, analyze others' behavior and motives, and supply explanations, stylized models, and narratives about the functioning of social life. Individuals regularly employ such forms of knowledge in their social interactions—which, in turn, also generate knowledge. The *presuppositions* members of a social group share, as well as the *meanings* attributed to their experiences and actions, also contribute to the community's stock of vernacular knowledge. This stock of knowledge is a soup of ideas, theories, quasi facts, and interpretations that may be seen as the community's "common sense." In part, society's hegemonic discourses also influence this accumulated intelligence.[3]

Lesbian and gay studies as a public discourse emerged from the movement's need to challenge the hegemonic cultural institutions and the specific forms of knowledge that they produced and disseminated. The psychiatric profession was the preeminent intellectual discourse that fed the homophobic complex during the middle third of the century. I can recall demonstrations and zaps (as quick, surprise confrontations were called) in the early 1970s at public forums about homosexuality in which gay activists carried signs declaring, "We are the experts."

Since 1987, lesbian and gay studies as an academic discipline has flourished in the United States. The number of books published on the subject each year has multiplied rapidly, numerous college courses exist all over the country, university departments increasingly seek faculty specializing in the field, and the 1994 *CLAGS Directory of Lesbian and Gay Studies* lists nearly six hundred scholars now working in the field in the United States.[4]

In the late 1980s, Martin Duberman, Esther Newton, and John Boswell among others sought—for the second time—to establish lesbian and gay studies programs.[5] Centers were established at the Graduate Center of The City University of New York, Yale, and the University of Toronto, and graduate seminars, courses, and scholarly conferences put lesbian and gay studies on the academic map across the country. A boom in lesbian and gay publishing has reinforced these academic developments. Such developments are only possible if there is a sophisticated and increasing audience of lesbians and gay men interested in the political and cultural issues of their lives. Making lesbian and gay studies into a formal academic discipline sets the stage for a potentially significant historical shift in the intellectual life of the lesbian and gay communities—the entry of the university into the communities' cultural development.

BEGINNINGS: GENERATIONS, POLITICS, AND COMMUNITY

Historical generations are not like families or political organizations, in which people are bound by kinship or commonly stated purposes. When a large group of people experience significant historical events at the beginning of their adult lives, it often creates a sense of shared identity. Although the demographic concept of *cohort* refers to a group of people born at the same time, that contemporaneity is not enough to forge a generational identity. Instead, that bond derives from a shared historical experience that creates a distinctive attitude toward life, a sensibility, and a collective state of mind.[6]

Frequently, people belong to certain generations in lesbian and gay life depending on when they came out, rather than how old they are. Important historical episodes such as the Stonewall riots, the advent of AIDS, or the influential political-cultural ideas of a period (lesbian-feminism between 1973 and 1980 or the antipornography debates between 1978 and 1984) define lesbian and gay generations. Together with social and political challenges from outside the lesbian and gay communities, cultural trends are very important. In some sense, lesbian or gay "generations" last only a short time (roughly five years) because the political and cultural atmosphere changes so quickly.

The Stonewall period of the late 1960s and early 1970s provided formative experiences for both women and men, although in somewhat different ways. The clash between the male-dominated gay liberation movement and lesbian-feminism deeply marked the women of the Stonewall generation. Lesbian-feminism created the context in which the next generation of lesbians came out in the mid-1970s. Later, the sex wars of the late 1970s established a new context in which women could come out; in this conflict, feminist sex radicals opposed lesbian-feminists leading an antipornography movement. Now there is a post–sex war generation of lesbians.

Gay male generations emerged in a somewhat different rhythm. The lesbian separatist impulse of the mid-1970s left the men of the Stonewall generation isolated from the political debates of the women's movement. Nevertheless, through women's studies courses and other public debates, feminism decisively influenced the next generation of gay men. Then the sex wars reopened intellectual exchange between gay men on the Left and the feminist sex radicals. With the advent of AIDS, there was a major watershed in gay male life, and to a lesser degree, in lesbian life. Many gay and lesbian participants in the sex wars became involved in AIDS activism and education.

Lesbian and gay studies is not exempt from the historical circumstances that have shaped the politics and culture of the lesbian and gay male communities. In the midst of the sweeping changes in the lives of lesbians and gay men, scholars, writers, and other intellectuals have strived to formulate theories of homosexual life that interpret both the historical changes and the texture of everyday life. The intellectual frameworks or paradigms that scholars and community intellectuals develop reflect the underlying cultural assumptions of the times and suggest concrete research programs. Research on lesbian and gay life takes place in most of the major disciplines of the humanities and social sciences, but a number of interdisciplinary theoretical paradigms have been very influential.

The recent effort to establish lesbian and gay studies as a discipline brings together several generations of scholars. One is the generation of writers and scholars who were mobilized by the gay liberation and the women's movements in the early 1970s. This generation responded to the profound cultural appeal for *personal authenticity* stirred by the influence of existentialism, the Beat generation, and feminism.[7] The quest for authenticity emphasized the unrealized potential for cultivating, directing, and understanding oneself, and for being creative.[8] Although the search for authenticity provided a feasible political framework for early homosexual liberation, the criterion of authenticity as an intellectual paradigm posed severe limits and inconsistencies. Important figures of this early generation included Jonathan Katz, Esther Newton, John D'Emilio, Karla Jay, Lillian Faderman, John De Cecco, James Saslow, and Martin Duberman.

The second wave of lesbian and gay studies (from 1987 to 1992) matured intellectually under a different set of cultural assumptions— one much more attuned to the importance of cultural codes and the signifying practices. In this framework, authenticity still has an appeal, although the terminology has shifted away from the existentialism of the late 1960s and favors a poststructuralist discourse instead. Among the scholars in this second generation, Eve Sedgwick, David Halperin, Diana Fuss, Thomas Yingling, Judith Butler, Douglas Crimp, Teresa de Lauretis, and Michael Moon are among the most eminent representatives.

Another group of writers and teachers, mostly women of color, bridges these two generations and has challenged lesbian and gay academics to confront the exclusion of race from intellectual and political discourse. This group includes poet Audre Lorde, playwright Cherríe Moraga, editor and publisher Barbara Smith, and writer Gloria Anzaldúa.

The work of each group or generation has markedly different intellectual styles. The Stonewall generation has created three influential intellectual perspectives that have framed research in lesbian and gay studies: a social-psychological model of authentic selfhood, the social-constructionist theory of homosexual identity, and essentialist theories of the woman-identified lesbian identity and gay identity. These three

paradigms are linked in their struggle to articulate the dialectic of authenticity and history—the interplay between the psychological sense
of true self or real desires and the cultural and historical process of
identity formation. The later generation was trained in literary and cultural criticism; it has developed an eclectic approach that emphasizes
the significance of interpretative strategies and cultural codes in gay
and lesbian life. The paradigm articulated by Audre Lorde, Cherríe
Moraga, Gloria Anzaldúa, and Barbara Smith, like those of the Stonewall generation, is rooted in the discovery of authentic selfhood, but it
explores the effects of hegemonic social patterns on the constitution of
social and personal identities. It challenges the exclusion of difference
and race from the approaches of the two generations.

Of course, some scholars do not seem to fit exactly into any generational grouping, and there are scholars, writers, and intellectuals who
have emerged before, in between, and after the main two waves of
lesbian and gay studies scholars. All of these individuals and groups,
though, inhabit a growing intellectual niche—lesbian and gay studies
as a book market, as a specialty within traditional departments, or even
as a separate program.

THE SEARCH FOR AUTHENTICITY, 1969 TO 1976

The generation of lesbians and gay men galvanized by Stonewall had
already witnessed five tumultuous years of intense political activity that
fundamentally challenged American values—the black civil rights
movement, the student antiwar movement, the women's movement,
and the emergence of the counterculture. The cultural atmosphere rang
with ideas of black power, sexual revolution, and liberation. Many of
the leading intellectual figures of the period promoted sexual liberation—Herbert Marcuse, Paul Goodman, James Baldwin, Susan Sontag,
and Allen Ginsberg. Of these, Goodman, Baldwin, and Ginsberg were
openly homosexual, and in *Eros and Civilization* Marcuse had explicitly
nominated homosexuals as cultural revolutionaries.

In *The Second Sex*, Simone de Beauvoir had written the first major feminist work of the postwar era in which she not only examined women's issues from an existentialist perspective but also penned a pioneering essay on lesbianism. Furthermore, Jean-Paul Sartre had explored the psychology of authentic identity in a string of influential works such as *Jew and Anti-Semite, Saint Genet*, the preface to Franz Fanon's *The Wretched of the Earth*, and chapters in *Being and Nothingness* on the authenticity and bad faith of the homosexual.[9] Sartre, Beauvoir, Paul Goodman, and others who wrote on the importance of being true to one's authentic self had a profound influence on the lesbian and gay writers, intellectuals, and young academics writing about gay liberation and feminism. The ideal of authenticity offered an intellectual framework with which they could emancipate themselves from a culture that stigmatized homosexuality. In a period when psychology was the dominant intellectual and therapeutic discipline in the public discourses on homosexuality, the existential psychology of authenticity provided a personal and even political alternative. The idea of authenticity allowed this generation to assert its homosexual desire—stigmatized and repressed by social forces—in opposition to the more biological Freudian presumption of universal bisexuality. The impulse to realize one's authentic self informed much of the thinking and action in the 1960s political and cultural movements. "Coming out"—so fundamental to the personal and political development of gay and lesbian identities—is a perfect illustration of an individual's experience of authentic selfhood.

Almost immediately after Stonewall, a flood of books, periodicals, and other publications found an eager audience who wanted to explore the political and cultural implications of feminism and gay liberation. During the first few years, intellectual debates among gay men and lesbians centered on psychological theories of homosexuality and the role of psychotherapy in stigmatizing and repressing homosexuality.[10]

The emphasis on authenticity and identity helped to undermine the assumption of bisexuality so prevalent among prominent homosexual writers of the previous generation—Paul Goodman, Lorraine Hansberry, Gore Vidal, and James Baldwin. Dennis Altman and Kate Millett, two of the authors most influential in the early gay movement, used the search for authenticity as a framework in their analysis of sexual oppression and liberation. Both Altman and Millett, like many other liberation theorists, promoted the discovery and expression of one's repressed self as the true or authentic self. At the same time, they remained committed to Freudian ideas about "polymorphous perversity" and the bisexuality of human desire.[11]

In the course of the public discussion about whether psychology's analysis of homosexuality was valid, George Weinberg, a gay-sympathetic psychologist, coined the term *homophobia* to designate the irrational fear of homosexual acts, persons, or sentiments.[12] Discussion of these issues largely took place outside the university among activists and community-based writers and intellectuals. Eventually, the debate directly engaged the psychiatric profession itself over the official designation of homosexuality as a mental illness in the American Psychiatric Association's *Diagnostic and Statistical Manual (DSM).*[13]

Between 1972 and 1978, Karla Jay and Allan Young published three anthologies that explored gay and lesbian history, psychological theories, the problems and possibilities of coming out, lesbian and gay culture before and after Stonewall, the gay movement's relation to the Left, the women's and black civil rights movements, sex roles, and the images of gay men and lesbians in the media.[14] These books were the locus of intellectual and political debate in the emerging gay and lesbian communities.

One of the earliest academic fields to experience this infusion of energy was literature. Louie Crew and Rictor Norton, a professor of English and a literary critic who edited the journal *College English*, assembled a special issue called "The Homosexual Imagination." They entitled their introduction to the issue "The Homophobic Imagination."[15] The special issue stimulated the rediscovery of lesbian and gay writers of the past: Christopher Isherwood, Vita Sackville-West, Jean Genet, Gertrude Stein, and Radclyffe Hall. Mass-market paperback editions of these and many other lesbian and gay authors' works were reissued during the 1970s.

The search for authenticity also fed the impulse that led gay and lesbian scholars to track down the history of homosexuals. In 1971, gay activist Jonathan Katz started doing research on gay history, working only from the presumption that gay American history actually existed.

In June 1972, he dramatized some of his early discoveries in a documentary play called *Coming Out*.[16] Eventually, Katz's research led to
two huge collections of lesbian and gay historical documents: *Gay American History* (1976) and *Gay/Lesbian Almanac* (1983). In the meantime,
Katz had served as the general editor of the Arno Press series Homosexuality: Lesbians and Gay Men in Society, History, and Literature, a
massive reprinting of over a hundred books that addressed homosexuality, from classics to the obscure, from both the nineteenth and twentieth centuries. Also in the early 1970s, John D'Emilio and James Steakley published pioneering explorations of homosexual emancipation
movements that took place during the 1940s and 1950s in the United
States and in pre-Nazi Germany.[17]

The 1976 publication of Jonathan Katz's *Gay American History* marked
the culmination of the early tradition of lesbian and gay scholarship
that worked within the loose intellectual paradigm rooted in the search
for authenticity. For various reasons, Katz included in *Gay American
History* people who could not clearly be called homosexual, and these
definitional ambiguities raised questions about what "homosexual"
meant in earlier periods and in different cultures. For example, Katz
included *berdache* (men who adopted the female role in Native American societies and engaged in sexual activities with their husbands); passionate friendships between pairs of men and women who probably
did not engage in sexual activity with each other; and women who
chose to pass and live as men, although some of these women may not
have had homoerotic desires. Most of these people did not seem to
resemble "homosexuals" in the usual sense of the word. Once scholars
and writers began to question these inclusions, and therefore to question the definition of a homosexual person, the idea of discovering the
history of authentic homosexuals seemed problematic. It was precisely
these questions that stimulated the emergence of a new paradigm.

THE SOCIAL CONSTRUCTION
OF IDENTITY, 1976 TO PRESENT

The outpouring of lesbian and gay social thought and history in the
early 1970s assumed that the homosexual experience in earlier periods

and in different cultures revolved around a type of personality called "the homosexual." This initial assumption soon gave way to the discovery, so influential toward the end of the 1960s, that phenomena such as gender roles and racial stereotypes were historically conditioned and socially constructed. The feminist work of Simone de Beauvoir, Kate Millett, Shulamith Firestone, and Germaine Greer influenced American lesbian and gay intellectuals, who began to challenge the way gender stereotypes were entangled in homosexual behavior.

The feminist strand of early social construction merged with the work of a group of left-wing British homosexual theorists and historians. The starting point was "The Homosexual Role," a paper that sociologist Mary McIntosh published in 1968. Basing her work on the empirical results of the Kinsey studies, McIntosh challenged the belief that there are two kinds of people in the world: "homosexuals" and "heterosexuals." She argued that the homosexual should be seen as a "social role" rather than as a natural or fixed "condition."[18] A group of young British intellectuals worked out the historical and political implications of McIntosh's theory in the journal *Gay Left* (1975 to 1979). In the pages of their journal, they synthesized Marxist social history and the "symbolic interactionist" school of sociology, which emphasized the importance of socially created meanings in everyday life.[19] This perspective on the historical emergence of the homosexual identity informed the work of Jeffrey Weeks in *Coming Out: Homosexual Politics in Britain from the Nineteenth Century to the Present*, and *Sex, Politics, and Society: The Regulation of Sexuality since 1800.*

The American version of the *Gay Left* theory of homosexual identity surfaced in the work of John D'Emilio. His pioneering article "Capitalism and Gay Identity" and his book *Sexual Politics, Sexual Communities* bring together this new theory of homosexual identity with the social history that grew out of the political movements of the 1960s. This approach to gay and lesbian history was eventually identified as the social-constructionist theory of homosexual identity. Michel Foucault's *History of Sexuality* (1978) developed a line of thought parallel to that of the *Gay Left* group's social-constructionist perspective on sexuality.[20] In addition, Foucault's work offered a full-scale philosophical critique of essentialism—the belief that "the homosexual identity" exists as a stable phenomenon throughout history. Although lesbian and gay studies emerged originally from the essentialist impulse—the search for authenticity and roots—the debate about the historical and social construction of the homosexual identity has increasingly framed the issues that lesbian and gay scholars have addressed.

The social-constructionist theory of sexuality and sexual identity played an important role in the political debates about pornography in the late 1970s and early 1980s. The antipornography movement and the work of its leading theorists—Andrea Dworkin, Susan Griffin, Adrienne Rich, Audre Lorde, and Catherine MacKinnon—often drew upon essentialist definitions of gender. Critics of the antipornography movement, such as Carole Vance, Gayle Rubin, Amber Hollibaugh, Ellen Willis, Joan Nestle, Deirdre English, and Cherríe Moraga, were social constructionists.[21] The political and intellectual debates on sexuality and feminism surfaced in a controversial conference at Barnard College in 1982. The papers from this conference were later published in an influential anthology called *Pleasure and Danger: Exploring Female Sexuality*, edited by Carole Vance, the conference organizer. Together with another anthology called *Powers of Desire*, which Ann Snitow, Christine Stansell, and Sharon Thompson edited, *Pleasure and Danger* made major contributions to social-constructionist thinking about sexuality, gender, and sexual identity.

The social-constructionist theory of homosexual identity has its own weaknesses, however. According to some evidence, sexual behavior is a continuum and varies over the life cycle. This evidence brings into doubt the fixedness or stability of people's sexual identities. In addition, homosexual-identified individuals seem to have existed before the modern homosexual identity was created. Steven Epstein explored some of these ambiguities in an influential essay called "Gay Politics, Ethnic Identity: The Limits of Social Constructionism," as did Diana Fuss in *Essentially Speaking* and the authors in Edward Stein's anthology *Forms of Desire: Sexual Orientation and the Social Constructionist Controversy*.[22] Despite the theory's ambiguities and limits, the social-constructionist interpretation of homosexual history is one of the major intellectual achievements of the Stonewall generation of lesbian and gay scholars.

ESSENTIAL IDENTITY:
LESBIAN EXISTENCE, GAY UNIVERSALS,
AND QUEER SCIENCE, 1975 TO PRESENT

The belief that the homosexual identity exists independently of historical, cultural, or social conditions is called *essentialism*. Most of us start our homosexual lives as essentialists—that is, when we first come out, we believe that Socrates and Sappho were "homosexuals" in the same way that lesbians or gay men of the late twentieth century are homosexuals. This belief is the naive form of essentialism. But essentialism as an intellectual program in lesbian and gay studies has two variants. The first one to develop was essentialism as a metaphysical or universal category of sexual identity, which might be called *identitarian essentialism*. The second variant to emerge focused on the biological explanation of sexual orientation and interpreted it as a naturalized category of behavior; this is *behavioral essentialism*.

Lesbian-feminism was the most thoroughly developed political philosophy to emerge from the heady days of early feminism and gay liberation. Through a series of popular and provocative writings, lesbian-feminists created an intellectual framework that posited such metaphysical and transhistorical categories of female identity as "woman" and "lesbian." This theory and intellectual paradigm was first publicly articulated in the pamphlet "The Woman-Identified Woman," which Radicalesbians published, and was elaborated more fully in Jill Johnston's *Lesbian Nation*.[23] Authors such as Mary Daly, Kathleen Barry, Susan Griffin, Diana Russell, Catherine MacKinnon, Lillian Faderman, and Adrienne Rich developed bold and vigorous interpretations of feminist politics, pornography, rape, lesbian culture, theology, and history.

Lesbian-feminist scholarship worked with the presupposition that male and female behavior was "essentially" different, politically opposed, and not very amenable to change. Patriarchy was seen as a trans-historical outcome of the male domination of women by means of compulsory heterosexuality. Within this paradigm, two of the most important theoretical essays were published in the early 1980s in *Signs:* Adrienne Rich's "Compulsory Heterosexuality and Lesbian Existence," and Catherine MacKinnon's "Feminism, Marxism, Method, and the State."[24] Although lesbian-feminism presupposed that gender was immutable, it did argue that heterosexuality was socially constructed. Its "essentialist" notion of gender was very important to the thinking of the antipornography movement in the late 1970s and early 1980s—particularly in the work of Susan Griffin, Andrea Dworkin, and Catherine MacKinnon.

If the early emphasis on authenticity reflected the coming-out experience, and social constructionism captured the discursive aspects of identity development, lesbian-feminism synthesized a growing revulsion toward male misogyny and the appeal of women's separatism. Lesbian-feminism was both a continuation of the search for authenticity—though in this case an authentic female identity—and a theory of the social construction of heterosexuality. According to lesbian-feminists, the rejection of heterosexuality and the acceptance of lesbian identity would lead to an authentic women's culture.

A variant of this identitarian essentialism is the assertion that gay or lesbian identities have existed throughout history and in different cultures. John Boswell and Will Roscoe have offered relatively sophisticated interpretations of gay history that find universal components of homosexual identities.[25] These versions of history are rooted in the history of religion. The earliest gay male version of the identitarian essentialism was published by Arthur Evans in *Fag Rag*, the radical political newspaper, and then in book form in *Witchcraft and the Gay Counterculture.* In this book, Evans linked the persecution of gay people to the repression of pagan witches. In contrast, John Boswell's 1980 history of "gay people" in the middle ages portrayed a more tolerant Christianity and gave the "new essentialism" academic respectability. Judy Grahn applied her skills as a poet and storyteller in a book called *In a Mother Tongue* to provide a unique brew of history, etymology, and fiction.[26]

Although lesbian-feminism and the very different versions of gay universalism of Boswell, Evans, and Grahn presuppose certain essential gender or sexual identities, they also assume that other aspects of homosexuality are socially constructed. Nevertheless, the intellectual program of essentialism implies that research in lesbian and gay studies must focus on realities or structures that span historical periods—patriarchy, spiritual identities, or the basis of sexual or gender identities in nature.

The second tradition—behavioral essentialism—focused on the biological origins of homosexuality, influenced, in part, by sociobiology. To some extent this work revives the tradition of Magnus Hirschfeld and others in the early German homosexual rights movement.[27]

One of the most influential pioneers in this intellectual current is Simon LeVay. In 1991, while on the faculty of the Salk Institute at the University of California at San Diego, he published a paper in the journal *Science* on differences in brain structure between heterosexual and homosexual men.[28] The reaction to this article, both in the mainstream media and among gay activists, made LeVay aware of the potential political significance of his research.

LeVay soon left his faculty position at the Salk Institute to found the Institute of Gay and Lesbian Education in West Hollywood. He has since developed his perspective in a series of books that explore the relationship between biological research and lesbian and gay studies: *The Sexual Brain, City of Friends: A Portrait of the Gay and Lesbian Community in America,* written with Elizabeth Nonas, and *Queer Science: The Use and Abuse of Research into Homosexuality.*[29] LeVay and other biological researchers have conducted studies exploring factors such as hormones, brain structure, and genetic differences as causes of homosexuality. One of the most important issues is whether homosexuality is defined as sexual orientation, specific behavior, or sexual identity. Early criticisms of this research centered on its naive use of social and cultural distinctions; some of those conducting biological research failed to distinguish between "identity" and "behavior," or they attributed "homosexuality" to gender-variant behavior. For example, when male rats, sheep, seagulls, and primates allow themselves to be mounted, some researchers called it "homosexuality."[30]

Most of the work on the biological origins of homosexual behavior has no intellectual or social relationship to the mainstream of lesbian and gay studies. LeVay is to some extent the exception. Although he has spent most of his career working as a neuroanatomist, his work at the Institute of Gay and Lesbian Education and his books reveal a serious effort to relate the biological research to the political and social needs of the lesbian and gay community.

RACE, DIFFERENCE, AND COLONIALISM: 1979 TO PRESENT

A radical challenge to what Adrienne Rich called the gay and women's movements' "white solipsism"—its tendency "to think, imagine, and speak as if whiteness described the world"—came most decisively from a group of women of color, including poets, essayists, and playwrights.[31] In a number of important speeches and essays, Audre Lorde criticized feminists' refusal to include differences of race and class in their analysis of male domination.[32] The anthology *This Bridge Called My Back*, edited by Cherríe Moraga and Gloria Anzaldúa, made a major contribution by exploring the discourse and expression of ethnically or racially mixed identities. The writers in this tradition have examined the fault lines and borders around which women of color have often built their identities—the generational differences between mother and daughter, language barriers, sexual identities, the specific cultural histories of different races, the physical bodies of women of color, and the diversity of work situations.[33]

This Bridge Called My Back was followed by other anthologies such as *Home Girls: A Black Feminist Anthology*, edited by Barbara Smith and published in 1983; Gloria Anzaldúa's 1990 sequel to *This Bridge Called My Back*, which was called *Making Face, Making Soul, Hacienda Caras*; and Carla Trujilla's 1991 *Chicana Lesbians*. Gloria Anzaldúa and Cherríe Moraga have both written in-depth autobiographical profiles of the multifaceted bridge identities of women of color. Gloria Anzaldúa explores her identity as "a border woman" in the 1987 work *Borderlands / La Frontera*. She maps the psychological, sexual, and spiritual border-

lands of her life in a work that switches "codes" from English to Cas-
tilian Spanish, a North Mexican dialect, Tex-Mex, and even Nahuatl.
Cherríe Moraga takes up a similar exploration in *Loving in the War
Years / Lo que nunca paso por sus labios*, published in 1983.

This Bridge Called My Back contributed an intellectual framework to
lesbian and gay studies by mapping identities that exist at the juncture
of different cultures and races. Gay male writers and scholars are just
beginning to explore this terrain.[34] Joseph Beam and Essex Hemphill
have published anthologies of essays and other work that analyze the
bridge identities of black gay men.[35]

Questions of representation figure significantly in the work in this
tradition. Scholars have raised this issue by asking whether depictions
of the homosexualities of people of color are culturally and artistically
adequate. In addition, they have questioned how the work affects the
political or legal representation of those communities.[36] Kobena Mercer
has also pointed out how the "restricted economy of minority representation in which one speaks for all" poses a burden on those selected
to represent (either culturally or politically) the black community or a
marginalized social group. They are "burdened with the impossible
task of speaking as 'representatives' "; with this responsibility of speaking for many different individuals and groups in their communities,
they are inhibited about even speaking for themselves.[37] This "burden
of representation" reflects the fact that because of racism, marginalized
communities have only limited access to public space.[38] In "The Spectacle of Blackness," Robert Reid-Pharr explores another aspect of this
burden of representation as he examines the interpretative schemes
through which white readers and observers view representations of
black homosexualities.[39]

One increasingly significant aspect of the interaction of race, ethnicity, and sexuality originates in the diaspora experience of migrants from
Latin America, Africa, and South and Southeast Asia. More recent work
about homosexualities within racial and ethnic communities has drawn
on British cultural studies and postcolonial theory. Paul Gilroy, for one,
has argued that sexuality and gender occupy a central place in the
contemporary discourse of race.[40] Many of Kobena Mercer's essays ex-

plore how a complex set of cultural exchanges between the Caribbean, Britain, Africa, and the United States mediates the life of black homosexuals in Africa, Europe, and the western hemisphere.[41]

The gay and lesbian movement in the United States, as well as the growing prominence of lesbian and gay studies in North America, has also had a noticeable impact on those with homosexual desires in Latin American and South Asian immigrant communities. The historical presence in the United States of communities from Central and South America and the frequent migratory flows back and forth between the United States and Latin American countries have led to interactions between the North American lesbian and gay experience and that of Latin American cultures. Joseph Carrier and Tomas Almaguer have documented some of the interactive patterns that have developed between the North American and Mexican homosexual experiences; for example, Mexican men who adopt the "gay" identity (incorporating both passive and active sexual roles in their sexual repertoires) are known as *internacionales*.[42] A number of writers and theorists have explored the relationship between race, gender, and sexual identity in Latino communities in the United States.[43]

By the mid-1980s, South Asian homosexual writers had begun to study the status of homosexuality in India, Pakistan, Sri Lanka, and Bangladesh. Newsletters and groups of homosexual intellectuals and activists emerged almost simultaneously all around the world: *Anamika*, *Trikon*, and *Shamakami* in the United States; *Khush Khayal* in Canada; *Shakti Khabar* in the United Kingdom, and *Bombay Dost* in India. Spurred by their repression in South Asian societies and by their invisibility in the white lesbian and gay communities of North America and Britain, these lesbian and gay intellectuals often emerged from the cultural crosscurrents of the South Asian diaspora experience. Young women and men growing up in South Asia or reared within traditional South Asian families often became aware of their homosexual desires and began the coming-out process when they encountered lesbian and gay communities in North America or Europe, possibly during their college years.[44]

The comparative study of cultural constructions of homosexuality in non-Western societies increasingly takes place in the context of global patterns of cultural exchange, and in many communities of color scholars must take into account the interplay between the corresponding racial or ethnic communities in the United States and their countries of origin. Recently, in the introduction to a special "queer" issue of *positions*, a journal of East Asian studies, the guest editor Ukiko Hanawa noted that studying homosexuality in Asian cultures was no longer "simply a matter of locating indigenous or local sexuality, whether in Asia or in Asian America, and identifying an appropriate lexicon of sexualities. Perhaps even more so than in other areas of inquiry . . . the terms by which the sexual-political economy gets defined is [*sic*] both local and global at the same time."[45]

One of most influential theoretical consequences of exploring the relationship between race and sexuality is the increased skepticism toward a unitary racial or ethnic identity and, instead, the validation of the hybrid or "bridge" identities forged among the overlapping communities of race, ethnicity, and sexuality. Given that it is impossible to speak for the community and to produce unambiguously positive images, intellectuals have looked to bridge identities to challenge the homogeneity of the modern homosexual identity presumed in early social-constructionist theories.[46] The women and men of color who explore homosexualities as scholars and intellectuals have drawn from the intellectual traditions of black and Latina feminists (for example, Audre Lorde, Cherríe Moraga, and Gloria Anzaldúa) as well as from postcolonial cultural studies (such as Kobena Mercer's *Welcome to the Jungle*) to make a complicated, double move of both invoking identity and contesting it.

QUEER THEORY: THE CULTURAL STUDIES PARADIGM, 1985 TO PRESENT

Scholars working within the cultural studies paradigm have explicitly built on the social-constructionist paradigm. They have extended it to include the interpretation of all kinds of texts, cultural codes, signifying practices, and modes of discourse that shape attitudes toward homosexuality and affect the formation of sexual or gender identities. As Thomas Yingling, a member of the new generation, has noted, "Gay writers seem often to have found literature less a matter of self-expression and more a matter of coding. The gay absorption into signs, meanings, interpretation and art is related to the fact that for the homosexual the 'problem of the homosexual' is in fact the problem of signs—homosexuality is a semiotic."[47]

Scholars who began writing on lesbian and gay issues in the wake of the late 1970s and early 1980s sex debates helped to create this intellectual shift in lesbian and gay studies. The new generation of lesbian and gay scholars has particularly flourished in the academic arena of cultural studies—an interdisciplinary synthesis of fields such as American studies, ethnic studies, and gender studies. Their intellectual framework derives from literary studies and the humanities and is influenced by cultural theorists such as Roland Barthes, Michel Foucault, Mikhail Bakhtin, Antonio Gramsci, Stuart Hall, Victor Turner, and Clifford Geertz.[48]

Representatives of this new approach include Eve Kosofsky Sedgwick, who has explored male homosexuality and homosocial desire in literature; Thomas Yingling, author of an original study of Hart Crane; Judith Butler, a philosopher who has published a book on the theory of gender identity; David Miller, author of a well-received book on the police in the Victorian novel; David Halperin, who has pioneered a new interpretation of homosexuality in ancient Greece; Diana Fuss, author of a collection of essays on essentialism and identity politics; Michael Moon, who has written on Walt Whitman; and Lee Edelman, who has published a string of brilliant papers on gay literature, including a famous essay on the ACT UP slogan Silence = Death.[49]

In an important theoretical statement of the cultural studies paradigm, Harold Beaver wrote:

> The homosexual is beset by signs, by the urge to interpret whatever transpires, between himself and chance acquaintance. He is a prodigious consumer of signs—of hidden meanings, hidden systems, hidden potentiality. Exclusion from the common code impels the frenzied quest: the momentary glimpse, the scrambled figure, the chance encounter, the reverse image, the sudden slippage, the lowered guard. In

a flash meanings may be disclosed, mysteries wrenched out and be-
trayed.[50]

Eve Sedgwick's magisterial *Epistemology of the Closet* is a major statement of the cultural studies paradigm. In it, she argues that "an understanding of virtually any aspect of modern Western culture must
be, not merely incomplete, but damaged in its central substance to the
degree that does not incorporate a critical analysis of modern homo/
heterosexual definition."[51]

The political implications of this model of cultural analysis have been
heatedly debated. In her book *Gender Trouble*, Judith Butler has "attempted to locate the political in the very signifying practices that establish, regulate, and deregulate identity."[52] Communication becomes
a form of identity politics because identity is made up of signs, symbols,
and performances. The practical application of this approach is clearly
demonstrated by the work of cultural activists on AIDS, especially
groups of artists and makers of films and videos. These works of propa-
ganda, education, and media criticism display great sophistication
about the cultural codes of sexual behavior, disease, and politics.[53]

THE POLITICS OF KNOWLEDGE AND AIDS

The advent of AIDS has spurred an enormous explosion of research on
homosexuality—though it is in many ways inadequate and is on a
much smaller scale relative to the significance of the epidemic. Initially,
most AIDS research was devoted to investigating the cause of the
breakdown of the immune system. This led to the discovery of the
human immunodeficiency virus (HIV), which causes the collection of
diseases called AIDS. Then, research focused on developing a test for
HIV. Consequently, most of the current medical research moved toward searching for a treatment or even a cure for AIDS (difficult though
that may be to develop).

A much smaller proportion of federal research dollars was devoted
to epidemiological research or work on the social and psychological

dynamics of prevention. Because most of the work published about AIDS and HIV is written in a scientific style and usually appears in scientific journals, there is not much likelihood that it will reach a general gay and lesbian audience—although recent books by Walt W. Odets and Gabriel Rotello, which are based on epidemiology and HIV prevention research, do manage to address a broader public.[54]

The grassroots politics of knowledge, honed during the gay and lesbian movement's battle with the American Psychiatric Association to remove homosexuality as a disease from its *Diagnostic and Statistical Manual (DSM)*, had a powerful effect on the conduct of AIDS research. AIDS activism, closely linked to the organized gay and lesbian community, focused on the medical research agenda. The story of this development is recounted in Steven Epstein's book *Impure Science*, a study of the AIDS movement's impact on biomedical research—and itself a major contribution to lesbian and gay studies.[55]

Medical and public health disciplines have shaped much of the research on AIDS and HIV. However, the intellectual perspectives developed within lesbian and gay studies influenced AIDS research in three areas: exploration of the cultural meanings of AIDS, the political and social construction of knowledge about AIDS, and the strategies and policies of HIV prevention.

The first significant development emerged when those working within the cultural studies paradigm explored the social meanings of AIDS. Douglas Crimp, an art critic and an AIDS activist, edited a special issue of the art journal *October* and called it "AIDS: Cultural Analysis, Cultural Activism." Subsequently published as a book, it was a collection of pieces that analyzed key words, homophobia, biomedical discourses, visual representations of people with AIDS, and the impact of cultural meanings on gay male sexual practices. In 1990, Crimp collaborated with artist Adam Rolston (both were members of the AIDS activist group ACT UP New York and were associated with its political graphics spin-off Gran Fury) to produce *AIDS Demo Graphics*, a documentation of political graphics produced by AIDS activists.[56]

Another group of intellectuals and scholars contributed to AIDS research by developing a strong social-constructionist analysis of AIDS knowledge. These authors came from disciplines such as sociology, history, and cultural studies. In a series of books, Cindy Patton has combined cultural analysis with the sociology of knowledge to offer a critique of epidemiology, the AIDS service industry, public policy, and HIV prevention education.[57] Like Cindy Patton, Paula Treichler has explored the overlapping discourses of science and culture.[58] Historians of science Elizabeth Fee and Daniel M. Fox have edited two anthologies of work by historians of medicine and science, as well as epidemiologists and sociologists. The anthologies offer historical comparisons of AIDS in relation to other epidemics and diseases.[59] In *Impure Science: AIDS, Activism, and the Politics of Knowledge,* Steven Epstein has written a detailed account of the relationship between AIDS activism and AIDS research.[60]

The third way in which lesbian and gay studies has had an impact on AIDS research has been through lesbian and gay intellectuals who, active in the sex debates of the late 1980s, have worked on AIDS education and HIV prevention. For instance, Amber Hollibaugh, Simon Watney, and Cindy Patton made contributions to the debates about pornography and the social construction of sexuality and, as activists, administrators, and writers, have helped to shape programs and policies for HIV prevention.[61]

Despite the linkages sketched above, the AIDS epidemic has stimulated a disproportionate share of all the social and behavioral research on male homosexuality. Most AIDS-related research has had no relationship to intellectual work explicitly considered to be lesbian and gay studies.

THE FUTURE OF LESBIAN AND GAY STUDIES

This chapter has examined five paradigms in lesbian and gay studies: the search for authenticity, the social construction of identity, essential identity, difference and race, and cultural studies. In addition, the AIDS epidemic stimulated a great deal of research on male homosexual behavior and culture, but most of it has been shaped by medical and public health paradigms. Although all five paradigms continue to have loyal adherents whose research and writing follows from the paradigms' core presuppositions, lesbian and gay studies is divided by the different cultural styles of various generations.

Many members of the Stonewall generation retain their commitment to the twin problems of authenticity and history—whether they are social constructionists or essentialists. Only the authenticity line of thought has failed to produce a major work of synthesis that claims to be an authoritative understanding of lesbian and gay life—although perhaps Andrew Sullivan's *Virtually Normal* could be considered as a contribution to this tradition.

The post-Stonewall generation came of age in a culture dominated by mass media and is acutely aware of the power of cultural codes. As post-Stonewall scholars enter the ranks of academics, the cultural studies paradigm has become increasingly influential. It is a flexible and eclectic framework that can incorporate elements from some of the other paradigms, but it is also stylistically more difficult and less accessible than most of the work produced in the other research traditions. Works in cultural studies run the risk of losing the readers and intellectuals in the community—those who have been the most supportive audience of work written by scholars in other frameworks.

6 INTELLECTUALS, IDENTITY POLITICS, AND THE CONTEST FOR CULTURAL AUTHORITY

Tensions and differences between intellectuals based primarily in the community and intellectuals working within the university are a persistent feature of cultural life in the lesbian and gay male communities. Similar tensions also haunt the activists and intellectuals of other movements and communities—for example, feminists, African Americans, and Chicanos.

The production of culture and the definition of identity are absolutely crucial to the formation and collective action of the new identity

This chapter was originally presented as a paper at a conference on Social Movements and Cultural Politics held at the University of California at Santa Cruz. A slightly different version was published in the volume of conference papers in Marci Danovsky, Barbara Epstein, and Richard Flacks, eds., *Social Movements and Cultural Politics* (Philadelphia: Temple University Press, 1995).

movements that have become an important feature of American political life.[1] Identity politics involves construction of shared knowledge and ethical norms and nurtures a new, affirmative sense of self. These social movements enable people to construct personal and collective identities through discourse and other social interactions. Membership and solidarity with the group develop in reaction to and relative to those outside the group's shared practices and knowledge. Identity and otherness are therefore established simultaneously.[2]

Intellectuals—and I refer to them in the broadest sense as people who formulate programs, strategies, and interpretations of their group's activities—are central to this process of articulating collective identities and forging a sense of group loyalty. Intellectuals facilitate this process both for already established groups who are seeking social recognition and for groups in the process of being established. Centrifugal forces in the cultural production of these communities complicates the important role that intellectuals play, however. Two dominant institutions of cultural legitimacy in our society—the university and the mass media—powerfully influence the framing and transmission of the minority discourses that help to establish and maintain these identities and communities.

Academic and community intellectuals each start out with different relations to the process with which their community creates collective representations. Because society generally does not accept the identities of new social movements, many intellectuals who help to enunciate collective representations operate outside the established, culturally legitimated institutions.

In identity politics, as in nationalism, there is a strong emphasis on inventing a new language and vocabulary and defining new bodies of knowledge. These new languages and knowledges would replace the institutionalized forms of knowledge that oppress certain communities or social groups. In this way, identity politics provides social and symbolic resources with which individuals can articulate the link between self-knowledge and the formation of social identities.[3]

Although collective action hinges on shared knowledge and beliefs, social and political movements often inspire the creation of knowledge.

Some movements have given rise to new scientific theories, new academic fields, and political and social identities.[4] Likewise, the lesbian and gay movements have provoked psychologists and other theorists to reformulate theories of sexual development and identity; the theory of discursive sexual identity formation, developed in part by participants of the gay and lesbian movements, has challenged traditional psychoanalytic theories of homosexuality.

This interplay between social movements, the construction of new knowledge, and cultural politics sets the stage for the complicated tensions between activists and intellectuals within social movements, on the one hand, and university intellectuals who also participate in their communities' political life, on the other. I will explore this charged terrain by examining how lesbian and gay culture and the production of knowledge create different political effects, both in the community and within universities.

CULTURAL POLITICS AND THE USES OF AUTHORITY

Tensions between social movements and the university take many forms, but a number of them involve contesting the forms of knowledge produced in the university and the value of those forms of knowledge to social movements and communities. For example, one concern of many gay and lesbian activists is the validity of research on the causes of homosexuality and the character of that knowledge. Research on the genetic basis of homosexuality might be interpreted as a fairly traditional form of disciplinary knowledge. Community intellectuals (as well as many academic ones) are passionately divided about the matter, however; some believe in the political value of seeing homosexuality as genetic (because it removes homosexuality from the realm of a moral or lifestyle "choice"), whereas some believe that such research has potential "eugenic" implications (because genetic engineering or selective genetic counseling could be used to reduce the possibility of giving birth to homosexual children).[5] Conflicting assessments of the knowledge generated in the course of everyday life, community organizing, and political discussions produce tensions.

Although the validity (what might be called "the truth effect" in Foucault's terms) of knowledge is certainly one of the key concerns of both scholars and political activists, I believe that political implications also divide activist-intellectuals from those in the university. Different ways of understanding and representing communities, movements, or political issues can have political effects (or "power effects," to use Foucault's language again).[6] The power effects of different forms of knowledge involve not only the legitimacy of that knowledge in communities or movements but also its effects on the political and intellectual leadership of movements and its strategic implications. The power effects of knowledge are important because they confer authority upon those who use it in their representations and interpretations of communities, movements, or issues in the course of political or social life; different forms of knowledge legitimate different activities.

The tensions between academic and community intellectuals also reflect differences in material resources. Academics usually earn salaries greater than those of activists and writers. In addition, academics have access to the university's benefits and privileges (such as health insurance, office space, free photocopying, a paid summer vacation, and so forth). Within the academy, however, scholars pursuing ethnic studies, women's studies, lesbian and gay studies, or leftist research face indifference if not outright hostility, a lack of institutional or professional recognition, and most likely underfunded programs. These inequalities themselves result from the lower status of the academic research that these scholars have chosen to pursue; that work has a lower status both within the university's institutional hierarchy of the university and within society at large. All the while, many such academics, particularly those who are younger and who do not have tenure, are under pressure to teach large classes and publish an enormous number of papers in order to keep their jobs or remain in their profession.

The intellectual commitments (the basic cognitive predispositions) of intellectuals and political activists determine the kinds of conduct they consider right and wrong, the kinds of phenomena they regard as puzzling or self-explanatory, the frameworks or "interpretative schemas" they use to understand their experience, and the kinds of intellectual arguments they consider cogent and plausible. Because our society has many different historical and cultural milieus, intellectuals and political activists face the question, What authority can be claimed, and by whom, in which social sphere or community?

Society values the disciplinary knowledge based in the university more than the vernacular knowledge of community intellectuals. This discrepancy yields unequal degrees of cultural authority or symbolic capital, and those differences in symbolic capital have distinct power effects. Community intellectuals produce knowledge to create *solidarity* within their community, whereas academic intellectuals create intellectual *legitimacy* (sanctioned by the institution—the primary source of intellectual authority in our society).[7] These highly charged differences create tensions between the kinds of intellectuals most often characterized as "academics" and "activists." One might describe this conflict as being between those with the "epistemic" authority of the university and those with the "charismatic" authority of everyday community experience.[8]

INTELLECTUALS AND THE EPISTEMOLOGY OF THE CLOSET

A deeply entrenched syndrome of invisibility, self-knowledge, and institutionalized ignorance that affects the personal and social development of homosexuals also shapes the identity politics of the lesbian and gay communities. Homosexuals are not born or reared in a community that recognizes our emotional and sexual interests. Instead, we establish lesbian and gay identities much later in life than people tend to develop their gender, ethnic, or racial identities.

Many of us do not feel that we choose our homoerotic desires (in fact, we grow up finding no positive reinforcement in the culture or community for homoerotic desires). We do, however, usually choose whether or not to come out and whether or not to participate in the lesbian or gay communities. An individual's struggle to come out often relies heavily on new ideas, critical reading, and, most important, on rejecting the heterosexual world's "knowledge" of homosexuality. Thus, in the life of lesbians and gay men, both *vernacular* and formal *disciplinary* knowledges play an important role (perhaps greater than for members of many other movements or communities).

This is true for a number of reasons. The closet is an institutionalized form of ignorance; it is a silence that surrounds any person's homoerotic desire.[9] Institutionalized forms of knowledge such as sex education; psychiatry and other forms of medicine; mainstream religion; electronic media and movies reinforce this ignorance through silence and stereotypes. Thus, coming out and forming gay and lesbian identities frequently depend on an individual's cultural and intellectual developments. When lesbians and gay men encounter each other, either through sexual relations, love affairs, or political activities, one of the most significant results is that they critically (discursively) evaluate stereotypes, misinformation, and social norms. Through this process, a sense of community is created. This is one of the reasons writers, journalists, librarians, booksellers, and other intellectuals play a particularly important role in lesbian and gay life.

Gay and lesbian communities, however, have not always existed. As with all communities, they are historical creations, imagined in the process of speaking, writing, and communicating publicly. Political activists, journalists, artists, and other community intellectuals articulate the vernacular knowledge of communal beliefs, practices, and norms in the course of political and everyday social activity. This vernacular knowledge is usually practical, very dependent on a social context, difficult to formalize (it is a form of personal knowledge), and transmitted casually to new members of the community. It is most rigorously tested in public discussion.

Two examples of lesbian and gay vernacular knowledge are the camp sensibility and the idea of safe sex. Camp originated among homosexuals many decades ago. Gay men widely appreciated it as a form of ironic commentary and broad humor that plays with the situation of a man's being sexually attracted to another man. ("Is a man attracted

to another really a woman?") A man would adopt feminine mannerisms and sometimes dress as a woman to comment ironically on male
homosexual life. In a fundamental way, camp builds on the idea that
gender is a role. Camp was therefore a very important form of vernacular knowledge (about the representation of gender, sexuality, and cultural coding) and cultural criticism in the gay and lesbian communities.

Although it received frequent expression in literary works, camp as
a form of humor and as an aesthetic sensibility existed for a long time
before intellectuals attempted to give a formal and coherent account of
it.[10] Susan Sontag and Esther Newton published two influential accounts of camp for audiences outside the gay community.[11] In her essay,
Sontag treated camp as an aesthetic sensibility that contributed to the
intellectual climate of the early 1960s. She saw camp as the forerunner
of a new "erotics of art" that downplayed art as a representation of
external reality and promoted a theory of art as subjective expression.
Newton's work on camp was a contribution to the urban ethnography
of contemporary America. Her book explored the life of female impersonators and camp's importance to them. For Newton, camp was, in
part, a profound vernacular commentary on the social construction of
gender and sexual roles.

In translating camp as a body of vernacular observations and practices into other intellectual frameworks, Sontag and Newton each formalized different "truths." Through their translations, camp moved
into other spheres of American society. As an aesthetic sensibility and
a commentary on gender roles and sexuality, camp had an impact outside the gay community. It entered the realms of disciplinary knowledge and was loosely formalized in literary criticism and anthropology.
This translation of vernacular to disciplinary knowledge illustrates perfectly how the two forms have differential power and truth effects.[12]
Sontag and Newton became authorities on camp to those outside the
world of drag queens and other practitioners of camp, whereas drag
queens remained authorities only in their own communities.

The social conditions that gave camp its existential punch changed
as an emerging lesbian and gay movement emphasized coming out of
the closet and insisted upon the social construction of gender and sexual roles. With these changes, camp lost some of its critical edge. Yet

disciplinary syntheses of camp forged by Sontag and Newton have proved useful to later generations of lesbians and gay men who never personally experienced anything like the camp culture of the 1950s. Thus, camp still exists—sustained by vernacular cultural traditions and the public disciplinary formulations of intellectuals such as Newton and Sontag—and is currently being reinterpreted by a younger generation of gay men and lesbians.[13]

The idea of safe sex served as another form of gay vernacular knowledge. This idea originated in the early days of the AIDS epidemic. Even before the virus was discovered, early epidemiological information suggested that AIDS was transmitted during sexual activity or through direct contact with the bloodstream. Most doctors recommended that gay men stop having sex altogether, except those in monogamous couples. Many men in the community felt, for both personal and political reasons, that it would be difficult to give up the sexual freedom achieved during the 1970s. Moreover, many gay men thought it was unrealistic to limit the spread of AIDS by calling for sexual abstinence.

In 1982, the Sisters of Perpetual Indulgence, a group of gay men in San Francisco who dressed in nuns' habits originally to protest the Catholic Church's position on homosexuality, began working with other activists to define safe sex. They developed a list of the prevalent sexual practices and classified them as high risk, moderately risky, and probably safe.[14] This was an important synthesis of vernacular knowledge and the available epidemiological information. The discovery of the human immunodeficiency virus in 1983 confirmed the reliability of most of the classifications of sexual practices in the early guidelines.

Safe-sex guidelines are the fundamental basis for AIDS education and for stopping the spread of HIV. As a result of these guidelines, the sexual practices of the gay male community have undergone social reconstruction.[15] The vernacular knowledge of sexual behavior, drawn upon by community intellectuals such as the Sisters of Perpetual Indulgence or Michael Callen and Richard Berkowitz, has helped to develop many important AIDS education strategies. These strategies have since been translated and reformulated into disciplinary frameworks of medicine, health education, cultural criticism, and sociology.[16]

The development of the camp sensibility and the idea of safe sex are powerful examples of the role of community intellectuals. Shifts in the forms of knowledge of camp and safe sex demonstrate that the cultural authority of vernacular knowledge is very unstable and limited. In part, this is true because of the economic fragility and limited life span of institutions that transmit vernacular knowledge to the lesbian and gay community (e.g., the drag bars where the camp sensibility thrived). These transient institutions have also supported the work of community intellectuals—lesbian and gay newspapers and magazines (the *Advocate*), art or drama collectives (groups such as Gran Fury and the Sisters of Perpetual Indulgence), history projects, civil rights law firms (National Center for Lesbian Rights and Lambda Legal Defense Funds), community-based AIDS research initiatives (the Treatment Issues Committee of ACT UP, the Community Research Initiative, *AIDS Treatment News*, or Project Inform) and political organizations (such as ACT UP, Queer Nation, and the lesbian and gay democratic clubs).

Another limitation originates in the belief that vernacular knowledge is spontaneous—that it emerges from the community almost directly. This "essentialism" belies the political and moral conflicts that often surround the development of vernacular knowledge. Vernacular knowledge is deeply embedded in the political and moral conflicts of the community. Its authority relies heavily on social pressure. Community members often cite vernacular knowledge when they criticize behavior and institutions that appear to transgress community norms. The context-dependence and normative priorities of vernacular knowledge (this does not mean disciplinary knowledge has no normative priorities of its own) severely limit the power it can have outside the community. Thus, as the producers of vernacular knowledge, lesbian and gay community intellectuals do not usually have much authority in the heterosexual world.

One interesting consequence of the political struggle over AIDS is that, contrary to the usual tendencies, gay intellectuals have acquired some authority outside the gay community. Gay AIDS activists have created major social service and educational institutions and have had a profound effect on AIDS policy.[17]

The power to articulate a collective identity, as with every other form of discourse, depends on the use of cultural capital. To inculcate in other minds a vision, a sense of self, and the recognition of new social possibilities, one must have acquired social authority in previous struggles. Cultural or symbolic capital is like credit; only those who have obtained significant recognition can legitimately demand more recognition. Representatives of a community or movement can only be chosen at the end of a long process of institutionalization, because a group gives its representatives the power to shape the group. Cultural authority or symbolic capital cannot be fabricated by fiat. Nor can it ever be effective if a social movement's vision of history is not based on existing social forces and developments.[18]

UNIVERSITY INTELLECTUALS AND IDENTITY POLITICS

As one of the major institutions that produces and legitimates knowledge in our society, the university gives lesbian and gay academics a different relationship to the production of knowledge and culture than the one community intellectuals and activists have.[19] Alvin Gouldner has characterized the university as having a culture of critical discourse.[20] Compared with the community, this culture depends less on context and is more formal, theoretical, and explicit about its underlying assumptions. Gouldner argues that this cultural style is also a form of cultural capital—this set of skills and achievements is economically rewarded within the professional and academic milieu. In addition, the social organization of universities shapes the forms of knowledge and their social usefulness. The intellectual norms of already established disciplines, the requirements of university curricula, and the power structure of educational institutions as they reflect the larger society all regulate the disciplinary knowledge produced at the university.[21] This institutional context is what differentiates the knowledge elaborated by academic intellectuals from that produced by community-based intellectuals.

Academics who are working to establish lesbian and gay studies as a legitimate field of teaching and research face enormous challenges. They not only must contend with the pervasive as well as subtle effects of homophobia but also must produce work that satisfies the norms of this culture of critical discourse. Lesbian and gay academics acquire disciplinary identities that are defined by two things: their status within the hierarchy of academic fields and departments, and the fact that lesbian and gay studies is only one distinct element of an "eclectic curriculum" that is not integrated into a coherent program.[22]

To construct knowledge within disciplinary boundaries prescribes certain methodologies, canonical texts, and acceptable research programs. Disciplines use certain conventions and norms to determine whether a particular intellectual contribution is legitimate and reliable knowledge. To give lesbian and gay studies legitimacy, the intellectual work of the new field must satisfy these conventions and norms. Whatever does not measure up to these standards—for example, some forms of the lesbian or gay community's vernacular knowledge—is marginalized and excluded.

Even the construction of acceptable disciplinary knowledge will not guarantee the incorporation of lesbian and gay studies into the university curriculum, however. The university is currently the battleground between rival political philosophies of education, and lesbian and gay studies (along with African American studies, women's studies, and ethnic studies) is at the center of the dispute.

The recent controversies over curriculum, the debate about the canon—this battle is about more than just reading lists and great books; it concerns different conceptions of social order.[23] Each vision of education implies a different academic professional identity.

Specialization within the eclectic curricula of most universities in the United States tends to encourage a strong subject loyalty that can serve as the basis for a professional identity. This "secular humanist" (as conservative cultural critics have labeled it) educational ideology incorporates new fields of knowledge and new intellectual identities into an open-ended eclectic curriculum that has no coherent educational philosophy.

In contrast, classical curricula such as the Great Books Program (at

St. John's College in Annapolis, Maryland, and Santa Fe, New Mexico) or those that emphasize the supposed coherence of Western civilization aim to develop individuals who have no strong loyalties to any particular discipline; these curricula therefore discourage disciplinary identities. Those on the Right, such as Allan Bloom, William Bennett, and the editors of the *New Criterion*, have exploited the canon debate in an attempt to establish a coherent educational philosophy and to block certain new disciplines from entering the curriculum. The conservative educational ideology definitively excludes those who they believe contribute to the "cultural decline of Western, male-dominated, family-based, capitalist civilization."[24]

In the debate about the humanities curriculum, communities or movements outside the university—African Americans, lesbians and gay men, Latinos, and women, for example—have challenged the disciplinary basis of education in the humanities, which has been communicated via strongly defined boundaries of subject matter.

To some extent, the academic hierarchy of disciplines and of the university shapes the identities of academic intellectuals. That is, as their careers progress, they know more and more about less and less, and thereby become distinct from everyone else. In the university, their intellectual (or disciplinary) identities are clearly marked and bounded.

This environment can insulate university intellectuals from their communities. Academic intellectuals who belong to the lesbian and gay communities must work within the structure of the university system, as must scholars who belong to any oppositional, ethnic, racial, or oppressed group. They must negotiate the overlapping demands of their academic lives and their political and social commitments. In the end, lesbian and gay academic intellectuals must address much of their intellectual work to other members of their academic disciplines in order to guarantee the work's intellectual credibility. Thus, lesbian and gay academics may do intellectual work that is potentially interesting to the community at large, but its disciplinary form inhibits their ability to communicate directly with a nonacademic lesbian or gay audience.[25]

The intellectual autonomy of academic disciplines that the American university encourages gives academic intellectuals a great deal of authority outside of their community. The authority rests ultimately on the status and resources of the university.[26] Community institutions cannot offer comparable conditions for carrying out intellectual work. Nor can they do much in the way of transmitting articulated and developed knowledge to new generations. Very few, if any, representatives of institutions within communities are able to address the larger society with the authority of a professor or assistant professor at Harvard, Stanford, or the University of California.

SOLIDARITY AND LEGITIMATION: INTELLECTUALS AND AUTHORITY IN THE PUBLIC SPHERE

Cultural politics become hegemonic through the slow building up of authority; the university, along with the mass media, is potentially one of the most powerful instruments of cultural legitimation. In contemporary American society, a great deal of our cultural politics originate when communities who are forging and reconstructing collective identities struggle for recognition and empowerment. These political struggles require both vernacular and disciplinary knowledge—both solidarity and legitimation. This is most forcefully illustrated by the battle against AIDS. Efforts to limit the transmission of HIV can only be effective if intellectuals and activists draw on the vernacular knowledge of the community affected—for example, the practices and beliefs of intravenous drug users—and combine that information with the disciplinary knowledge of epidemiology and medicine.

The *legitimation* that accrues to disciplinary knowledge about a marginalized or stigmatized community's life contributes to the social acceptance of that community. Academic intellectuals who are committed to such a community depend on community intellectuals and activists to articulate the meanings and values, relationships, and practices that are continually being created.

What is at stake in the tensions between academics and activist-intellectuals is control of the very grounds on which knowledge is produced and legitimated. The question of cultural authority involves the issue of *who* gets to "represent" the community, both politically and intellectually.

Community and academic intellectuals often have different orientations toward theory, and they need to acknowledge those differences. Community intellectuals resist theory, because they recognize the virtue of vernacular knowledge's context-dependence, but academics often insist that theory (which is not closely bound to its social context) is nevertheless necessary to make very explicit the links between social institutions and interpretative strategies.

Although community and activist-intellectuals often have greater access to the community public sphere—performance and gallery spaces, cabarets, local gay press, national magazines, theater companies and film festivals—academic intellectuals have the potential backing of one of our society's major institutions of cultural legitimacy, as well as greater access to institutional security. From the university, lesbian and gay academics can often speak with greater authority to the rest of society.

Currently, hardly any kind of institutional framework encompasses both community and academic intellectuals.[27] In the United States, the lesbian and gay community does have a relatively diverse and lively public sphere, but there are few public forums for academic research. There is an annual lesbian and gay studies conference (which has taken place at Yale, Harvard, and Rutgers). A number of lesbian and gay studies centers also sponsor seminars, panels, and conferences. In terms of publishing venues, there is one established journal (the *Journal of Homosexuality*), a new one (*GLQ*), and a growing number of mainstream academic publications (such as the *Journal of the History of Sexuality*) that will publish research on homosexuality.

Despite the lack of interlocking public spheres for community and academic intellectuals, there are rarely any efforts to exclude members of either category from the activities of both arenas. Yet lesbian and gay scholars' investments in the academic cultural capital (i.e., the "privileges" of the university) have led Eve Sedgwick to caution that "the extreme difficulty, not at all to say impossibility, of doing or thinking coalition politics at more than a superficial level" may be reinforced by the fact that "relative privilege in our mode of labor is inevitably going to oppose to [sic] most of our investment of real creativity, courage, and steadfastness in a class-based analysis."[28]

Creating some form of interlocking public spheres can modify the scholars' psychological investments and academic privileges and activist-intellectuals' charismatic authority in order to produce knowledge that draws from both vernacular and disciplinary sources.[29] The validity (the truth effects) and eventually the authority (the power effects) of each kind of knowledge must be tested through debate, analysis, and social experimentation. Without a mutual encounter in public life, both forms of knowledge are trivialized and socially limited.

Whether in academia or in the community, knowledge is a product of collective debate. This is evident in a number of ways, such as in the evolution of safe-sex guidelines, in the development of post-Stonewall therapeutic understanding of lesbian and gay relationships, and in the intellectual recognition of the social construction of identity. For dialogue and negotiation to take place between the community and academia, there need to be cultural intermediaries such as publishing houses, journals, conferences (the International AIDS conferences are good examples of such institutions).

According to Michel Foucault and many others, the intellectual who speaks for a universal and abstract idea of human rights is no longer politically acceptable. Rather, Foucault has argued that the "specific intellectual," as he named the role, is the appropriate example for our time. That conception of the specific intellectual most closely resembles what I have described here as the academic or disciplinary intellectual who uses specialized knowledge to the social good.[30] In contrast, the community intellectual most resembles Antonio Gramsci's organic intellectual.[31] Without creating a real institutional framework of interlocking public spheres along the lines suggested by Nancy Fraser, all of these models of intellectual activity are limited and inadequate.

The first step in creating a dialogue between the university and community is for both types of intellectuals to test and debate vernacular and disciplinary knowledges. Intellectuals have complex loyalties to overlapping identities of gender, generation, political orientation, ethnicity, and so on. The cultural authority of specific or organic intellectuals is subject to criticism. Therefore, they must adopt a new role—one deeply hybridized by the multiple sources of knowledge and authority in cultural life. This is the responsibility of intellectuals in contemporary society—to become public intellectuals.

PESSIMISM OF THE MIND

Universities and the Decline of Public Discourse

My mind is pessimistic, but my will is optimistic.

ANTONIO GRAMSCI, *Letters from Prison*

You can only beat an idea with another idea, and the
war of ideas and ideologies will be won or lost within
"the new class," not against it.

IRVING KRISTOL,
"On Corporate Philanthropy"

Ideas have always been important in American political life, and perhaps never more so than now.[1] Ironically, though, there are a growing number of complaints about the decline of public discourse in the United States—from Left, Right, and Center. Over the last decade, a constant stream of books and articles has analyzed the declining quality of American public life.[2] In 1987, two authors offered bold and dashing assessments of the current state of American intellectual life. Allan Bloom's *The Closing of the American Mind* and Russell Jacoby's *The Last Intellectuals* share a preoccupation with the role of Left intellectuals

This chapter is an updated and revised version of "Intellectuals, Universities and the Left," a review of Allan Bloom's *The Closing of the American Mind* and Russell Jacoby's *The Last Intellectuals* that appeared in *Socialist Review* no. 1 (January–March 1988).

within the university, but these authors approach their subjects from opposite ends of the political spectrum.

The growing dissatisfaction with the quality of public life came near the end of a decade in which the power of economic elites sharply increased and the balance of power in the United States underwent a major shift. This transfer of power, which started before Reagan's election to the presidency in 1980, coincided with a broad realignment of public policy and intellectual life. Behind this realignment of public life lay an elite of conservative intellectuals, situated in foundations, journals, and think tanks, who were lavishly funded by major corporations.[3]

Throughout this period, Left intellectuals were less and less able to engage constructively in national debates about political values, cultural issues, and public policy; the cultural hegemony of the Right increasingly constrained the terms of debate. The Right achieved this intellectual domination through its gross economic advantage. As business and economic elites seized control over public policy, they channeled millions of dollars into conservative think tanks, journals, and educational institutions.

THE ADVERSARY CULTURE AND THE UNIVERSITY

Since the mid-1970s, conservatives worked to reclaim American culture from the Left's supposed "domination" and to reverse the influence of "minorities," feminists, and "Marxists" on American public life and culture. It has long been a dogma of conservatives that Marxists and leftists dominate the humanities and social sciences in American universities.[4]

Allan Bloom's phenomenal best-seller, *The Closing of the American Mind*, took up the conservative critique of American intellectual life. Bloom places the blame for the lamentable state of public discourse squarely on the university, which is corrupted by relativism, egalitarianism, and leftist cultural criticism. Bloom's book is a rambling, ranting, and vulgarly snobbish analysis of the current state of American higher education. After twenty-nine weeks on the *New York Times* best-seller list, after selling almost 445,000 copies, and after making its author a millionaire, the book decisively affected the fundamental terms of debate about American education.[5] The Right's cultural policies seem likely to have a long-lasting intellectual impact. *The Closing of the American Mind*, like the owl of Minerva, took wing at the Reagan era's dusk.

The neoconservative analysis of the intellectual in recent American history owes its earliest formulation to Lionel Trilling. In the 1960s, he introduced the notion of an adversary culture in his dismay with his students' willingness to engage in "the socialization of the anti-social, or the acculturation of the anti-cultural, or the legitimization of the subversive"[6] under the influence of modernism in literature and art. What Trilling called the adversary culture had become "modernism in the streets," an early naming of what soon became the counterculture, and later postmodernism. Even more alarming, however, the adversary culture had become institutionalized in the universities.

Both Daniel Bell and Irving Kristol elaborated on Trilling's analysis of the adversary culture in subsequent works. For Bell, modernism had become the culture of capitalism. The adversary culture dominated the postindustrial society with three results: (1) modernist intellectuals had become so numerous that they no longer required a "bohemian enclave," (2) the majority of the population no longer had an intellectually respectable culture of its own, and (3) the protagonists of the adversary culture came close to dominating the cultural establishments—"the publishing houses, museums and galleries; the major news, picture and cultural weeklies and monthlies; the theater, the cinema, and the universities."

Adding to Trilling's and Bell's analysis of the adversary culture, Kristol cited Joseph Schumpeter's theory that capitalism stimulates the creation of intellectuals whose "restless rationalism" and criticism eventually undermine the legitimacy of capitalism as an economic system. For Kristol, modernism's "moral and spiritual hegemony" resulted from "the tremendous expansion—especially after World War II—of postsecondary education [which] provided a powerful institutional milieu for modernist tastes and attitudes among the mass of both teachers and students."[7]

In somewhat different terms, Bloom's book explores in detail the impact of the adversary culture on American universities. *The Closing of the American Mind* is ostensibly a critique of the university—it is subtitled *How Higher Education Has Failed Democracy and Impoverished the Souls of Today's Students.* Bloom's primary concern is political, however, and his basic thesis is that cultural relativism (and its political correlate, egalitarianism) is the prevailing ideology of American life.[8] Furthermore, he argues, this "relativism of truth and values" has made democracy impossible and has corrupted the moral character of the American people.

Shockingly, the book received incredibly generous treatment from reviewers and educators. Even critical reviewers discussed Bloom's arguments as though they are intellectually serious. Yet throughout his book Bloom makes many questionable generalizations and more than a few ridiculous assertions. The writing is slapdash and strident. The book is rife with glib and crude misinterpretations of Rousseau, Nietzsche, Marx, and that demon of American culture, Martin Heidegger.[9] One of the harshest critics, conservative educator Mortimer Adler, shared Bloom's interest in the "Great Books" approach to education but dismissed the book as "just silly."[10] Indeed, the book is silly, as well as stupid and vicious.

In the book, Bloom catalogues the "vices" of contemporary college students—their corruption by rock and roll, sexual freedom, racial tolerance, and feminism.[11] He then links those "vices" to the nefarious influence of German philosophy on American culture since World War II. The importation of Nietzsche, Freud, and Max Weber have promoted a "value relativism." Bloom argues that these ideas created "Nihilism—American Style," which is to say "nihilism with a happy ending."[12]

The image of this astonishing Americanization of the German pathos can be seen in the smiling face of Louis Armstrong as he belts out the words of his great hit, "Mack the Knife" . . . a translation of the song "Mackie Messer" from *The Threepenny Opera*, a monument of Weimar Republic popular culture, written by two heroes of the artistic Left, Bertolt Brecht and Kurt Weill. . . . This image can be seen in our intellectual history, if only one substitutes Mary McCarthy for Louis Armstrong and Hannah Arendt for Lotte Lenya, or David Reisman for Armstrong and Erich Fromm for Lenya and so on through the honor roll of American intellectuals. Our stars are singing a song they do not understand, translated from a German original. . . . But behind it all, the master lyricists are Nietzsche and Heidegger.[13]

For Bloom, one of the most significant effects of this German influence has been the "Nietzscheanization of the left," which refers to the way Lukács, Marcuse, Adorno, Sartre, and Merleau-Ponty (all under the influence of Weber, Freud, and Heidegger) have refashioned Marxism from an economic ideology to a form of "cultural criticism of life in the Western democracies." Under the influence of this left-wing Nietzscheanism, the 1960s were an "an unmitigated disaster" for American universities.[14]

Bloom devotes the last third of the book to exploring the university's role in a democratic society. He argues that the Enlightenment's original conception of the modern university was "to provide a publicly respectable place—and a means of support—for theoretical men, of whom at best there are only a few in any nation, to meet, exchange their thoughts and train young persons in the ways of science."[15] That German philosophy—primarily the influence again of Nietzsche and Heidegger—corrupted the university, however. For example, Heidegger made a famous speech as rector of the University of Heidelberg in which he urged his listeners to devote "the life of the mind to an emerging revelation of being, incarnated in a mass movement"—Heidegger meant National Socialism, of course. Thus, for Bloom, all the ills of American university life stem from the influence of mass movements on the life of the mind. Extending this logic, he announces that "the crisis of the German university . . . is the crisis of the university everywhere." From this follows the story of higher education during the 1960s and 1970s—the destruction of American universities by a mass movement seeking to "stamp out racism, sexism and elitism (the peculiar crimes of our democratic society)."[16]

Perhaps the most dangerous effect of Bloom's analysis has been the introduction of his political assumptions into the debate about higher education. Bloom's interpretation of the history of political philosophy has been profoundly influenced by his teacher Leo Strauss, whose *Natural Right and History* criticizes "modern" political philosophy and the idea of "natural rights."[17] Political philosophy and educational thinking, in the tradition of Leo Strauss, privilege "the ancients" over "the moderns."[18] Bloom thus marries a traditionalist concept of education based on Western European "great books" with the neoconservative critique of the adversary culture of postindustrial capitalist societies.

Bloom does not make explicit recommendations, but his strong arguments have obvious implications—ones which, pernicious though they are, he is able to avoid defending. The educational policy implied by Bloom's analysis rejects political and cultural values not already embodied in the "great books" of Western Europe. Seemingly, even the "great books" after Machiavelli—such as Kant, Rousseau, Hegel, Marx, or Nietzsche—must be excluded! What kind of educational philosophy is this? Bloom also argues that university education should be available only to an elite. Furthermore, Bloom implies that Left intellectuals should be eliminated from university teaching jobs because Left, minority, and feminist academics promote egalitarianism and, by Bloom's definition, "relativism." Bloom's vision of education is a reactionary nightmare.

THE MISSING GENERATION
OF PUBLIC INTELLECTUALS

Although the belief of right-wing intellectuals that Marxists, minorities, and feminists dominate universities is ridiculous,[19] it does reflect the distorted perception of an important fact—that Left intellectuals almost exclusively depend on academic jobs for their economic and intellectual livelihoods. Very few Left intellectuals make their livings outside academia. This corresponds with the broader trend that less and less of American intellectual life takes place outside the university.

If Bloom blames the decline of the university on the Left, in *The Last Intellectuals*, Russell Jacoby blames the decline of the Left on the university. Jacoby's examination of this matter derives from the larger question of the decline in the quality of American public discourse. Unfortunately, however, he interprets this broad concern much more narrowly. He asks, "Where are our intellectuals?" With "our," he means "the Left" or "the generation of the 1960s." By "intellectuals," he means "public" intellectuals.

Once one accepts these limits in Jacoby's analysis, one sees that his argument has a certain plausibility. He asserts that there have been three key changes:

1.   urban neighborhoods with cheap rents and residential concentrations of low-income intellectuals have disappeared;
2.   university employment has increased;
3.   Left intellectuals have moved into academic employment and adopted academic intellectual standards.

These developments, according to Jacoby, have created a missing generation of "public intellectuals" (that is, intellectuals who address a general educated audience).

The "missing generation" came of age during the 1960s and 1970s. The men and women of this generation are missing from public life because they entered academia. They became professors because it was difficult to earn a living as an intellectual outside the university. Once they took university jobs, they gradually ceased to address a larger public. Instead, they wrote for professional journals and explored the intellectual problems of academic disciplines rather than the public issues of the day.

In addition to this tale of generational woe, Jacoby argues that suburbanization and gentrification have destroyed the bohemian enclaves that allowed intellectuals to live cheaply and near other writers and intellectuals.[20] This, however, is Jacoby's least plausible argument (although it is politically and culturally attractive). Urban bohemias and their cultural radicalism have rarely been important environments for public intellectuals. In American history, only two notable groups of public intellectuals have come out of a bohemian culture—the social critics and intellectuals working with Randolph Bourne, Max Eastman,

and Lewis Mumford on the journals *Seven Arts* and the *Masses* in the
early 1900s; and the New York intellectuals centered on the *Partisan
Review* in the 1930s and 1940s.[21]

Some varieties of cultural radicalism have been important to the political development of intellectuals involved in social movements. For
example, the 1960s counterculture, black culture, and lesbian and gay
male cultures have all played a role in the political life of our times.
Jacoby is most convincing, however, when he argues that the academ-
icization of Left intellectuals explains their political isolation and their
retreat into obscure disciplinary issues.

THE RISE OF NEOINTELLECTUALS AND THE
EXCLUSION OF COMMUNITY INTELLECTUALS
FROM THE PUBLIC SPHERE

Jacoby's parochial emphasis on *Left* intellectuals obscures the political
and economic forces currently reshaping the American public sphere.
Can we really understand these changes by restricting our analysis to
Left intellectuals? Are there really no "public intellectuals" under forty-
five? Are there no Left intellectuals outside the university? If we answer
these questions, we will interpret the shifts in contemporary intellectual
life quite differently than Jacoby has.[22]

There is no doubt that the university has captured most of the intellectual life since World War II. In addition, Jacoby correctly assesses
the impact of academic hegemony on American public life. By focusing
on the university, however, Jacoby has missed some of the fundamental
changes that have shaped public intellectual life. One of the most important shifts is that "think tank" intellectuals, predominantly neoconservatives, have a growing influence in the public sphere. Another is
that a fragile intellectual life has emerged from social movements and
minority communities over the past twenty years.

Left intellectuals do not have an exclusive monopoly on the role of
"public" intellectual. There *are* public intellectuals in the United States
today. Both neoconservative and neoliberal intellectuals regularly ad-

dress broad issues of social values and public policy. Many of these intellectuals are not university professors. We must therefore ask two additional questions: Why are the neointellectuals[23] able to address a broader public than Left intellectuals? Furthermore, what institutions support the neointellectuals if they are not regularly attached to universities?

By refusing to recognize the significance of neoconservative intellectuals, Jacoby misses one of the most significant changes in American public life; a powerful new institution of intellectual life—the think tank—has emerged.[24] By ignoring the neoliberals, Jacoby misses a group of public intellectuals who most resemble his models—Lewis Mumford, C. Wright Mills, and Edmund Wilson. Many of the leading neoliberal intellectuals—James Fallows, Sidney Blumenthal, Charles Peters, and Michael Kinsley—are young journalists associated with the *Washington Monthly* (where most neoliberal journalists have been trained), the *Atlantic*, the *Texas Monthly*, and the *New Republic*.[25]

Most of the neointellectuals may not be highbrow by academic standards, but university intellectuals have held in contempt many public intellectuals, such as Lewis Mumford or Edmund Wilson. If one identifies a wider spectrum of public intellectuals, however, it becomes obvious these groups have vastly different sources of patronage. Many conservative intellectual institutions—the Heritage Foundation, the Institute for Contemporary Studies, the *New Criterion*, and the Committee on the Present Danger—are well funded by big corporations and right-wing foundations. Many neoliberal intellectuals work as journalists, although a few are professors. Left intellectuals depend almost exclusively, however, on the university for their economic livelihoods.

By failing to recognize the important role of neoconservatives as public intellectuals, Jacoby also misses an important shift in public life during the 1980s. Business elites mobilized politically by creating a conservative intellectual agenda. The think tanks and other intellectual institutions funded by corporations and conservative foundations hammered out this agenda.

The promotion of *Losing Ground*, Charles Murray's book on welfare policy, is a perfect example of this development. Funded by conservative foundations, Murray wrote the book while he was senior research fellow at the Manhattan Institute for Public Policy. The institute spent almost $15,000 distributing seven hundred free copies to academics, journalists, and policymakers—including members of Margaret Thatcher's cabinet. Intellectuals and journalists with influence on policy received honoraria ranging from $500 to $1000 to attend a seminar on Murray's book at the exclusive New York Athletic Club. The conservative backers hired a public relations specialist, who ensured that the author appeared on television and met with editors and academics.[26]

The Left cannot mobilize comparable resources to promote its policy recommendations. Elliott Currie wrote his award-winning book *Confronting Crime* on a publisher's advance without any institutional support. Murray's book *Losing Ground* has been called the most important work on poverty and social policy since Michael Harrington's *The Other America* in 1962, but Harrington's book became influential without any corporate funding.

Although think tanks have promulgated conservative points of view to a broad public, the political effectiveness of these institutions hinges on the private discussion that takes place between the intellectual elite and policymakers. The rise of the think tanks, which often exist outside the public sphere and independent of the market, impoverishes the public debate so essential to a democracy.

Jacoby ignores another important dynamic of American intellectual life—the emergence of intellectuals within social movements. Intellectuals in the black community, the women's movement, the lesbian and gay communities, or the environmental movement participate in intellectual and political debates within these communities and frequently represent them in mainstream arenas. Some of these intellectual activists work in community organizations. Many write, edit, or regularly discuss the ideas and analyses published in the movement publications.[27] Although these intellectuals may not identify as "socialists," many do identify themselves broadly as "progressives" or "leftists." How do these intellectuals relate to American public life and to the university?

African American intellectuals have a long and complex history of a communal public life independent of the university.[28] In the 1960s and 1970s, however, black intellectuals increasingly worked in American universities, as did Left intellectuals. Some of the differences between African American academics and black public intellectuals clearly reflect the same processes that Jacoby analyzes for white Left intellectuals. Essays by Cornel West, Martin Kilson, and Greg Tate explore the emergence of a new wave of black intellectuals (such as Ntozake Shange, Maya Angelou, Spike Lee, Julius Lester, Larry Neal, Alice Walker, and Henry Louis Gates). These thinkers bridge the black cultural nationalism institutionalized in black studies programs and a new cultural pluralism recognizing the competing social identities that many intellectuals, writers, and activists experience. These new developments promise to create the basis for an intellectual life that includes both academics and community intellectuals.[29]

Kilson develops this theme against the experience of the Harlem Renaissance:

> Black intellectuals have nonetheless packaged their pluralism in intricate varieties. For example, while the Harlem Renaissance or New Negro movement among the post–World War I generation represented the first assertion . . . of blackness vis-à-vis white America, this movement was also a milieu or agency through which Afro-American intellectuals gained some creative autonomy vis-à-vis their own ethnic group.
>
> While coming together under the umbrella of the Harlem Renaissance movement, some black intellectuals simultaneously latched onto a homosexual subculture (Countee Cullen); some reached out to the political Left, both socialist and communist (Claude McKay); some nested with elite bohemian circles (Zora Neale Hurston); and some flirted with all of these (Langston Hughes).[30]

Kilson identifies two obstacles preventing African American intellectuals from participation in American public life. One is that black intellectuals usually depend on employment in black studies programs. Another obstacle (also echoed by Tate) is the lack of "a major journal that could serve as a forum for discussion, appraisal, and prescription."[31]

Public intellectuals will always be at a disadvantage compared with university intellectuals until some kind of institutions exist outside the university. Such institutions have been established, but for financial reasons, they usually combine their intellectual work with other community projects. One such example is the Center for Third World Organizing in Oakland. Although it primarily trains community organizers, it also has a publishing program and holds conferences, which convene academics and activists to discuss political and cultural issues.

In recent years, lesbian and gay intellectuals have also worked to establish an intellectual life within their communities. Even almost thirty years after the emergence of the gay movement, there are few openly gay or lesbian university professors.[32] One of the most important intellectual developments within the lesbian and gay male communities has been the work done in the history of homosexuals. Between 1970 and 1984, much of the research, writing, and public presentation of lesbian and gay history has been done by nonacademic intellectuals (Jonathan Ned Katz, Allan Bérubé, Joan Nestle) and by the members of community history organizations located across the country. These "history projects" have included the Lesbian Herstory Archives in New York (founded in 1975), the San Francisco Lesbian and Gay History Project (which began in 1978), the Buffalo Oral History Project, and the Boston Area History Project. What is distinctive about the history projects is that their members are volunteers; few of them are professional historians.[33]

Lesbian and gay history has been politically important because it provides a means for exploring crucial issues of identity, sexual socialization, and community development that previously were studied very little, if at all. Gay and lesbian history has had not only a strong influence on gay political thinking but also a visible impact on the feminist and public policy debates over whether pornography contributes to violence against women. Many feminists who criticized the antipornography movement were active in the lesbian and gay history movement.[34] Gay historians also published historical analyses as contributions to the debate over closing the bathhouses in the early years of the AIDS epidemic.[35]

Community intellectuals have not been able to mobilize the resources to establish stable, long-lived institutions that can support work directly addressing the community. Although such intellectuals often play important roles in their own communities, they rarely have the chance to address a broader public. During the 1960s and early 1970s, community intellectuals frequently participated in public discussions. Their exclusion from the public sphere is largely the result of growing conservative hegemony over what is discussed in public. Conservatives exercise this dominance by creating new intellectual institutions, such as think tanks, which have the money to develop and promote cultural activities and public policies.

Jacoby's narrow focus on the traditional Left and the university makes it difficult to identify the changes in American public life. Both the visibility of neointellectuals and the exclusion of community intellectuals result from business elites' momentous entrance into the U.S. political arena. The Right's reshaped government policies on the economy, defense, and social spending largely by establishing think tanks and lobbying groups. The business campaign of the 1980s has helped make economic policy one of the pivotal themes of American public life. Since 1980, these conservative campaigns have channeled enormous resources toward formulating and promoting their vision of public policy.

THE DECLINE OF PUBLIC DISCOURSE

Since the 1960s, the university has been an ideological and cultural battlefield. Jacoby and Bloom examined the results of that long historical process. Whereas Bloom sees the university as overrun by barbarians, Jacoby believes that intellectual guerrillas are missing in action. In a sense, Bloom is right that the university is overwhelmed by the heterogeneous discourses of social movements and modern America's cultural diversity. The university has failed to provide a discursive framework within which different social groups can address each other. Outside the university, American society has also failed to create a public sphere in which different ideological and social groups can democratically debate social and economic policy. Instead, the conservative hegemony has reduced the vigorous striving of American public life.

Jacoby's critique of Left academics is also accurate in some respects. A distinctive feature of the university is what Alvin Gouldner has called "the culture of critical discourse" (CCD).[36] This culture constrains the language with which academic intellectuals can address their communities or a larger public. Some of CCD's traits—for instance, terms that are abstract or relatively independent of context, or the legitimation of intellectual claims without reference to a speaker's social role—reduce the value of an academic's contribution to debates outside the university.[37]

Since World War II, social scientists have extended CCD to social and cultural thought, thus excluding discussions of historical context, cultural values, and ethical norms. The institutions of the academic labor market (publish or perish, tenure, peer review, and so forth) and the federal research funding process enforce CCD's hold on intellectuals who are committed to thinking about public issues. Community intellectual institutions (such as journals, theater companies, study groups, book publishers, and music clubs) rarely have the resources to compete with the system of higher education. Yet the university rarely provides opportunities for the intellectuals on their faculties to address a broad public audience.

Although universities' culture of critical discourse limits the salience (for Jacoby) of intellectuals' contributions to public debates, conservative intellectuals (following Leo Strauss's criticism of modern political theory) view CCD as subverting the moral and spiritual values of mainstream American culture. Both Bloom and Jacoby have focused on only one of the institutions that significantly affect the quality of public discourse. I have pointed to how the rise of conservative elites has transformed the public sphere. No diagnosis of the declining public sphere, however, should overlook the powerful influence of mass media.

In 1985, Neil Postman—a well-known author and social critic—published *Amusing Ourselves to Death: Public Discourse in the Age of Show Business*, one of the first essays on the declining quality of public discourse. In his book, Postman argued that "we have reached . . . a critical mass in that electronic media have decisively and irreversibly changed the character of our symbolic environment. We are now a culture whose information, ideas, and epistemology are given by television, not by the printed word." Postman overstates his case, but there is little reason to doubt the influence of television on American public discourse. As with the influence of academic culture, television and the mass media pose a threat to the public sphere by excluding political and cultural diversity.

Having vital intellectual institutions outside the university is a crucial part of having a democratic public sphere. The existence of numerous journals of critical opinion, bookstores, community radio stations, socialist schools, and study groups helps to create a culture that thinks critically. In such a culture, people examine and discuss the ideas and philosophies that shape government policies and the solutions to social problems.[38]

Public discourse has declined because powerful forces have restricted the terms of debate. Political debate in a democracy relies on the clash of values and differences. Heterogeneous political discourses and various speech communities (including professional jargons, generational slangs, and minority dialects) should enter the public sphere in a lively dialogue. Public life should encourage community and movement intellectuals to address specific issues and concerns that cut across different communities. Public intellectuals should respond to the issues and concerns of many communities. In the public sphere, the cultural differences and social values of diverse communities should help fashion public policies and political goals.

8 UNDER THE SIGN OF THE QUEER

Cultural Studies and Social Theory

For several years now, lesbian and gay studies has found a growing place in the academy. Increasingly, work in literary theory and cultural studies has defined this field. More recently, lesbian and gay studies has gone by the name of "queer theory," in which scholars have tended to focus on representations of homosexuality in literature, film, and popular culture.

A new paradigm of cultural studies, queer theory draws on the work of theorists such as Michel Foucault, Jacques Lacan, Jacques Derrida, and Roland Barthes. Queer theory differs from the writing and research of earlier scholars in lesbian and gay studies because it emphasizes the

This chapter is a slightly revised version of a review of Michael Warner's *Fear of a Queer Planet* that originally appeared in *Found Object* (fall 1994).

close analysis of texts, popular culture, and the media. The earlier generation focused on historical, social, and anthropological analysis of documents, movements, and social structures—supplemented by the recovery of lost and forgotten authors, historical figures, and pioneering political activities.

Although the term "queer" reflects a revolution in lesbian and gay studies, it also marks the emergence of a new generation of political activists. The 1991 founding of the group Queer Nation underlined this development. The term "queer" plays on the double entendre of its pejorative meaning in relation to homosexuals and its more benign implication of "odd" or "marginal"; together, the two types of connotations assert the relation of the stigmatized "queer" to the dominant "normal." The name "queer theory" appeals to those in the field because it moves away from the simple assertion of identity politics indicated by the name "lesbian and gay studies," and includes all hybrid forms of identity that are different from hegemonic heterosexual identities.

"Queer" includes those who identify as homosexual, lesbian, or gay; those men (who may not identify as homosexuals) who have sex with men, and those women who have sex with women; bisexuals; transvestites, transsexuals, and transgendered people; sadomasochists and leather people; and all those who have a sexual preference that is not normative. "Queer" can signify the mere eccentric, as well as the sexual pervert (the word has long been used to identify—and stigmatize—deviants). "Queer" privileges that which is "not normal"—it defends the different, the marginal, and the oppositional.

It is not always clear whether queer theory and the politics of groups such as Queer Nation seek to transform existing social norms (thus replacing oppressive norms with new, liberating ones), or whether they strive to resist the social process of normalization *tout court*. The latter strategy is hopelessly romantic—that is, sociologically impossible. No form of social life exists without some sort of norms.

To theorize under the sign of "queer" is to critique lesbian and gay politics as a form of social mobilization predicated on a stable social identity. Queer politics, Michael Warner has argued, avoids the binary logic of member/nonmember, a polarization that plays a key part in the identity politics of race and gender. Although both gender and race remain important distinctions, queer politics offers a way of cutting across race and gender lines. It rejects the minority group pursuit of social acceptance or proper representation. Instead, queer politics represents inclusion. Specifically, queers resist the regimes of the normal. It implies that we redefine the problem of homosexual liberation so that we no longer fight *intolerance* but resist *normalization*. We need to stand firm against *heteronormalization*—the domination of norms that support, reinforce, and reproduce heterosexual social forms. To assert that *normalization* rather than *intolerance* is the aversion of queer politics overwhelmingly suggests that homophobia expresses itself not through repression and physical violence alone but also through normalizing moral and scientific discourses.

Michel Foucault provided the theoretical foundation for this form of homosexual politics. In the first volume of his *History of Sexuality*, Foucault challenged the "repression hypothesis"—the notion held by theorists such as Freud and Wilhelm Reich that modern societies required a high degree of repression in order to function effectively. Foucault argued that in the modern era, power was no longer centered predominantly in the sovereign state but was dispersed throughout civil society. Foucault thought we could not comprehend the implications of such a momentous historical shift if we continued to think of the subject's relationship to power solely in terms of repression. He posited that resisting repression and violent domination no longer exclusively shaped the modern subject so much as the power of discourse.

There is no doubt that the normalizing discourses of medicine, psychiatry, religion, popular culture, and even advertising have had a significant impact on homosexual oppression in American and European societies. However, a social theory that exclusively focuses on the discursive regimes of power/knowledge can offer only limited guidance in developing political strategies and achieving long-term social change.

In *Fear of a Queer Planet*, Michael Warner has edited a collection of essays that seeks to spell out the implication of queer politics for the writing of social theory. In this essay, I will focus on the vision of social theory revealed by the authors in Warner's collection. In his introduction to the book, Warner notes that the Foucault-inspired social-constructionist perspective of queer theory has encouraged a growing skepticism about rights discourse and forms of universalism in gay politics. In the wake of such doubts, queer theorists have replaced the universalizing discourse of rights and gay identity with new theories of political interest or sexual difference.[1] As Cindy Patton argues in that volume, "The crucial battle . . . is not achieving democratic *representation* but *wresting control over the discourses*."[2]

How do we wrest control over the discourses? Discursive formations are pervasive, highly elastic, thoroughly interlocking social structures. Can political and social movements (or even power elites) do anything more than try to shape the fundamental discourses of any social system? If we must try to wrest control over the discourses, is that a politically realistic strategy?

PERFORMATIVE AS POLITICAL

What are the theoretical foundations of queer theory? The work of Eve Kosofsky Sedgwick and Judith Butler, in addition to that of Jacques Lacan and Michel Foucault, looms over most of the pieces in *Fear of a Queer Planet*, and their operative assumptions have significant implications for queer social theory as represented in Warner's book. Sedgwick and Butler's works extend and work out the social-constructionist agenda that Michel Foucault pioneered.[3] Their work explores the productive and mobilizing effects of discourse. In the work of these queer theorists, like that of Foucault, the subject is the product of complex regimes of power/knowledge that function in and through discourse.

Eve Kosofsky Sedgwick is perhaps the most creative and original theorist of queer studies. Nonetheless, the relation between the texts she studies and the real historical processes that have shaped those texts remains obscure. She makes the radical claim that by the end of the nineteenth century, no one could avoid categorizing himself or herself as heterosexual or homosexual. The emergence of such a choice—between categorizing oneself as homosexual or heterosexual—obviously resulted from profound historical changes. It provides the historical context within which Sedgwick examines a series of literary texts. Yet, she neither explains nor empirically demonstrates the genesis and development of this choice.

Sedgwick has developed two complex lines of argument that have significant social implications. The first one, which she elaborates in her 1985 book, *Between Men*, is that homosocial forms of domination partly result from men's repudiation of homoerotic bonds.[4] As they shun these homoerotic feelings, they project them onto the marginalized figure of the homosexual man. In the Victorian period, both class identity and male domination rested on homosociality—the sex-segregated forms of social life. The second argument, which she makes in *Epistemology of the Closet*, is that in Western societies, separated but related forms of knowledge (science, coded vernacular knowledges, open secrets, the unsayable) have established a medium of domination unlike any other. Sedgwick's arguments identify powerful ways in which society represses and marginalizes homosexuality.

Judith Butler's contribution to queer discourse has less to do with constituting queer studies as a discipline than with working out a theory about how gender and sexuality are forms of subjectivity. In her book *Gender Trouble* and in the essays collected in *Bodies That Matter*, Butler has explored gender and sexual identity as constituted through performativity. This notion of the performative comes from speech-act theory. According to this theory, judicial sentences, baptisms, inaugurations, legal contracts, declarations of ownership, and marriage ceremonies would all be performative acts. In her work, Butler has expanded the notion of performativity. People construct gender and sexual identities, Butler argues, through a reiterative process by which the power of discourse can produce the phenomenon that it "names" or categorizes. In other words, if one acts queer in enough ways, one acquires a queer identity.

Following in the footsteps of kindred political theorists such as

Chantal Mouffe, Ernesto Laclau, and Slavoj Žižek, Butler identifies the performative character of discourse as a prerequisite for political mobilization.⁵ According to this theory of performatives, political signifiers are only contingently related, whether they are identities, ideologies, or symbols. Thus, political mobilization (whether it involves building a coalition or establishing hegemony) requires a perpetual interweaving of these political signifiers.

Cindy Patton's essay "Tremble Hetero Swine" provides a good example of this theoretical approach by precisely exploring how political signifiers are defined and constituted contingently. Patton argues that the lesbian and gay movement and the Religious Right have focused on each other, which has helped both groups to consolidate their internal identities. They have each publicly *dis-identified* with the other, which makes the two movements "allies" in a sense, or perhaps more accurately "codependents."

THE DISAPPEARANCE OF THE SOCIAL

Cindy Patton argues that our ability to understand the social *"constitution* of identities in the civil sphere lags behind the techniques for deconstructing them." For instance, "the 'social,' " as Patton says, "is deconstructed and evacuated, but a 'cultural' . . . is reinserted in the same place."⁶ In other words, Patton sums up well the dilemma that Warner and many of the contributors face.

Patton's diagnosis is right on the nose, but ironically, her own essay is trapped in the rhetorical theorizing that she seems to want to escape. The truth is that, compared with the social or political theories that are currently available, the cultural and textual theories of homosexuality and identity *are* much more sophisticated, subtle, and extensive.

For example, when Patton explores the state's significance for queers, she does not discuss policies, institutions, or material effects of the government's actions, but identities, discourses, and the space of queerness. Patton's analysis is intelligent and might be true, but it remains too much at the highest levels of abstraction about discursive formations.

This aspect is compatible, however, with her claim that our political goal should be *"wresting control over the discourses."*[7] Queer theorists never recover the social because the empirical detail of institutions and social structures is never examined. Identifying potential political strategies primarily by wresting control over the discourses leads only to cultural politics—certainly a valid form of political activity but not sufficient for achieving many political goals.

Lauren Berlant and Elizabeth Freeman's study of Queer Nation shows just how elusive "the social" remains and just how dominant "the cultural" is in its presence. Their article demonstrates the limits of both queer politics and queer theory as political analysis. Berlant and Freeman's survey of Queer Nation's political activities reveals a politics of symbolic gestures, many of which are nothing more than intellectually creative cultural provocations: posters, T-shirts, kiss-ins at malls, or "queer nights out" at local singles bars. Only the Queer Nation offshoot, the Pink Panthers (modeled on the Guardian Angels), directly uses physical or institutional forms of domination. Berlant and Freeman interpret most of Queer Nation's actions as theoretically suggestive forms of resistance to the cultural hegemony of heterosexuality—to the process, as Warner said, of heteronormalization.[8]

The queer moment did not emerge from nowhere; it grew out of AIDS activism. As with being queer, being infected with HIV cuts across numerous social categories such as sexual identity, race, and gender. Those with AIDS are stigmatized by the normalizing discourses of morality, medicine, and politics. Queer politics thus owes something to AIDS activism.

The AIDS movement pioneered new and sophisticated forms of cultural politics—the large dramatic and well-planned demonstrations on Wall Street, at the Food and Drug Administration, and at St. Patrick's Cathedral, along with the political posters by the activist art groups Gran Fury and Gang. The movement was also politically successful; it forced the federal government to modify its policies about testing AIDS treatments and about the direction of AIDS research and education. AIDS activism has successfully combined media-savvy cultural politics with hard-headed realpolitik. Queer theory has been much more interested in being media savvy than in the politics of governmental reform. Douglas Crimp's AIDS activism work acknowledges both dimensions of the movement's political strategy, but he has nonetheless tended to focus his argument on cultural politics.[9]

Cultural politics is the form of political action that queer theory and its conception of heteronormalization imply. Some queer political activists discount as naive and assimilationist any interpretation of civil life that emphasizes legal rights, political representation, community development, and identity politics as necessary for homosexual emancipation.

THE HETERONORMATIVITY OF GRAND THEORY

In *Fear of a Queer Planet*, Michael Warner makes the powerful and fruitful claim that because of the centrality of heterosexual norms in the work of the most contemporary social theorists (Jurgen Habermas, Pierre Bourdieu, Ernesto Laclau, and Chantal Mouffe), this work has minimal relevance for queer activists and intellectuals. These thinkers have not only frequently failed to incorporate sexuality into their theories, but if they do, they almost never account for the central role of *homosexuality* in North American and European societies. In contrast, queer theory has produced a solid body of work that shows homosexuality's centrality—in *Epistemology of the Closet* Eve Sedgwick has argued that "an understanding of virtually any aspect of modern Western culture must be, not merely incomplete, but damaged in its central substance to the degree that does not incorporate a critical analysis of modern homo/heterosexual definition."[10]

Heteronormativity, in Warner's interpretation, is not merely an intellectual or normative "bias" in the work of social theorists; it is embodied in social systems.[11] Heteronormativity permeates the powerful discursive formation—what Gayle Rubin has called "the sex/gender system"—that codes everything from social class to race into a particular set of sexual and gender identities and roles.[12] Warner's account of heteronormativity offers an original and radical critique of the social ontologies of contemporary social theorists. He takes "queer" as the fundamental recognition of difference. To ignore queer sexuality is to deny the queer nature of the world and the production of difference.

Following the lead of Monique Wittig, Warner identifies heterosexuality itself as "the social contract." This implicitly heteronormative political fiction has a supplementary idea—a reproductivist conception of the social. The institutions of heterosexual reproduction (marriage, kinship), institutions of socialization (schools, sports, families), and heterosexual hegemony (family law and the heterosexual assumption) all contribute to this notion. The heterosexual social contract and the reproductivist conception of the social shape the political and moral discourses that normalize sexual perversities.[13]

Is it possible to have a society that is not founded on a reproductivist conception of the social or heteronormativity? Herbert Marcuse in *Eros and Civilization*, Norman O. Brown in *Life against Death*, and Gilles Deleuze and Felix Guattari in *Anti-Oedipus* and *A Thousand Plateaus* have all tried to articulate conceptions of the social that are not reproductivist or heteronormative.[14]

Identifying the heteronormativity implicit in works of social theory is extremely important for developing homo positive social theorizing. A third of *Queer Planet* consists of valuable studies of the heteronormative bias in important works of social thought. Andrew Parker explores the homoerotic and homophobic dynamics underlying Marx and Engels's collaboration, which effectively challenges them as authors and castigates their homophobic reaction to the nineteenth-century German homosexual emancipation movement.

Queer Planet does not take on any of the major figures of contemporary social theory. An examination of heteronormativity in the work of Habermas, John Rawls, Ronald Dworkin, or Pierre Bourdieu would be extremely valuable to homo theorists. Moreover, none of the *Queer Planet* authors examine the work of social theorists who do include queer and homosexual themes. For example, in several of his latest books, including *Modernity and Self-Identity* and *The Transformation of Intimacy*, Anthony Giddens has identified lesbians and gay men as creating new forms of intimate relationships.[15]

Several feminist social theorists have developed powerful critiques of heteronormativity, including Kate Millett, Adrienne Rich, and Monique Wittig. Gayle Rubin undertakes the most important deconstruction of heteronormativity in social theory (she draws on Claude Lévi-Strauss and Jacques Lacan) in her landmark essay "The Traffic in Women." By analyzing the sex/gender system as the infrastructure of discursive formations that map "biological capacities into symbolic and social patterns that constitute our lives as gendered and sexual human beings" and that privilege heterosexuality, Rubin contributes significantly to nonheteronormative social theorizing.[16]

Warner notes in passing Herbert Marcuse's important contribution to a social theory of sexuality and homosexuality. It would be a shame, however, to forget that in *Eros and Civilization*, Marcuse managed to escape heteronormativity to some extent. Arguing that homosexuality was a revolutionary form of sexuality, he championed "polymorphous perversity" as a utopian form of sexuality free from procreative demands. Although we might have reservations about Marcuse's theoretical assumptions and terminology, he does try to explain the capitalist organization of libidinal gratification. Marcuse points to the double-edged aspect of consumption—its liberatory as well as its repressive role—and discusses how the emergence of a late-capitalist consumer economy increased the search for sexual gratification within new normalized limits. He characterized this heightened but constrained desire as "repressive desublimation."[17] To some extent, the theoretical writing of the Gay Left Collective, Jeffrey Weeks, Dennis Altman, and John D'Emilio in the late 1970s and early 1980s derives from Marcuse's example.

One of the contemporary homo social theorist's most important projects would be to deconstruct the heteronormative in our social thinking. The heteronormativity of most influential social theories is partly what makes *normalization* the primary focus of queer theory. The stress on the issue of normalization, or the "wresting control over the discourses," makes cultural politics a major component of homosexual politics. With this emphasis, however, lesbian and gay theorists and activists find it difficult to develop political strategies promoting the acceptance of sexual diversity in American life. Cultural politics and its reconfiguring of cultural representations can have a discernible impact, but they can't help us defeat those who resist changes in public consciousness.

The gay and lesbian movement failed to counter homophobic representations of homosexuals' serving in the military. In addition, the movement could not exert the raw economic and political power needed to force the Senate Armed Services Committee to hold fair hearings on the question. The movement's stress on cultural politics and the critique of heteronormativity showed that it was not prepared or willing to organize institutional and electoral resources. Ultimately, this political failure resulted from both the continued hegemony of normalizing discourses *and* the movement's inability to mobilize political and electoral power.

CULTURE WARS AND THE PROBLEM OF HEGEMONY

Fear of a Queer Planet does not situate the queer, the homosexual, and the sexual pervert in a broader political and social context. Although Warner and many other queer theorists believe that the word "queer" overlaps many other identities, being queer does not necessarily mean that one can escape other institutionalized social identities. The discursive formations that shape the queer, the homosexual, and the sexual perversions do not stand alone. They are embedded in a whole network of discursive processes that generate a spectrum of American social identities—racial, gendered, religious, regional, ethnic, and generational.

Queer politics and social theory need to be placed in the larger political framework in order to articulate the movement's political project and its relationships to other communities and identity groups. Despite the homophobia that pervades American life, no single hegemonic discourse precludes the queer. Instead, society is deeply divided between a vaguely liberal inclusiveness and a hostile conservative fundamentalism.[18] Unfortunately, the idea of inclusiveness—multiculturalism— does not really provide an effective counterhegemonic framework for a political analysis of queer and sexual issues. At best, this eclectic, expressive form of pluralism offers a loose umbrella under which many groups can define a social space for themselves. Multiculturalism does not imply a clear-cut agenda for politically reorganizing American public life. Nor does it provide a realistic basis for a political coalition; no societywide consensus exists for establishing an institutional framework for multicultural political representation. Nevertheless, an important component of any queer political or social theory is to locate homosexuality in a larger social framework.

In queer theory and cultural studies, intellectuals are mapping the discursive regimes of power/knowledge that constitute the queer, the homosexual, and the sexual pervert. These regimes of cultural hegemony are immensely powerful, but a discursive politics alone will not weaken the forms of domination that shape the lives of homosexuals and other sexual perverts. Although Foucault was right to critique the "repression hypothesis" as the exclusive explanation of stigmatized identities or sexualities, he explicitly noted that repression remained a component of domination.[19]

The state and the material force of economic life remain central institutions of repression, enmeshed as they are in normalizing discourses and bodies of knowledge. Homo social theory must incorporate the larger historical structures of the economy, institutions, and the state in order to complement queer theory's maps of discursive formations. In doing so, homo social theorists must elaborate the relationships between discursive formations and the other aspects of social-historical systems. Discursive formations help both to explain *and* to interpret people's actions, intentions, and beliefs, whereas social-historical systems explain the institutions, social structures, and normative patterns within which people operate.

Fear of a Queer Planet marks the emergence of a new style of homosexual politics and theorizing under the sign of "queer." The book also denotes a revival of interest in the construction of social theory that integrates sexuality, homosexuality, and the queer as constituent elements. These developments are particularly valuable in this period of escalating political-cultural strife—the primary aim of the Religious Right is to eliminate homosexual rights (which barely exist in most places) in the coming years.

Fear of a Queer Planet joins the tradition of political and social theory that Dennis Altman, Gayle Rubin, Radicalesbians, John D'Emilio, Jeffrey Weeks, Kate Millett, Jill Johnston, Guy Hocquenghem, and Mario Mieli established in the first twenty years after Stonewall. The question that the book addresses, and that none of the contributions resolve, is, What is the relation between queer theory and knowledge of society? Queer theory has emerged from the work of scholars in literary and cultural studies, while lesbian and gay studies increasingly devalues knowledge based on empirical research and theory in the social sciences and history. The essays in *Fear of a Queer Planet* attempt to develop social theory within a theoretical paradigm that privileges cultural politics.

Part Three

From Identity Politics to
Radical Democracy

Throughout the chaotic and manifold surges of the sexual revolution, new political projects, identities, and social movements have emerged to stake claims and secure rights. At the same time, other social actors have fought to limit those claims and revoke any new rights. Feminists fought for the legalization of abortion; religious conservatives tried to restrict those rights. Lesbians and gay men made "coming out" a political act; Anita Bryant led a campaign by religious conservatives to push homosexuals back into the closet, to retract the laws against discrimination that city councils had passed. Through this dialectic, the sexual revolution has been one of the pivotal historical processes shaping American culture since World War II.[1]

During the tumultuous 1960s and 1970s, many social movements and communities adopted identity politics. This strategy emerged by incorporating cultural change as part of a political project; it enabled a movement's participants to transform their cultural identities while seeking recognition of their civil rights.[2] Identity politics, however, reifies and institutionalizes personal and social identities, with the help of market dynamics; the politicized and culturally transformed self acquires the consistency and inflexibility of an object.[3]

Moments of desire, the pleasure of sexual adventure, and the thrill of transgression repeatedly introduce new representations into the historical process, therefore, forcing changed definitions of identity to surface; this "perverse dynamic" undercuts the reified identities.[4] Political actions, social images, and sexual experiences all interact vigorously.

Throughout the many battles of the sexual revolution, the political project of lesbians and gay men has undergone numerous redefinitions. Each new vocabulary implied an updated conception not only of homosexual emancipation but even of sexuality. Before the Stonewall riots, the tiny bands of homosexual activists called themselves "homophiles." After 1969, when the politics of coming out mobilized thousands, they adopted "gay." Then, after divisive conflicts between men and women, they included the term "lesbian."

Homophile activists battled over the significance of cultural differences. Were homosexuals just like heterosexuals except for their sexual preferences, or had homosexuals actually created a distinctive and viable culture? Transvestites, S/M, leather, butch/femme, transgender, the clone, the gym body, lipstick lesbians, men who have sex with men, bisexuality, the sexualities of different racial and ethnic communities and of classes—each reconfigures and deconstructs the fantasy of a unitary homosexual identity. The proliferation of "differences" found a political outlet in 1988 when Queer Nation was founded and "queer" became the new banner term—all queers were "different," so the term applied to everyone whose identity reflected a sexual difference. Each change in nomenclature reflected new distinctions—and each change in conception provoked new formulations of political goals.

Buffeted by both the proliferation of difference and the perverse dynamic (in which sexual limits are transgressed), identity politics enables self-expression and cultural transformation as a political goal. Then each new identity group strives to achieve representation within "the rainbow of identities," but in the process it encounters limits. The multicultural project can only offer each new group limited space. Each identity group arrives, however, with huge investments in its "definition" and in its social boundaries. Thus, these groups' political agendas are usually quite rigidly determined. They remain fixed until new differences emerge within the identity group to burst it open and disperse its offshoots. Group identities can change in response to interactions with other groups; without those changes, no broad coalitions of identity and minority movements are possible.

Chapter 9, "The Limits of Multiculturalism," grew out of my experiences of working at OUT/LOOK magazine and organizing conferences. It was quite common for both editors and conference organizers to be criticized if they did not adequately represent groups who felt excluded or ignored. At OUT/LOOK and in organizing the first two national lesbian and gay writers' conferences, we adopted rigid guidelines to guarantee the representation of women and people of color. Although such schemes were well intentioned and worked with the groups designated, they usually failed to represent other groups adequately.

In such circumstances, time and space limitations create zero-sum situations—everyone must compete for a place in the sun. In addition, these problems impose what Kobena Mercer has called the "burden of representation" in which one voice, one image, or one person speaks for the whole group; this both burdens the voice who must represent the community and represents the others inadequately.[5]

The essay examines how both political and cultural forms of representation create tensions and ambiguities in a multicultural project. Coalitions between different communities or movements cannot form without a public sphere in which the participants can communicate. A public sphere must be constructed that encourages dialogue between the various communities engaged in the multicultural project.

In the late 1980s, a new style of politics surfaced within the lesbian and gay communities. A movement called Queer Nation promoted a politics of "difference" as though it were a form of nationalism. Allan Bérubé and I wrote a short piece on Queer Nation to introduce a series of articles on this new political trend; this piece is now chapter 10, "Reflections on Queer Nation." This brief note tried to situate Queer Nation in the history of homosexual politics.

All the essays in this book were written against the background of religious conservatives' vast campaign to eliminate the homosexual presence from American life. Chapter 11, "Culture Wars and Identity Politics," assesses different forms of gay and lesbian political activity—traditional post-Stonewall identity politics, AIDS activism, and Queer Nation—in relation to the political challenge posed by the Religious Right. None of the existing forms of gay and lesbian politics are adequate. Instead, the community needs to engage in a broader counterhegemonic politics, and it must be willing to show initiative and leadership in forging a broad political response to the Religious Right.

_9_ THE LIMITS OF MULTICULTURALISM

Identity Politics and the
Transformation of the Public Sphere

At the end of the twentieth century, U.S. society is becoming more racially and ethnically diverse; more polarized along class lines; more alarmed by lesbians, gay men, and other sexual minorities; more conscious of gender differences; and as a result, increasingly preoccupied with issues of representation.[1] I mean "representation" in two senses: "political" representation—that is, the role of a delegate or a spokesperson for a particular community; and "cultural" representation—that is, how particular social groups are portrayed in fiction, in movies, or on television. Both meanings of the word involve communicating something about a particular group to the larger society.

Representational issues surface in a number of different contexts,

This chapter is a slightly revised version of an essay that originally appeared in _Socialist Review_ 21, nos. 3/4 (July–December 1991).

ranging from affirmative action hiring programs, concern about the effects of "political correctness," the composition of panels at conferences,
college curricula and what "great books" are included in the canon,
expressions of hatred on college campuses, stereotypes, and defamation
in the public media. These examples originate in a society with an enormous array of culturally diverse, politicized communities. When the
dominant political or cultural institutions do not accept the legitimacy
of these communities, they make political demands in which they emphasize their strong collective identities.

Identity politics is a kind of cultural politics. The politics of identity
can only exist in a culture that can create new and affirmative conceptions of the self, articulate collective identities, and forge a sense of group
loyalty. In identity politics, as in nationalism, there is a strong emphasis
on inventing a new language and vocabulary.[2] As with nationalism,
however, identity politics requires strongly defined boundaries between
those who share particular collective identities and those who do not.

These questions of representation reflect a broader crisis. We no
longer have any societywide framework of representation to which the
majority of the population consents. The traditional modes of representation that functioned in this society until the 1960s (for example, the
way various institutions assigned "slots"—such as jobs, delegates, or
even token roles—to minorities and majorities [e.g., blacks and whites])
may not have been fair, but most of the political struggles up until the
1960s took place within that widely accepted political and cultural
framework. It is increasingly clear, however, that the classic schemas
of political representation in the United States have collapsed.[3]

Multiculturalism is a loose ideological framework that offers a new
model of representation. I believe, though, that the multicultural project
can only provide limited representation unless it creates a framework
that allows new political identities to emerge.

"BRIDGING" IDENTITIES

Political mobilization based on ethnic and group identity has characterized the United States since the late nineteenth century. Ethnic urban
politics of the late nineteenth and early twentieth centuries—for ex-

ample, the urban machine politics of New York's Tammany Hall—was not ideological. The new forms that have emerged since the 1960s, however, are more based on ideological conceptions of identity. One of the earliest and most influential expressions of this new identity-based politics was the black power movement that came out of the civil rights struggle of the late 1950s and 1960s.[4] The women's movement, the gay and lesbian liberation movement, Chicano politics, and the environmental movement have adopted similar ideological and political forms, as illustrated by rhetorical appeals such as Sisterhood Is Powerful or Gay Power.[5] This new form of discursively constituted identity politics, reinforced by the postindustrial reorganization of U.S. society, has led to the breakdown of the classical paradigms of representation in U.S. politics.[6]

The vision of a multicultural society has long been a political current in U.S. history (for example, Randolph Bourne and Horace Kallen in the early twentieth century), especially on the Left (the Rainbow Coalition).[7] Although the multicultural project rests on the expectation that different communities retain their cultural integrity within the coalition, it seems to offer a mode of social representation—so far mostly in the cultural arena. It also makes several social-psychological assumptions that limit its capability as a new mode of representation.

The very term "multicultural" assumes enduring and distinct cultural identities—both personal and collective. These collectively constructed identities require strong boundaries, however, to protect the values embodied in them from the powerful influences of the hegemonic culture looming outside. Because a community's values are embedded in their personal identities, other community members experience any modification of the normative boundaries of individual identities as a personal threat.

Those of us in the lesbian and gay community experience this phenomenon when someone we consider part of the lesbian or gay community forms a heterosexual relationship. Many lesbians and gay men view such an action as a form of social and personal abandonment. Thus, bisexuality is widely perceived as a "political" threat, as well as a personal one. For lesbians or gay men, the personal construction of sexual identity is a difficult and drawn-out process involving heavy emotional and social costs. The implicit challenge of bisexuality serves as a reminder of the potential fluidity of sexual identity. Interracial relationships also challenge a community of color's sense of identity and solidarity. Spike Lee's movie *Jungle Fever* portrays these very concerns.

When emotional stakes and investments are so high, it is difficult to accept the complicated desires of bisexuality or interracial attractions without responding. Thus, the community will often respond to such "abandonment" with moral denunciation, frequently combined with social exclusion and emotional rejection. A community centered on identity politics that has relatively weak institutions of public life (compared with the larger hegemonic culture) tends to rely on such psychological defenses.

Those who envision a multicultural society assume that this society will recognize and accept very different cultural norms, social needs, and forms of social interaction. This imagined society is not the one invoked with the image of the melting pot; this early-twentieth-century metaphor was used to dispel the fears of native-born U.S. whites that the hordes of immigrants from eastern and southern Europe would not overwhelm their way of life. Nevertheless, the melting pot image does have a lot of validity; it reflects the ability of powerful institutions such as the educational system and the mass media to socialize second-generation immigrants into the hegemonic values of white American society. The vision of a multicultural society must rest on a belief that some of these powerful homogenizing forces can be neutralized. A politics of identity emerged in the first place to defend the values and needs of stigmatized or oppressed communities from the enormous power of these homogenizing institutions.

One major limitation of identity politics and its representation in multiculturalism is that we are all born within a web of overlapping identities and group affiliations.[8] Cherríe Moraga and Gloria Anzaldúa explored this experience in the anthology they edited, *This Bridge Called My Back*. More recently Norma Alarcon exemplified their perspective in three sentences: "We are colored in a white feminist movement. We are the feminists among the people of our culture. We are often lesbians among the straight." *This Bridge Called My Back* remains a model for clarifying some of the dilemmas of multiculturalism.[9]

Although the women who contributed to the anthology have varied attitudes toward identity politics, many of the authors remain aware that they are inextricably at the nexus of several identity discourses. *Bridge* implicitly critiques a politics of unity based on any single dimension, such as gender, race, class, or sexual identity, and demonstrates that the self is multiple. Many of the writers in *Bridge* have continued to explore this terrain in hybrid literary forms combining poetry, essay, memoir, and drama.[10] Moraga in *Loving in the War Years*, Anzaldúa in *Borderlands*, and Audre Lorde in *Zami* all incorporate what Bakhtin called "heteroglossia"—dialogue between different cultural voices.[11]

Moraga, Lorde, Anzaldúa, Alarcon, and many other authors writing from the perspective of "bridge" identities recognize that identity is not the result of an isolated community's discourse but the interaction of people bound to each other in many different ways. The self takes it shape from a continuous process of discourse and communication— between people of different races, genders, classes, generations, social roles, and sexualities. People with multiple loyalties can only be meaningfully included in their communities through public dialogue.

The work of British-Pakistani writer Hanif Kureishi explores the contradictions and possibilities of this terrain. In his essay about the contradictions of his own complex identity, he criticizes conservative philosopher Roger Scruton's justification of racism's "illiberal sentiments" as nothing more than the desire for "the company of one's kind."[12] Kureishi writes:

> What a feeble, bloodless, narrow conception of human relationships and the possibilities of love and communication. . . . One does seek the company of one's kind. . . . But the idea that these are the only people one can get along with or identify with . . . leads to the denigration of those unlike oneself. It leads to the idea that others have less humanity than oneself or one's own group or "kind"; and to the idea of the Enemy, of the alien, of the Other. As Baldwin says: "this inevitably leads to murder."[13]

ANOTHER COUNTRY: REPRESENTATION AND
THE TRANSFORMATION OF THE PUBLIC SPHERE

Living on the boundaries of different communities and finding oneself within overlapping identities makes one see how inadequate the existing forms of political and cultural representation are. Cultural forms have shown certain possibilities of sophistication—as Moraga's plays, Anzaldúa's and Lorde's essays, and Kureishi's films illustrate—but it is not clear how to represent complex identities politically.

Most of the cultural institutions in the United States (television, universities, and the recording industry, for example) are still governed by traditional schemas of representation, which limit the number and kind of minority communities represented. Unfortunately, these institutions remain indispensable instruments for producing ideas and legitimating practices. This holds true whether they offer a fictional representation of everyday life, as with television dramas and situation comedies, or whether they are the major institutions in our society that legitimate knowledge, as with universities.

Overall, the electronic media dominate American public life through the talk show (Oprah Winfrey, Phil Donahue, Geraldo Rivera, Sally Jessy Raphael, Ted Koppel) and the news magazine–format show (*Sixty Minutes*, the *Today* show, *Fresh Air*). The public life reflected in book and magazine publishing and in the university reaches a smaller, select audience. Publishing and academia are also more permeable and less monolithic than the electronic media. Despite these differences, the global media conglomerates (for example, Pearson PLC (Penguin Putnam), Viacom, Bertelmanns, Murdoch's News Corporation, Walt Disney Co., Time-Warner, and Sony) and the universities function together to frame public discourse in American life.[14] Nevertheless, significant and lively debate also takes place in the communities excluded from mainstream U.S. public life. It is often these communities that have been galvanized by the politics of identity.

The politicization of personal and collective identities is the basis for several significant changes in the characteristics of public debate. The new "multicultural" public sphere demands representation in the form of speakers, political delegates, cultural figures, and role models. Most of the communities that have adopted identity politics—for example, the Chicano, African American, lesbian and gay, and feminist communities—are underrepresented in positions of power and visibility relative to their proportions in the population. Increasingly, members of these communities insist on access to the institutions of public discourse, such as television, radio, universities, publishing, movies, and music.

The adequacy of representation in cultural forms is also a contested issue. There is still an abundance of stereotypes, invidious narrative conventions (for example, the homosexual who dies in the story), inauthentic language (using terms such as "fellatio" rather than "sucking cock" in safe-sex literature aimed at street hustlers), and value-laden metaphors ("innocent victims" for people who were infected with HIV through blood transfusions rather than sexual activity or intravenous drug use). One hopes that more complex and sophisticated representations of stigmatized or excluded communities will go a long way toward reducing the distorted communications that currently exist between mainstream U.S. society and marginalized communities.

Probably the most highly publicized effect of identity politics on public discourse is the notion of "politically correct" speech. Most communities have the used the term "politically correct" for years in an ironic and self-deprecatory way. Fundamentally, it implied an awareness that community members had residual feelings and opinions that conflicted with their ostensible political identities. In addition, the term implicitly acknowledged the value of political etiquette. Community members used "political correctness" ironically because they had long experienced political moralism (on the Left and in the women's movement), as well as strong community pressures to conform.[15] Thus, jokes about political incorrectness marked either emotional ambivalence or quiet disagreement with prevailing political attitudes.

Recently, conservatives and the mass media have taken up the term "political correctness" and used it to attack the Left. They have called politically correct speech the "new McCarthyism." Although conservatives appear to be targeting the political moralism that actually does characterize many forms of identity politics, they intend their campaign against political correctness and the cultural Left to close down the debate about the very issues of representation that multiculturalism raises.

Representation poses a problem even within movements committed to multiculturalism. In the public life of the lesbian and gay communities, the issues of multicultural representation are widely discussed. There are good reasons that multicultural representation is such an active issue within these communities. Almost no lesbian or gay man is raised in a family of other homosexuals. Instead, most lesbians and gay men enter the homosexual community through self-conscious choices that they make as adults. The lesbian and gay communities consist of men and women who leave, even if only temporarily, the cultures of their primary socialization to engage in sexual, political, or social activities in a different community. To function effectively, the lesbian and gay communities must acknowledge their participants' diverse cultural backgrounds. Of course, this process is neither automatic nor conflict-free.

Questions of representation regularly arose among the planners of OutWrite '91 and '92, the national lesbian and gay writers' conferences that *OUT/LOOK* magazine sponsored. For a long time, the publishing industry has clearly favored white males over women, people of color, or sexual minorities as authors. Conference organizers wanted to honor pioneering homosexual authors (the majority of whom have been white men), but this desire sometimes clashed with the explicit commitment to recognize contemporary writers from communities of color or with previously marginalized experiences (such as writers from the S/M or transgender communities).[16]

Aspiring to have a conference that adequately represents the real and complex diversity of the lesbian and gay communities quite legitimately creates an endless process of negotiation. Because there are so many different and conflicting perspectives, conference planners will inevitably fall short of full inclusion. Among the many communities that the planning committee of OutWrite '92 sought to represent were ethnic and racial communities such as Latinos, African Americans, Native Americans, Asian Americans; sexual minorities such as bisexuals, transsexuals, and S/M; people with AIDS; and lesbian and gay writers from Latin America and Canada. Some communities were represented by specific panels, whereas others were represented on several different panels. Of course, we did not always succeed in adequately representing every perspective or community. Defining the appropriate representation often poses new questions. For example, our commitment to representing people of color on all panels raised interesting questions for the panel on Jewish writing—in addition to having Ashkenazim, should we encourage the presence of Sephardim, or Jews from the Middle East or Africa?

As Louise Sloan wrote in the *Bay Guardian* when she reported on the conference, "One thing that became very clear . . . is that speaking for anyone else or claiming any community as absolutely one's own are highly problematic, if not impossible undertakings." Also, as that realization implies, there is no "universal" point of view that rises above the multicultural diversity of perspectives.[17]

Identity politics as we practice it in this country is competitive—partly because different communities are vying for limited space in public life. At each new level of political mobilization, we must proliferate identities to guarantee further representation. This competitive struggle for representation undercuts the multicultural project.

Although writers such as Moraga, Anzaldúa, Lorde, Kureishi, and Baldwin have developed more adequate models of cultural representation, the forms of political representation remain deep in crisis. There is still minimal representation of women, people of color, homosexuals, and other marginalized groups within our major political institutions. It is time to work out forms of multicultural coalition politics that do not rely only on the existing formulas of representation.

We need public dialogue, with all its attendant risks, so that we can create a multicultural political project. As Bernice Reagon says, "We've pretty much come to the end of a time when you have a space that is 'yours only.' "[18] Dialogue is the primary medium through which we can construct political coalitions and a multicultural project.

MAKING DIALOGUE POSSIBLE

No vision of a multicultural society is viable without a commitment to dialogue—candid and engaged, risky and painful, but ideally thoughtful and fair. Dialogue is only the first step in sharing public life. It is not the same thing as an exchange of power, and it is not the only necessary form of political agency. Dialogue, however, helps individuals modify their political understandings without force or violence.

The multicultural project can provide a new model of representation only if we are responsive to people from other cultural communities—if we can give up some of the rigid boundaries that differentiate social identities and become permeable selves. This openness is what makes the public discussion of politically tense questions so risky and personally frightening. The risk for individuals is worthwhile, however, because of the benefits for the community. Public discussion offers a form of social objectivity and makes the participants accountable to the communities engaged.

Inequalities of power threaten every attempt to establish the social conditions of dialogue. We should not see these inequalities as insurmountable obstacles, however; they mean that we should try to redistribute power within the public sphere. One step toward reducing power inequalities is to create institutions that consciously embody multicultural ideals—that is, cultural intermediaries such as alternative publishing houses, journals, and conferences.[19]

The intensity and bitterness of many debates involving multiculturalism have exposed the participants' emotional, cultural, and political vulnerability. Those who have been excluded from public feel vulnerable when they publicly express the anger and pain of their exclusion from the dominant culture. Ironically, those who were raised within the hegemonic WASP culture also experience vulnerability when they relinquish privileges and power; it is painful for them to lose emotionally significant forms of expression.

This social and psychological vulnerability underlies our fear of public debate on the shape of multicultural society. Much of the reaction to political correctness stems from the pain that people on all sides of the question have experienced. Every participant enters the public arena with differing degrees of power and privilege. Those who come from communities that are represented in mainstream public life or those who have traditionally had greater access to political and cultural institutions must enter the dialogue prepared to treat other perspectives as equal.

To create a multicultural public sphere in which dialogue can take place, people should take the following social and psychological guidelines into account:

1. None of us is immutable. The risk of dialogue is that we learn something new about ourselves and others. Once dialogue starts, we become open to change.

2. There is no universal position. All dialogue involves interpretation. We might even say all dialogue involves "misinterpretation." Although a lack of understanding is unavoidable, it should not be taken lightly. Such a situation creates an important role for theory, for the systematic examination of our assumptions, for framing questions, and for learning what we don't know. Everything is always open to criticism. Nothing should remain unexamined. (We recognize no power or privileges.) We discover how our assumptions may be mistaken.

3. Stoicism is necessary in public debate. No one enjoys being humiliated in public. Participation in public dialogue will not be fruitful if we do not learn to accept conflict, pain, and hurt feelings. Some of the detrimental effect of political correctness stems from the fear of being criticized or misrepresented in public. Expressions of anger and hostility should be expected.

4. There is no closure. No debate or political discussion is ever final. There will be no end to debate. The question will always be reopened.

The debate about multiculturalism has been emotionally painful, partly because it challenges the cultural basis of one's sense of self-worth, and partly because the social stakes are high. We are battling over the terms of inclusion and exclusion in American life. The psychological vulnerability that most of us have felt in the debate on multiculturalism makes the conflicts over representation increasingly futile and bitter. There are no widely accepted political frameworks that will help us resolve these questions. By itself, dialogue is not the answer, but we must have dialogue and debate so that we can develop a coalition on the Left. This coalition will provide a basis for social inclusion, cultural autonomy, and political solidarity.

10 REFLECTIONS ON QUEER NATION

with Allan Bérubé

A new generation of activists is here. They have come out into communities devastated by the HIV epidemic and into political consciousness through the struggle against AIDS. But AIDS is not their main focus.

This new generation calls itself *queer*, not *lesbian, gay, and bisexual*—awkward, narrow, and perhaps compromised words. *Queer* is meant to be confrontational—opposed to gay assimilationists and straight oppressors while inclusive of people who have been marginalized by anyone in power. Queer Nationals are undertaking an awesome task. They

This chapter, written with Allan Bérubé, was published in *OUT/LOOK* 3, no. 3 (winter 1991). One of the first essays to characterize Queer Nation, it has not been revised for this volume.

are trying to combine contradictory impulses: to bring together people who have been made to feel perverse, queer, odd, outcast, different and deviant, and to affirm sameness by defining a common identity on the fringes. They are inclusive, but within boundaries that threaten to marginalize those whose difference doesn't conform to the new nation. These contradictions are locked in the name Queer Nation:

QUEER = DIFFERENCE

NATION = SAMENESS

Queer Nation meetings are thick with tensions—tensions between consensus, with its attention to marginalized minorities, conflicts with the temptation of majority rule, with its efficiency in getting things done, tensions between taking sharply defined political positions and establishing an open forum for imaginative tactics and free discussion. Queer Nationals are torn between affirming a new identity—"I am queer"—and rejecting restrictive identities—"I reject your categories," between rejecting assimilation—"I don't need your approval, just get out of my face"—and wanting to be recognized by mainstream society—"We queers are gonna get in your face."

Queer nationalism's actions play on the politics of cultural subversion: theatrical demonstrations, infiltrations of shopping malls and straight bars, kiss-ins and be-ins. Rather than a strategic politics that confronts powerful institutions directly or uses lobbying and electoral campaigns to bring about change, Queer Nation takes to the street wearing "QUEER" stickers and badges on their jackets, fighting to keep queer turf safe from bashings. At times, they look like queer urban street gangs.

These queers are constructing a new culture and identity by combining old and new elements that don't usually go together. They may be the first wave of activists to embrace retrofuture/classic contemporary styles of postmodernism. They are building their identity from old and new elements—borrowing styles and tactics from popular culture, communities of color, hippies, AIDS activists, the antinuclear movement, MTV, feminists, and early gay liberationists. Their new culture is slick, quick, anarchic, transgressive, ironic. They are dead serious, but they also just wanna have fun. If they manage not to blow up in contradiction or get bogged down in the process, they may lead the way into new forms of activism for the 1990s.

11 CULTURE WARS AND IDENTITY POLITICS

The Religious Right and the
Cultural Politics of Homosexuality

Since the 1970s,[1] American political and cultural life has become polarized between secular liberalism—increasingly identified with multiculturalism, pluralism, and the politics of diversity—and religious conservatism.[2] The Religious Right is engaged in a campaign to achieve political and cultural hegemony in American life, and it has built this campaign on the revival of supposedly traditional "family values." Homosexuality is currently a major target of this hegemonic project.

Gay and lesbian activists have long sought acceptance within a liberal framework of tolerance and equal treatment. They have modeled

This chapter is a slightly revised version of an essay that originally appeared in David Trend, ed., *Radical Democracy: Identity, Citizenship, and the State* (New York: Routledge, 1996).

this quest on the black civil rights movement and the assimilation of other ethnic groups. I will argue that the framework of this "ethnic model" (increasingly characterized as "identity politics") is too limited to mobilize the cultural and political resources necessary to defeat the Religious Right's agenda. Existing alternatives modeled on AIDS activism and queer politics can supplement but not replace identity politics. The only strategy that offers reasonable hope is a radical democratic politics that appeals to the disorganized bloc of Americans who remain opposed to conservative orthodoxy.

The culture wars of the last decade originated in the battles of the 1960s and 1970s: the black civil rights and black power movements, protests against the Vietnam War, the counterculture, the sexual revolution, the rise of feminism, and the emergence of the gay and lesbian movements. Each of these movements encountered resistance from a broad body of Americans. The spread of black civil rights activity made a growing number of whites aware of their own racism. The antiwar movement flew in the face of those who believed that communism threatened the American way of life. The counterculture disseminated its powerful brew of drugs, sex, and rock music to young people across the country.[3]

By the mid-1970s, the energies that fed these movements had begun to wane. Black political movements, such as the civil rights movement, Black Muslims, and the Black Panthers, were increasingly the targets of violent responses—the assassinations of Malcolm X in 1965 and Martin Luther King, Jr., in 1968. Black communities rioted in response to long-standing injustices and antiblack violence. Although the social struggles of the 1960s reinvigorated the Left, which reached its peak in the early 1970s, the 1976 U.S. withdrawal from Vietnam eliminated a major source of discontent—one which had fueled the leftist movement.

Among the movements that emerged from the political struggles of the 1960s, three continued to grow throughout the 1970s and into the 1980s. The environmental movement has had an enormous impact. Both the women's movement and the gay rights movement also flourished throughout the 1970s, making more and more people aware of issues such as the ERA, abortion, and gay rights. The AIDS epidemic aroused new political energies in the gay and lesbian community.[4]

Originally, the conservatives who opposed the movements of the 1960s and 1970s formed an amorphous group; they had no coherent identity. Political leaders and intellectuals sought to organize this conservative opposition. They called it, among other things, "the silent majority." The Religious Right began to participate in American politics during the 1970s.[5] With Reagan's election in 1980, the New Right that emerged victorious was an alliance of traditional conservatives primarily preoccupied with communism and economic issues and religious fundamentalists such as Jerry Falwell.[6]

For many on the Right, multiculturalism is replacing communism as the evil force currently threatening "the American way of life." In 1993, Irving Kristol, the so-called Godfather of American conservatism, wrote, "There is no 'after the Cold War' for me. So far from having ended, my cold war has increased in intensity, as sector after sector of American life has been ruthlessly corrupted by the liberal ethos. . . . Now that the other 'Cold War' is over, the real cold war has begun. We are far less prepared for this cold war, far more vulnerable to our enemy, than was the case with our victorious war against a global Communist threat."[7] This new "cold war" is a political-cultural struggle over the shape of American democracy.

In the 1970s, conservative opposition to this peculiar conflation of "liberalism" and the descendants of the counterculture increasingly found common ground in the "family values" agenda. Targeting anything that seemed to challenge the idealized nuclear family, this agenda appeals to many Americans who feel strained by conjugal commitments and who fear a loss of authority over their children. Drugs, violence in the schools, the social dominance of television, and particularly the risks of teenage sexuality (for example, pregnancy and AIDS) lurk as threats to their children.[8] Conservatives use family values as the basis for both religious proselytizing and political mobilizing (including fundraising, lobbying, and electoral politics). The Right has placed their family values agenda at the cultural center of their hegemonic project and have supplemented it with other planks of conservative ideology, such as dismantling the welfare state, privatizing public services, reviving prayer in the schools, adding a balanced budget amendment to the Constitution, and reinstituting the death penalty.

THE RELIGIOUS RIGHT'S ''GAY AGENDA''

Abortion has been one of the most divisive social issues in American politics. As the linchpin of women's reproductive rights, it is intimately connected with a whole range of other issues (such as sex education, teenage pregnancy, and distributing condoms to teenagers) that assume the individual's freedom of sexual choice. The abortion issue has united fundamentalists across the spectrum—from Roman Catholicism, Protestant fundamentalism, and Orthodox Judaism. The conservative anti-abortion movement has waged an extremely confrontational and even violent war against abortion clinics and doctors who perform abortions. Although a large minority (20 percent) of the American population opposes abortion on moral grounds, most Americans reject government interference in women's reproductive rights. The fundamentalists' momentum in the battle against abortion has stalemated. Thus, the Religious Right has turned to the other key plank in its crusade to shore up "family values"—the defeat of gay and lesbian rights.

The growing visibility of the lesbian and gay community throughout the 1970s forced conservative fundamentalists to take notice of homosexuality. Fundamentalist churches felt compelled to assert that the Judeo-Christian tradition views homosexuals as "sodomites" who engage in "unnatural practices." Fundamentalists also viewed homosexuality as one of a number of threats to the traditional nuclear family. Christian fundamentalists launched their first electoral campaign against gay rights in 1977; Anita Bryant's "Save Our Children" crusade aimed to repeal gay rights legislation in Dade County, Florida.

The Religious Right's project to reconstitute traditional Christian values in American culture is increasingly dominant. It has had an enormous effect on the mass media, it has captured the Republican Party, and it swayed many voters in the 1994 elections. By the mid-1990s, gay issues became the one social issue—even more than abortion—that most polarizes the American electorate. Homosexuals are now the primary target of many fundamentalist organizing activities.

Can gay and lesbian political organizations meet that challenge? Do lesbians and gay men have the cultural and symbolic resources to organize an effective political strategy? Identity politics as a type of political mobilization cannot defeat the Religious Right's agenda—nor can politics modeled on AIDS activism or queer nationalism replace identity politics. Lesbians and gay men need a new political strategy—one more far-reaching—to combat the Religious Right's project.

CIVIL RIGHTS, IDENTITY POLITICS, AND COMMUNITY ECONOMIC DEVELOPMENT

At the end of the 1960s, gay political activity exploded in the wake of the Stonewall riots.[9] Publicly declaring one's homosexuality was the decisive innovation of the post-Stonewall gay and lesbian liberation movement. This "coming-out strategy" demonstrated that there was a sizable group of people engaged in primarily homosexual behavior. Gay and lesbian political organizers gained an identifiable population, one could almost say a "quantifiable" goal, which provided the basis for residential and economic community building and political mobilization in the form of demonstrations, marches, and voting. "Coming out of the closet" became the essential precondition for gay and lesbian political advancement.

Early homophile (the term adopted by the pre-Stonewall homosexual civil rights movement) activists had never even conceived of a coming-out strategy before. Many homosexuals in the period prior to Stonewall tended to think of their homosexuality as only one component of their identities. In that spirit, Gore Vidal has always insisted that "homosexual" is an adjective, not a noun. In effect, however, coming out as a political-cultural strategy has tended to reify homosexual identities, although it also initiated a public discursive process of identification.[10] Stigmatization and repression contributed to this reification of homosexual identity. The gay and lesbian movement's emphasis on coming out, nevertheless, did not totally dismantle the closet. Nor did it spontaneously cause the stigma or repressive laws to disappear.

The publicness of the new homosexual identity encouraged new forms of community building and organizing. Openly lesbian and gay activists demonstrated in public places for increased tolerance and civil rights, particularly in housing and employment. As the number of gay and lesbian political organizations proliferated, lesbians and gay men created businesses to supply their communities with news and litera- ture (newspapers, publishers, and bookstores), consumer goods (cloth- ing, jewelry, and sexual commodities), meeting places (coffee houses, restaurants, and bathhouses), and social services (psychological coun- seling centers). Gay neighborhoods formed around the old pre- Stonewall sexual zones, bars, and community-owned businesses. The economic development would have been impossible without the dis- cursive reconstruction of homosexual identity based on coming out.

Ironically, this strategy allowed many members of the lesbian and gay communities to be public about their homosexuality in limited ways. They were able to remain in the closet at work or with their families, but they could be "out" in the protected environment of urban gay enclaves. The heightened visibility of the community protected in- dividual members. It was not necessary for everyone who engaged in homosexual behavior to come out unequivocally. The visibility possible in the lesbian and gay communities and the economic development provided a framework in which homosexuals could identify as lesbian or gay without paying the price of full public disclosure.

As lesbian- and gay-owned small businesses flourished, gay and les- bian political activity drew on this community development. The for- mation of Gay Democratic Clubs and their success in local elections reinforced the process of community development—a process that was jointly discursive and economic. Harvey Milk's 1976 election to the San Francisco Board of Supervisors represented, in part, the consolidation of the Castro district as a gay neighborhood; many small business own- ers in the community had financed his campaign.[11]

Once the coming-out strategy unleashed the potentialities of gay and lesbian economic development, the community stratified economically along the lines of class, race, and gender—just as in mainstream Amer- ican society. This division limited the political and cultural possibilities of those who did not or were not able to participate in the predomi- nantly white, middle-class, and male enclaves.

Whatever economic development occurred by the late 1970s had never been equitably balanced between lesbians and gay men. As women, lesbians had many fewer economic resources at their disposal than gay men. Lesbians and gay men had also specialized in different kinds of businesses and had often lived in different neighborhoods. Lesbian political developments created different economic priorities; lesbian community building and economic development reflected different needs and agendas. In the mid- to late 1970s, lesbians entered a separatist phase, partly in an effort to build women's communities and businesses, and partly because gay men were no less chauvinist than straight ones.[12] Homosexual women and men began to share a political and economic community in response to a series of outside threats— the right-wing initiatives to erase gay rights legislation, which began in 1977, and the AIDS crisis, which started in the early 1980s.

These economic and political developments did not fully include homosexuals of color. It has been primarily white gay men and lesbians who have settled in gay neighborhoods and owned businesses serving the community. Lesbians and gay men of color often reside in their ethnic or racial neighborhoods. Gay people of color must commute to the gay community districts in order to participate in the gay community—and they often encounter discrimination.

The development of gay and lesbian identity politics results from the combined effects of discursive identification and economic development. Discursive identification occurs through the process of coming out and requires cultural reinforcements, such as "the coming-out novel" as a genre, the use of lesbian or gay consumer goods, residence in a lesbian or gay neighborhood, and participation on lesbian softball teams or in gay choirs. The community's small businesses supply those cultural reinforcements in the form of commodities. Discursive identification and economic development are inseparable elements in the history of the post-Stonewall homosexual community.

The joint play of these elements has encouraged some political leaders to think of the gay and lesbian community as an "ethnic group." This trope enables those leaders to situate gay and lesbian identity politics in American political history. Lesbians and gay men follow in the footsteps of the Irish, Italians, Jews, Poles, and Scandinavians—the construction of communities, political machines, and eventually "assimilation."

What disrupts this comfortable perspective, however, is that some members of the lesbian and gay community are not easily assimilated. Those deviant members include: homosexuals of color, kindred sexual minorities such as the leather community, bisexuals and other sexual perverts, and those resisting the norms of gender conformity, such as drag queens, transgendered people, and transsexuals. The irony is that communities using identity politics both resist assimilation (by insisting that their identities are each different) and strive for assimilation (by claiming that their identities are compatible with those of other American groups).

The gay and lesbian community's identity politics, built on economic-cultural foundations resembling the classic American ethnic model, cannot offer an effective political response to the Religious Right's hegemonic project of reconstituting family values as an official American ideology. If the Right characterizes homosexuals as morally corrupt and irresponsible, as wealthier and better educated than the average American, adopting a fortress mentality only to protect existing economic and cultural enclaves could potentially isolate the lesbian and gay communities.[13]

THE AIDS CRISIS: THE BREAKDOWN
OF IDENTITY POLITICS

As the 1980s progressed, the gay and lesbian community increasingly realized the devastating impact of AIDS on gay men. Fostered by the economic-cultural "ethnic model" of community development, gay and lesbian identity politics was unable to cope with this situation.

The complex of diseases called AIDS was first discovered among gay men in 1981. From the first moment the gay male community became aware of AIDS (which was first called GRID—gay-related immune deficiency), it responded politically. By the end of the summer in 1981, a group of gay men had already met at author Larry Kramer's apartment in New York City and had established the Gay Men's Health Crisis (GMHC)—the largest AIDS organization in the country today.[14]

In the late 1970s, homosexuals had been under attack from the Religious Right and other conservatives. Lesbian and gay communities had just barely fought off conservative attacks not only in Dade County, Florida, but also in St. Paul, Minnesota; Eugene, Oregon; and statewide in California with Proposition 6. In the midst of these campaigns, a disgruntled conservative politician assassinated Harvey Milk. When Milk's murderer was convicted of manslaughter and received a light sentence, San Francisco's gay community erupted in a riot outside City Hall.[15]

Gay activists realized that an epidemic of a fatal, sexually transmitted disease originating in the gay male community was politically explosive. People might take drastic political action against the gay community. Homophobic conservatives could demonize homosexuals and promulgate an antisexual morality. Doctors initially advised gay men to stop having sex. In addition, it soon became apparent that the public health authorities were less responsive to the epidemic than had been the case in previous fatal outbreaks, such as Legionnaires' disease in Philadelphia in 1976.

As the number of deaths in the gay community skyrocketed, the inadequate response of federal and local authorities provoked increasing despair and anger.[16] Soon, gay men banded together to try to deal with the epidemic more effectively. Even before the human immunodeficiency virus (HIV) itself was discovered, the epidemiological evidence suggested that the disease was probably transmitted through blood and sperm. Groups of activists in New York and San Francisco focused on education as a way to retard the epidemic. They developed safe-sex guidelines and established organizations to circulate information about the epidemic and counsel people who feared exposure.[17]

The epidemic's dimensions seemed to expand enormously. It affected other communities, such as Haitians, African Americans, hemophiliacs, the recipients of blood transfusions, and intravenous drug users. The incubation period seemed to be growing longer. The gay community's own organizing efforts, important and valuable though they were, fell far short of what was required with an epidemic of such huge proportions.

It became increasingly clear that a more forceful political response was needed. In the fall of 1987, activists formed ACT UP (AIDS Coalition to Unleash Power) in New York. Soon afterward, they organized groups in cities across the country. ACT UP revitalized a style of radical political activity that had flourished in the early days of the gay liberation movement. Grassroots and confrontational, it had a flair for imaginative tactics that captured media attention.[18] ACT UP demanded that the Food and Drug Administration accelerate the approval of AIDS drugs, that pharmaceutical firms lower drug prices, and that the National Institutes of Health expand its research on AIDS. In addition, ACT UP attacked public indifference, which hindered AIDS education and enabled employers, landlords, and insurance companies to discriminate against people with AIDS.

The growing impact of AIDS on the American population forced activists to broaden their constituency. ACT UP groups around the country primarily consisted of gay white men, but the need to reflect AIDS's epidemiology and to build alliances with other communities affected by AIDS led to a politics that strived to be more inclusive and more open to building coalitions. It was never a smooth process. Various communities affected by AIDS sometimes had little else in common. Some of the groups were also socially stigmatized and had even fewer resources than the gay community. Occasionally, they had segments who voiced their discomfort with or disapproval of homosexuality. When it came to matters of strategy, AIDS activists even had increasing conflicts with gay and lesbian political elites within the community over political priorities.[19]

The politics of AIDS activism forced gay and lesbian activists to have increased interaction with federal, state, and local governments, thereby transforming the lesbian and gay community's relation with the state. Community-based organizations received government funding and participated in policymaking to a much greater extent than ever before. The AIDS movement has had a significant impact on government research, public health policies, and government funding of treatment, care, and education. This government funding has created large-scale institutions with jobs and career possibilities that did not exist in the lesbian and gay communities before the epidemic.

These economic and institutional developments have had two major effects on the gay and lesbian communities. First, they have encouraged lesbian and gay political institutions to engage more with other communities, governmental agencies, and mainstream institutions. Second, they have transformed the class structure of gay and lesbian leadership. The new jobs and career possibilities attracted a generation of leaders who were upwardly mobile and educated at elite universities and colleges. In the past, gay men such as this might have pursued conventional careers. Now, though, many of them were infected with the virus that causes AIDS and took up AIDS activism to fight for their lives. The older generation of leaders had chosen gay political life as an alternative to mainstream careers. Very early on in the epidemic, however, AIDS devastated the founding generation both physically and emotionally. A new generation soon displaced the older one.

AIDS had decimated the gay male community, had forced it to reach out to other communities, and had seriously undermined its economic and cultural self-sufficiency. The countervailing pressures of gay and lesbian identity politics and of AIDS activism produced a political situation that required a new perspective—one that conceived of identity as stable, but also recognized the incredible diversity within the community. The perspective needed to account for the kinship of all sexual minorities and the range of possible gender roles, ethnic, and racial identities. In this moment, Queer Nation was born.

QUEER POLITICS AND CULTURAL RADICALISM

Lesbian and gay identity politics was grounded in an appeal to liberal beliefs in equal treatment and tolerance. The Right, however, has always attacked civil rights for lesbians and gay men—whether through the antigay initiatives in 1976 and 1977 or with the siege that began in

1991 and continues today. Neither the increasing numbers and growth of visible gay and lesbian communities in most major U.S. cities nor the increasing size of a measurable lesbian and gay electorate nor the opening up of a lucrative gay market for major brand-name consumer products has seemed to contribute to the acceptance of homosexuals in American life.

Because many other activists felt frustrated that lesbian and gay identity politics could not achieve even the liberal benefits of tolerance and equal treatment and that AIDS activism had diluted gay and lesbian concerns, a new movement called Queer Nation emerged in the spring of 1990.[20] After a wave of homophobic violence occurred in New York City, Queer Nation formed, growing out of a demonstration against the violence. A broadside at the protest that announced "I Hate Straights" inspired the group.[21] It brought together many people who had been active in ACT UP New York and who felt frustrated by compromises on gay issues during coalition work. Queer Nation groups soon sprang up across the United States.

Queer Nation spurred new tactics and revived the politics of visibility. In his column in the New York–based magazine *Outweek,* AIDS activist and journalist Michelangelo Signorile introduced a new tactic called "outing," which extended the coming-out strategy of the early gay movement. Whereas coming out had been a voluntary personal and political act that contributed to lesbian and gay visibility, outing was a political agenda to expose closeted homosexuals who were famous or politically conservative. Outing was a punishment for remaining in the closet—and many activists thought it particularly appropriate to expose gay men or lesbians on the Right.[22]

Queer Nation was an openly militant challenge to the identity politics of the lesbian and gay communities. It rejected the traditional liberal goals of equal treatment and tolerance, criticizing those ideals as assimilationist. "We're here, we're queer, get used to it," was one of its slogans. The name "Queer Nation" brought together an extremely complicated notion of identity. By adopting the term "queer," it expanded the definition of the community that it sought to represent; Queer Nation embraced anyone who differed from the white heterosexual norm, such as lesbians, gay men, bisexuals, transsexuals, transgendered people, and sexual perverts, especially if members of these groups had hybrid identities of class, race, and ethnicity. By calling themselves a "nation," queer activists appealed to an exclusive sort of nationalism, almost a separatism. Thus, queer activists sought to combine seemingly contradictory notions of difference and identity into "an oxymoronic community of difference."[23]

Most of the Queer Nation groups have since ceased to exist. Their contradictory mission caused them to founder. Yet queer politics remains a normative ideal, and queer theory has emerged in academia to focus on the cultural impact of normalized heterosexuality.[24]

Potentially, queer politics will help keep gay and lesbian identity politics honest about the diversity of racial and sexual differences and their significance. Queer politics can also help forge links between lesbian and gay politics and the broad agenda of multiculturalism. Queer politics, however, cannot serve as a basis for fighting the Religious Right about issues such as AIDS education and funding, gay-positive school curricula, or civil rights because queer politics cannot advance the community's engagement with the state or provide the institutional and economic resources necessary to overcome opponents.[25] In contrast, lesbian and gay identity politics and AIDS activism have provided those benefits. The lesbian and gay communities must win over a broad spectrum of the American population; the Religious Right will ask that same segment of people to support the repeal of already existing laws and to limit social tolerance. None of the existing political models that lesbians and gay men have developed are adequate, either separately or together. Activists need to devise a new strategy.

FAMILY VALUES, GAY RIGHTS, AND RADICAL DEMOCRACY

The Religious Right's ambitious project to make the ideology of "family values" hegemonic violates long-standing American political beliefs. The campaign seeks to subvert the separation of church and state and to mobilize class resentments against lesbians and gay men. Ironically, the class structure of the homosexual community does not differ significantly from that of American society as a whole. The lesbian and gay community can oppose this project only by expanding the narrow focus of identity politics or by shifting its emphasis away from queer politics. The gay movement should aim to participate in a radical democratic project with other communities and groups.[26]

The Religious Right began its campaign against homosexuality with an antihomosexual interpretation of biblical texts. Now, it also portrays homosexuality as a social cause of the breakdown of the family. The Religious Right disapproves of open homosexuality because it implies a nonreproductive sexuality; fundamentalists see procreative sexuality as the basis of the family, so homosexuality appears to be a rejection of the family. When young people come out, it demonstrates that families have no control over youthful sexuality. The Religious Right interprets homosexuality in "moral" terms—as a choice to defy religious laws.

On one level, religious fundamentalists have a right to think whatever they want. Lesbians and gay men object to the Religious Right, however, because it is disseminating inaccurate information. Apart from differing over interpretations of biblical and religious texts, lesbians and gay men do not feel that they choose, by and large, to be homosexual. The Right's religious injunctions cause enormous (and unnecessary) pain to those whose families believe that homosexuality is sinful and evil. Homosexuals are not inherently unethical or evil people. Therefore, homosexuality should not be the basis for stigmatization, discrimination, or abuse against a significant minority in our multicultural and multireligious society.

These intellectual and ethical differences would not have any political significance if the Religious Right were not tapping into homophobia to garner support for changing laws and public policies. The Religious Right has adopted two basic approaches to achieve its goals. Lesbian activist and lawyer Nan Hunter has identified the two different types of campaigns as either "No Promo Homo" or "No Special Rights."[27]

The "No Promo Homo" strategy strives to ensure that it is illegal to promote the tolerance or acceptance of homosexuality. For religious fundamentalists, this translates into "the promotion of homosexuality." Many of the most bitterly fought campaigns against lesbians and gay men illustrate this tactic. The other strategy is to argue that homosexuals need no "special" legal protections, that society does not discriminate against homosexuals. To supplement this argument, fundamentalists usually appeal to class resentment by adding that gay men and lesbians are wealthier and better educated than most Americans and therefore do not need "special" protections. Both of these political strategies draw on the large pool of homophobia that Americans already have.

Both strategies also appeal to populist sentiments, to long-standing American beliefs among even liberal and nonreligious people. Americans distrust "proselytizing" and fear that lesbians and gays will try to "convert" other people. Suspicion of proselytizing was the basis for the separation of church and state in the Bill of Rights. Americans also resent underground minorities who have economic power and who are not completely visible.

The appeal is ironic precisely because the Religious Right's tactics actually violate each of these beliefs. It proselytizes continually. The "No Promo Homo" campaigns infringe on the separation of church and state; the Religious Right is attempting to turn fundamentalist Christian beliefs into law.

The "No Special Rights" campaigns, of course, obscure the fact that openly gay men and women suffer discrimination and denigration. They usually earn less than their counterparts by age and occupation.[28] The Religious Right and their conservative allies have dramatically shifted the distribution of wealth so that less than 10 percent of the population has almost 50 percent of the money.

This implies that gay and lesbian political strategies should focus more on the separation of church and state *and* on economic issues. With these issues, activists can relate the more narrow political interests of the lesbian and gay communities to the concerns of the rest of the country. AIDS activists have used that strategy, promoting the needs of people with AIDS by arguing that the whole country would benefit from national health insurance. As Michael Nava and Robert Dawidoff have argued in their eloquent and forceful book, "Americans will have to recognize their gay family, friends, and neighbors as fellow citizens to protect their own individual freedom, not to mention traditional American democratic pluralism."[29]

The lesbian and gay movement can adopt two broad political strategies to combat the Religious Right's hegemonic project. One strategy, proposed by Bruce Bawer, Marshall Kirk, Hunter Madsen, and other gay conservatives (or "moderates" as they wish to be called), would require a major reconstruction of gay and lesbian politics, in particular a rejection of the "ethnic model" or identity politics. This "moderate" strategy focuses on redressing "the ignorance that makes straight people fear homosexuality and consider it a threat to American society."[30] Bawer and his associates wish to embark on an educational and public relations campaign—partly to undo the negative effects of the gay subculture's radicalism and flamboyance, but mostly because they fail to understand how the Religious Right's hegemonic political project deliberately employs false and misleading representations and violates basic political guarantees such as the separation of church and state.

A more realistic—but incredibly difficult—political strategy is to follow in the footsteps of the Rainbow Coalition. The gay and lesbian movement would work with political groups from other communities— racial and ethnic minorities, the economically disadvantaged—to create a radical democratic politics.

Currently, the Rainbow Coalition is moribund—many of its constituent movements fragmented, tensions between groups remained unresolved, and it may have been tied too closely to Jesse Jackson's candidacy. Such a radical democratic coalition must nevertheless be revived in order to counter the Religious Right. Lesbian and gay political leaders must not wait for others to take the initiative—they must reach out to other communities and build coalitions.

No coalition politics will ever succeed without a concomitant learning process. This means that the lesbian and gay communities must be willing to learn about issues important to other coalition members and to incorporate that knowledge into their political common sense. Other members must do the same. The lesbian and gay movement, as well as other currents on the Left, must also reach out to and work with churches and religious groups in the progressive religious tradition.[31]

It is important to recognize that although the Religious Right wants to keep homosexuality at bay, it also intends to use the issue of gay and lesbian rights to destroy "liberalism," which many conservatives identify with "multiculturalism." Protecting liberal gains such as civil rights legislation and Medicare is an important component of the radical democratic project. The lesbian and gay movement will only defeat the Religious Right in its hegemonic ambitions if it can join with its allies to provide a counterhegemonic project—a radical democracy that is open, pluralistic, and practical.

CONCLUSION

Meditations in an Emergency

The crisis consists precisely in the fact that
the old is dying and the new cannot be born;
in this interregnum a great variety of morbid
symptoms appear.

ANTONIO GRAMSCI, *The Prison Notebooks*

The "state of emergency" in which we live is not
the exception but the rule.

WALTER BENJAMIN,
"Theses on the Philosophy of History"

In May 1996, the United States Supreme Court struck down an amendment to the Colorado state constitution. The amendment had nullified any existing antidiscrimination ordinances in the state but had also barred the passage of any gay and lesbian civil rights laws in Colorado.

The Supreme Court's decision to overturn Amendment 2 of the Colorado Constitution marked a turning point in the history of homosexuality in the United States. The decision represents a subtle shift in public discourse. Fewer people now believe that homosexuality is an evil and that society is justified in adopting severe forms of repression and disallowance (such as the Court upheld in *Bowers v. Hardwick* just ten years before). These days, people tend to define homosexuality as a quotidian trait or as a characteristic of human behavior that lawmakers, judges, and citizens should treat in a socially responsible manner.

This transition takes the status of lesbians and gay men from sexual outlaws to citizens.[1]

American society, which had for so long exhibited the complex historical intertwinement of homoeroticism and homophobia that signifies *American homo*, now has an explicit public discourse dedicated to the status of homosexuality in American life. The public discourse links the conversations of ordinary men and women, gay or straight, to the institutional discourses of churches, legislatures, and the Supreme Court. People commonly debate homosexual issues, including the rights of gay men and lesbians to serve in the military, the right to privacy (*Bowers v. Hardwick*), the legitimacy of civil rights legislation (the Colorado decision), and the right to same-sex marriages. The public discourse is highly contested, characterized by sexual latitudinarism as well as homophobic populism, but homosexuality is no longer a taboo subject in society.

Justice Anthony Kennedy wrote the majority opinion in the Colorado decision, arguing that the provision under consideration, which singled out Colorado's homosexuals, violates the U.S. Constitution's equal protection guarantee that "[a] state cannot so deem a class of persons a stranger to its laws." Such a designation would have established a legal disability so sweeping that the majority of the Court concluded that Amendment 2 was otherwise inexplicable except for simple hatred—"animus" in the Court's language. The language of Amendment 2 almost resembled that of the laws that the Nazis passed to disenfranchise German Jews. The opening of Justice Scalia's dissenting opinion reinforced this comparison: "The Court has mistaken a Kulturkampf for a fit of spite. The constitutional amendment before us here is not the manifestation of a 'bare . . . desire to harm homosexuals,' . . . but rather a modest attempt by seemingly tolerant Coloradans to preserve traditional sexual mores against the efforts of a politically powerful minority to revise those mores through the use of laws."[2] Both opinions acknowledge, in different ways, the ongoing culture wars that have placed homosexuality at the center of American political life.[3]

One of the historical ironies is that the AIDS epidemic has helped open homosexuals to participate in the process of government—primarily by forming policies about medical and epidemiological research on HIV, HIV prevention plans, and the treatment and care of people with AIDS.

After representatives of gay men and women began to help formulate policies and, perhaps even more significantly, after the details of gay men's sexual practices became the subject of epidemiological and prevention discourses, it became increasingly difficult for political leaders to avoid confronting other issues raised by the gay and lesbian communities. The infamous Helms amendment attempts to shun such subjects. The amendment insists on excluding from all federally funded HIV prevention literature any nonjudgmental information about homosexuality; obviously, such a law would prohibit an honest description of gay men's sexual practices.[4]

Storming such "sacred institutions" as the military and marriage by demanding the same rights as heterosexuals seems almost like an unexceptional stage in consolidating lesbian and gay citizenship. At the same time, the gay movement (as well as the AIDS movement) has become increasingly dependent on the state.

The Supreme Court's Colorado decision is only the latest episode in the culture wars over homosexuality, which have been waged continuously since 1977. Before then, they erupted only intermittently, such as during the McCarthy scare in the 1950s. Homosexuality represents a historically complex entanglement of religion, politics, and culture. Gay and lesbian identity politics is, only in part, about the social status of self-identified homosexuals; it is also about the meaning of sexuality, gender, the family, and even community in our society.

The transformation from sexual outlaw to citizen challenges groups both outside the lesbian and gay communities and inside them. Religious fundamentalists, of course, abhor the social acceptance of a group they see as sinful and morally decadent, a community that seems to transgress some of their most treasured values.[5] The lesbian and gay communities, however, have considerable ambivalence toward the campaign for citizenship, because the outlaw status of homosexuals is historically very significant. It originally spurred the creation of the gay and lesbian movement, stimulated cultural creativity, and helped to mobilize the building of lesbian and gay communities across the nation.

Queer politics in the late 1980s and early 1990s celebrated the otherness, the differentness, and the marginality of the homosexual, whereas the gay politics of citizenship acknowledges the satisfactions of conforming, passing, belonging, and being accepted. We have suffered from the stigma, the exclusion from society, and the homophobia that made lesbians and gay men pariahs. At the same time, we have rights as citizens, rights that we earned by fulfilling the same duties as "straight" citizens—we pay taxes, we fight in wars, we vote in elections.

The increased participation of lesbians and gay men in the political and governing process bears one fundamental and risky irony.[6] Disciplinary mechanisms and normative processes shape the political identities of citizens (e.g., as punctual, economically self-sufficient, knowledgeable, law-abiding individuals), as well as enabling their political participation. But the democratic participation of those same citizens also masks disciplinary and normative procedures. At the same time that citizens exercise their political freedom, they have also been trained, counseled, and disciplined in order to qualify as citizens. The normative expectation is that the gay man as sexual outlaw must give up his public sex in the park in order to become the sexual citizen who qualifies for the right to serve openly in the military.

Similarly, the corporate effort to expand the lesbian and gay market has a "regulatory" or "disciplinary" effect. It represents an improvement in some respects by offering new goods and services—but it also shapes the psychological and physical needs that those goods satisfy. It fixes or reifies those needs and limits satisfaction to that provided by those commodities available in the gay marketplace. Needs that are not met are marginalized, sometimes even stigmatized. In addition, social acceptance and the recognition of political rights ensure the accessibility of the good gay citizen to various normalizing and regulatory practices. As Foucault bitterly observed, every institutionalized form of political rights (a positive achievement) also enables disciplinary and normalizing forms of domination (not necessarily good things). Yet, only the active exercise of democratic rights allows a group to resist, modify, or restructure the forms of domination operating through discipline and normalization.[7]

Lesbian and gay activists have characterized this complicated and double-edged process as "mainstreaming." Like a struggle in quicksand, the effort to define political rights may only make the lesbian and gay communities sink further into a morass of normalizing discipline. Homosexuals cannot, however, just walk away from this messy and contradictory aspect of civil life.

No one can ever completely step outside of the society in which they were reared. Not even by emigrating to another country can we escape our socialization and language, nor can we consent to our society's stigmatization of homosexuality. Deciding neither to step outside the arena nor to accept its prevalent mores is a surefire formula for conflict but it is unavoidable—so many different things divide the terrain of social life.[8] There are no transcendent solutions to the ambivalence of identity—our only consolations are the "concrete social structures of friendship, love and pity."[9] The powers of sexual perversity *and* community nurture these structures.[10]

Politically, the only viable strategy will be to create a sense of community, form alliances with other social groups and movements, and then take direct political action. In our society, this is the only way to build political and cultural hegemony. This triangular strategy of community building, direct action, and political alliance resembles the strategy that Italian political theorist Antonio Gramsci formulated. He argued that in Europe's and North America's highly developed civil and market societies, an oppositional political movement must wage both a war of position (for example, by building communities) and a war of maneuver (direct action plus political alliances). In this way, the movement can resist hegemonic institutions and ideologies, such as the heterosexual, male-centered, and reproductivist cultural norms and institutions that stigmatize homosexuality.[11]

When building communities, gay and lesbian activists must include the full range of economic, cultural, and political institutions. In contrast, when they take direct action, activists can target particular issues and specific enemies. Finally, lesbians and gay men must forge political alliances that allow the gay movement to engage in negotiations, and make viable compromises, with other communities and movements.

NOTES

INTRODUCTION

1.   I want to thank the following friends for their comments and suggestions on this introduction: Chris Bull, E. G. Crichton, Jim Green, Amber Hollibaugh, Robert Hughes, Terrence Kissack, Loring McAlpin, Molly McGarry, Kevin Murphy, Matt Rottnek, Andrew Spieldenner, and Leith ter Meulen. I would especially like to thank Matthew Lore, who guided me through its many drafts. I remain responsible for its shortcomings.

2.   These structures reflect the temporality of the *longue durée*—the slower, often hidden social developments, as opposed to the temporality of current events. See p. 31 of Fernand Braudel, "History and the Social Sciences: The *Longue Durée*," in his book of essays *On History* (Chicago: University of Chicago Press, 1980). See also Raymond Williams on structures of feeling in *Marxism and Literature* (New York: Oxford University Press, 1977), pp. 128–35.

3.   For a rare first-person account of a homosexual life originally published in 1901, see Claude Hartland, *The Story of a Life* (San Francisco: Grey Fox Press, 1985). See also the documents in Jonathan Ned Katz, *Gay American History:*

Lesbians and Gay Men in the U.S.A. (New York: Crowell, 1976), and in Martin Bauml Duberman, *About Time: Exploring the Gay Past* (New York: Gay Press of New York, 1986), pp. 5–48.

4. Barbara Welter, "The Cult of True Womanhood: 1820–1860," in *The American Family in Social-Historical Perspective,* ed. Michael Gordon (New York: St. Martin's Press, 1973); Carol Smith-Rosenberg, "The World of Love and Ritual," in *Disorderly Conduct: Visions of Gender in Victorian America* (New York: Knopf, 1985); and Lillian Faderman, *Surpassing the Love of Men: Romantic Friendship and Love between Women from the Renaissance to the Present* (New York: Morrow, 1981).

5. Ben Barker-Benfield, "The Spermatic Economy: A Nineteenth-Century View of Sexuality," in *American Family,* ed. M. Gordon.

6. See Eve Kosofsky Sedgwick, *Between Men: English Literature and Male Homosocial Desire* (New York: Columbia University Press, 1985), pp. 83–96.

7. For example, see Estelle B. Freedman, *Maternal Justice: Miriam van Waters and the Female Reform Tradition* (Chicago: University of Chicago Press, 1996); and John D'Emilio, "Homophobia and the Trajectory of Postwar American Radicalism: The Case of Bayard Rustin," *Radical History Review,* no. 62 (spring 1995).

8. See Edward Carpenter, "The Intermediate Sex," in *Selected Writings,* vol. 1, *Sex* (1908; reprint, London: Gay Men's Press, 1984), pp. 217–19. See also John Addington Symonds, *A Problem in Modern Ethics,* reprinted along with Symonds's letters to Carpenter in *Male Love: A Problem in Greek Ethics and Other Writings* (New York: Pagan Press, 1983), pp. 93–103, 153–54. For a fuller sense of the historical background and Walt Whitman's role, see Sheila Rowbotham and Jeffrey Weeks, *Socialism and the New Life: The Personal Politics of Edward Carpenter and Havelock Ellis* (London: Pluto Press, 1977).

9. My view of homoeroticism as an American cultural semiotic was suggested by Houston A. Baker's study of blues as a cultural semiotic in *Blues, Ideology, and Afro-American Literature: A Vernacular Theory* (Chicago: University of Chicago Press, 1984), pp. 1–14; and from Thomas E. Yingling's discussion of homosexuality as a cultural semiotic (he cites Baker) in *Hart Crane and the Homosexual Text* (Chicago: University of Chicago Press, 1990), pp. 1–23.

10. Michael Moon, "Disseminating Whitman," *South Atlantic Quarterly* 88, no. 1 (winter 1989): 248.

11. Ibid., p. 251.

12. For a pioneering discussion of the social implications of this mix of dread and desire from the perspective of French philosophers of desire Gilles Deleuze and Felix Guattari, see Guy Hocquenghem, *The Problem Is Not So Much Homosexual Desire as the Fear of Homosexuality* (London: Allison & Busby, 1978; reprint, Durham, N.C.: Duke University Press, 1994).

13.   See the two documentary histories that Jonathan Ned Katz edited. One section of *Gay American History* ("Trouble: 1566–1966," pp. 11–128) documents the repression of homosexual behavior throughout U.S. history. A more focused exploration of repression during the colonial period appears in *Gay/Lesbian Almanac: A New Documentary* (New York: Harper & Row, 1983), pp. 66–133.

14.   George Chauncey documents Roosevelt's investigation of sexual perversion in the Navy. See Chauncey, "Christian Brotherhood or Sexual Perversion? Homosexual Identities and the Construction of Social Boundaries in the World War I Era," in *Hidden from History: Reclaiming the Gay and Lesbian Past*, ed. Martin Bauml Duberman, Martha Vicinus, and George Chauncey, Jr. (New York: New American Library, 1989), pp. 294–317.

In addition to the findings in lesbian and gay history, works of broad cultural interpretation reveal a powerful current of homoeroticism in American culture and history. See especially Leslie A. Fiedler, *Love and Death in the American Novel* (New York: Criterion Books, 1960). See also F. O. Mathiessen's correspondence with his lover Russell Cheney: *Rat and the Devil: Journal Letters of F. O. Mathiessen and Russell Cheney*, ed. Louis Hyde (Hamden, Conn.: Archon Books, 1978) on the homosexual background to Mathiessen's magnum opus, *American Renaissance: Art and Expression in the Age of Emerson and Whitman* (New York: Oxford University Press, 1941). For other historical work documenting American homoeroticism, see the following: Steven Watson, *The Harlem Renaissance: Hub of African-American Culture, 1920–1930* (New York: Pantheon Books, 1995); Georges-Michel Sarotte, *Like a Brother, Like a Lover: Male Homosexuality in the American Novel and Theatre from Herman Melville to James Baldwin* (New York: Anchor Press, 1978); and Sandra M. Gilbert and Susan Gubar, *No Man's Land: The Place of the Woman Writer in the Twentieth Century* (New Haven: Yale University Press, 1988–89). Texts documenting the history of homophobia are somewhat scarcer, but see again works of lesbian and gay history, particularly Katz's documentary histories, *Gay American History* and *Gay/Lesbian Almanac*.

15.   In *Between Men*, Sedgwick explores a similar pattern of interlocking social structures—homosocial desire and homophobia—in the hundred years between the mid-eighteenth century and the mid-nineteenth century.

16.   *New York Times*, February 11, 1996. See also Frank Rich's op-ed piece "Bashing to Victory," *New York Times*, February 14, 1996.

17.   Jonathan Ned Katz, *The Invention of Heterosexuality* (New York: Dutton, 1995).

18.   Herbert Marcuse, *Eros and Civilization: A Philosophical Inquiry into Freud* (Boston: Beacon Press, 1966); and Norman O. Brown, *Life against Death: The Psychoanalytical Meaning of History* (Middletown, Conn.: Wesleyan University Press, 1959).

19.   Karl Marx, "The Eighteenth Brumaire of Louis Napoleon," in *Surveys from Exile: Political Writings* (New York: Penguin Books, 1973), 2:146.

20.   Paul Berman discusses this phenomenon in *A Tale of Two Utopias: The Political Journey of the Generation of 1968* (New York: Norton, 1996).

21.   See Marshall Berman, *The Politics of Authenticity: Radical Individualism and the Emergence of Modern Society* (New York: Atheneum, 1972); James Miller, *Democracy Is in the Streets* (New York: Simon & Schuster, 1987); and Lionel Trilling, *Sincerity and Authenticity* (Cambridge: Harvard University Press, 1971).

22.   Frederick A. Olafson, "Authenticity and Obligation," in *Sartre: A Collection of Critical Essays*, ed. Mary Warnock (New York: Doubleday Anchor Books, 1971), p. 138.

23.   See Jean-Luc Nancy, *The Inoperative Community* (Minneapolis: University of Minnesota Press, 1991); and The Miami Theory Collective, eds., *Community at Loose Ends* (Minneapolis: University of Minnesota Press, 1991).

24.   Berman, *Politics of Authenticity*, pp. 284–320.

25.   Gerald Early, ed., *Lure and Loathing: Essays on Race, Identity, and the Ambivalence of Assimilation* (New York: Allen Lane, 1993). This collection of essays explores W.E.B. DuBois's notion of the "double consciousness" of African-Americans.

26.   Bruce Bawer, *A Place at the Table: The Gay Individual in American Society* (New York: Poseidon Press, 1993). Other writers share many of Bawer's positions, including Andrew Sullivan, *Virtually Normal: An Argument about Homosexuality* (New York: Knopf, 1995), and Marshall Kirk and Hunter Madsen, *After the Ball: How America Will Conquer Its Fear and Hatred of Gays in the Nineties* (New York: Doubleday, 1989).

27.   Urvashi Vaid, *Virtual Equality: The Mainstreaming of Gay and Lesbian Liberation* (New York: Anchor Books, 1995), p. 3.

28.   See "Queer/Nation," the brief article I wrote with Allan Bérubé. See also articles on Queer Nation in *OUT/LOOK: National Lesbian and Gay Quarterly*, no. 11 (winter 1992); and Lauren Berlandt and Elizabeth Freeman, "Queer Nationality," in *Fear of a Queer Planet: Queer Politics and Social Theory*, ed. Michael Warner (Minneapolis: University of Minnesota Press, 1993), pp. 193–229.

29.   Warner, introduction to *Fear of a Queer Planet*, p. xxvi. See also Steven Seidman, "Deconstructing Queer Theory or the Under-Theorization of the Social and the Ethical," in *Social Postmodernism: Beyond Identity Politics*, ed. Linda Nicholson and Steven Seidman (Cambridge, England: Cambridge University Press, 1995), pp. 123–31.

30.   Warner, introduction to *Fear of a Queer Planet*, p. xxvii.

31.   For a discussion of queer theory, see chapter 8 in this volume: "Under the Sign of the Queer."

32.   Hocquenghem, *Problem Is Not Desire*, p. 36.

33.   Sigmund Freud, *Three Essays on Sexuality* (New York: Basic Books, 1962). See also Freud's 1908 essay " 'Civilized' Sexual Morality and Modern Nervousness," in a collection of his essays, *Sexuality and the Psychology of Love*, ed. Philip Reiff (New York: Collier Books, 1963), pp. 20–40.

34.   Sigmund Freud, *Civilization and Its Discontents* (New York: Norton, 1961).

35.   In a series of essays and books, Leo Bersani has explored the significance of perverse, transgressive sexuality. See Bersani, *The Freudian Body: Psychoanalysis and Art* (New York: Columbia University Press, 1986); idem, "Is the Rectum a Grave?" in *AIDS: Cultural Analysis, Cultural Activism,* ed. Douglas Crimp (Cambridge: MIT Press, 1988); idem, *The Culture of Redemption* (Cambridge: Harvard University Press, 1990); and idem, *Homos* (Cambridge: Harvard University Press, 1995). Jonathan Dollimore has also explored these issues in *Sexual Dissidence: Augustine to Wilde, Freud to Foucault* (Oxford, England: Clarendon Press, 1991).

36.   Roland Barthes, *The Pleasure of the Text* (New York: Farrar, Straus & Giroux, 1975), p. 19. The "perverse," or polymorphous perversity, represents what might also be called "the homosexual sublime," which Yingling examines in *Hart Crane*, pp. 145–85. Fredric Jameson characterizes the sublime as "something like the pleasure in pain" in his essay "Baudelaire as Modernist and Postmodernist," in *Lyric Poetry: Beyond New Criticism*, ed. C. Hosek and P. Park (Ithaca, N.Y.: Cornell University Press, 1985), p. 262.

37.   John Rechy, *Sexual Outlaw* (New York: Grove Press, 1977).

38.   Bersani, *Freudian Body*, pp. 81–106, and *Culture of Redemption*, pp. 29–46.

39.   Bersani, *Homos*, pp. 2–3.

40.   Ibid., p. 4.

41.   Ibid., p. 4.

42.   Ibid., p. 69.

43.   Tony Kushner, *Thinking about the Longstanding Problems of Virtue and Happiness: Essays, a Play, Two Poems, and a Prayer* (New York: Theatre Communications Group, 1995), p. 78.

44.   Erving Goffman explored identity ambivalence in *Stigma: Notes on the Management of Spoiled Identity* (Englewood Cliffs, N.J.: Prentice Hall, 1963).

45.   Hannah Arendt developed a post-Holocaust theoretical framework within which to examine Jewish identity politics. See Ron H. Feldman, ed., *The Jew as Pariah: Jewish Identity and Politics in the Modern Age* (New York: Grove Press, 1978).

PART ONE

1.   Jean-François Lyotard, *The Postmodern Condition: A Report on Knowledge* (Minneapolis: University of Minnesota Press, 1984), pp. 37–41.

2.   There is a small body of work on the term *sexual revolution*. I have adopted the argument that Gayle Rubin made in "Thinking Sex: Notes for a Radical Theory of the Politics of Sex," in *Pleasure and Danger: Exploring Female Sexuality*, ed. Carole Vance (Boston: Routledge, 1984). See also Jeffrey Weeks, *Sexuality and Its Discontents* (London: Routledge, 1985), esp. pp. 15–32. More recently, Weeks discusses the sexual revolution as an interrupted historical process in "An Unfinished Revolution: Sexuality in the Twentieth Century," in *Pleasure Principles: Politics, Sexuality, and Ethics*, ed. Victoria Harwood, David Oswell, Kay Parkinson, and Anna Ward (London: Lawrence and Wishart, 1993). See the use of the term in Barbara Ehrenreich, Elizabeth Hess, and Gloria Jacobs, *Remaking Love: The Feminization of Sex* (Garden City, N.Y.: Anchor Press, 1986). On the historical evidence for a sexual revolution, see Daniel Scott Smith, "The Dating of the American Sexual Revolution: Evidence and Interpretation," in *American Family* (2d ed.), ed. M. Gordon. For an argument against using the term *sexual revolution*, see Albert D. Klassen et al., *Sex and Morality in the U.S.* (Middletown, Conn.: Wesleyan University Press, 1989), pp. 3–16.

3.   Perry Anderson, *Lineages of the Absolute State* (London: New Left Books, 1974), p. 8.

4.   Gayle Rubin, "The Traffic in Women: Notes on the 'Political Economy' of Sex," in *Toward an Anthropology of Women*, ed. Rayna R. Reiter (New York: Monthly Review Press, 1975). See also John Gagnon and William Simon, *Sexual Conduct: The Social Sources of Human Sexuality* (Chicago: Aldine, 1973), pp. 287–88.

5.   Gagnon and Simon, *Sexual Conduct*, pp. 287–307.

6.   Weeks, *Sexuality and Its Discontents*, p. 16.

CHAPTER 1

1.   I would never have written this essay without the constant encouragement of four people: Dick Bunce, Mark Leger, Ilene Philipson, and Gayle Rubin. In addition to thanking them, I would like to thank Dennis Altman, Jeanne Bergman, Allan Bérubé, George Chauncey, Donald Lowe, William Simon, Howard Winant, and the Bay Area Socialist Review Collective for their extensive comments and suggestions. I owe a special debt to the students in my course on homosexuality and social change at the University of California, Berkeley, during the summer and fall of 1983; their critical, passionate, and intelligent arguments helped me develop many of the ideas in this essay.

2.   For a theoretical discussion of the political ontology of identities, see Ernesto Laclau and Chantal Mouffe, *Hegemony and Socialist Strategy: Towards a Radical Democratic Politics* (London: Verso, 1985), pp. 114–22.

3. Rubin, "Traffic in Women," pp. 159, 199–200. Recently, Rubin has modified her earlier formulation to distinguish between the sex and gender components of the sex/gender system and to outline a model of "sexual transformation." See Rubin, "Thinking Sex," pp. 284–87, on sexual transformation; and see pp. 307–9 for modifications to her conceptualization of the sex/gender system.

George Chauncey, Jr., has also used the sex/gender system as an analytical framework in his history of medical theories of gender deviance and homosexuality. See George Chauncey, Jr., "From Sexual Inversion to Homosexuality: Medicine and the Changing Conceptualization of Female Deviance," *Salmagundi*, nos. 58–99 (fall 1982–winter 1983): 114–46. Chantal Mouffe has argued that the sex/gender paradigm is more useful than concepts of "patriarchy" or the "social relations of reproduction" for understanding the different practices, discourses, and institutions by which women's subordination is constructed. See Mouffe, "The Sex/Gender System and the Discursive Construction of Women's Subordination," in *Rethinking Ideology: A Marxist Debate*, ed. I. Bessenyei et al. (New York: International General/IMMRC, 1983), pp. 139–43.

4. Anthony Giddens's analysis specifies these three dimensions (domination, normative regulation, and coding) as aspects of social reproduction. See his *Central Problems in Social Theory: Action, Structure, and Contradiction in Social Analysis* (Berkeley: University of California Press, 1979), esp. pp. 96–115 and 225–33, for his discussion of the analysis I draw on here.

5. For an account of racial formation, see Michael Omi and Howard Winant, "By the Rivers of Babylon: Race in the United States," *Socialist Review*, no. 71 (September–October); no. 72 (November–December 1983). For an analysis of class formation in the same spirit, see Adam Przeworski, "Proletariat into a Class: The Process of Class Formation from Karl Kautsky's *The Class Struggle* to Recent Controversies," *Politics and Society* 7, no. 4 (1977). Authors who have mapped some of the interactions of the sex/gender system with other sectors of society include Jeffrey Weeks, *Sex, Politics, and Society: The Regulation of Sexuality since 1800* (London: Longman, 1981), pp. 12–16; and Gagnon and Simon, in their pioneering work *Sexual Conduct*, pp. 287–307.

6. Michel Foucault, *The History of Sexuality*, vol. 1, *An Introduction* (New York: Pantheon Books, 1978), pp. 15–50.

7. Clellon S. Ford and Frank A. Beach, *Patterns of Sexual Behavior* (New York: Harper & Row, 1951).

8. K. J. Dover, *Greek Homosexuality* (New York: Vintage Books, 1980), pp. 39–57.

9. Will Roscoe, *Zuni Man-Woman* (Albuquerque: University of New Mexico Press, 1991).

10. Jeffrey Weeks, *Coming Out: Homosexual Politics in Britain, from the Nine-

teenth Century to the Present (London: Quartet Books, 1977); John D'Emilio, *Sexual Politics, Sexual Communities: The Making of a Homosexual Minority in the United States, 1940–1970* (Chicago: University of Chicago Press, 1983); Kenneth Plummer, ed., *The Making of the Modern Homosexual* (London: Hutchinson, 1981).

11.   Lionel Trilling, "The Kinsey Report," in *The Liberal Imagination* (New York: Anchor Books, 1953), p. 234.

12.   Alfred C. Kinsey, Wardell B. Pomeroy, and Clyde E. Martin, *Sexual Behavior in the Human Male* (Philadelphia: Saunders, 1948), and Alfred C. Kinsey et al., *Sexual Behavior in the Human Female* (Philadelphia: Saunders, 1953), p. 10.

13.   Paul Robinson, *The Modernization of Sex* (New York: Harper & Row, 1976), p. 51.

14.   Ibid., pp. 49–51, 115–19.

15.   Ira L. Reiss, "Standards of Sexual Behavior," in *The Encyclopedia of Sexual Behavior*, ed. Albert Ellis and Albert Abarbanel (New York: Hawthorn Books, 1961). This was calculated from unpublished data from the Institute for Sex Research, which were quoted in D. Smith, "Dating of the American Sexual Revolution"; also Linda Gordon discusses the dating of sexual behavioral changes in *Woman's Body, Woman's Right: Birth Control in America* (New York: Penguin, 1977), p. 193.

16.   Lewis M. Terman, *Psychological Factors in Marital Happiness* (New York: McGraw-Hill, 1938), quoted in L. Gordon, *Woman's Body, Woman's Right*, p. 193.

17.   For discussions of the distinction between homosexual persons and homosexual acts, see Claude J. Summers on Gore Vidal, in *Gay Fictions: Wilde to Stonewall* (New York: Continuum, 1990), p. 113; and Richard Goldstein's interview with James Baldwin in Goldstein, "Go the Way Your Blood Beats," *Village Voice*, June 26, 1984, p. 14.

18.   D'Emilio, *Sexual Politics*, pp. 57–91.

19.   Two books by Robert J. Corber explore the connection between anticommunism and homophobia. See *In the Name of National Security: Hitchcock and the Political Construction of Gender in Postwar America* (Durham, N.C.: Duke University Press, 1993); and *Homosexuality in Cold War America: Resistance and the Crisis of Masculinity* (Durham, N.C.: Duke University Press, 1997).

20.   Recently, Daniel Harris has explored the role of gay culture as the basis for group consciousness. See Harris, *The Rise and Fall of Gay Culture* (New York: Hyperion, 1997).

21.   The quotations from and material about the Mattachine Society are from D'Emilio, *Sexual Politics*, pp. 65, 77–91.

22.   Donald Webster Cory, *The Homosexual in America: A Subjective Approach* (New York: Castle Books, 1951; reprint, 1960).

23.   Ira L. Reiss, *Premarital Sexual Standards in America* (New York: Free Press,

1960); Robert R. Bell, *Premarital Sex in Changing Society* (Englewood Cliffs, N.J.: Prentice Hall, 1966).

24. Barbara Ehrenreich, *The Hearts of Men* (New York: Doubleday/Anchor, 1984), pp. 42–51.

25. H. W. Arndt, *The Rise and Fall of Economic Growth* (Chicago: University of Chicago Press, 1984), p. 27.

26. Samuel Bowles and Herbert Gintis, "The Crisis of Liberal Democratic Capitalism: The Case of the United States," *Politics and Society* 11, no. 1 (1982): 65–66.

27. Richard A. Easterlin, "What Will 1984 Be Like? Socioeconomic Implications of Recent Twists in Age Structure," *Demography* 15, no. 4 (November 1978). See also idem, "American Population since 1940," in *The American Economy in Transition,* ed. Martin Feldstein (Chicago: University of Chicago Press, 1980).

28. Robert A. Gordon, *Economic Instability and Growth: The American Record* (New York: Harper & Row, 1974), pp. 105–7; Harry N. Scheiber, Harold G. Vatter, and Harold Underwood Faulkner, *American Economic History* (New York: Harper & Row, 1976), pp. 422–27.

29. See Ruth Milkman, "Organizing the Sexual Division of Labor: Historical Perspectives on Women's Work and the American Labor Movement," *Socialist Review,* no. 49 (vol. 10, no. 1; January–February 1980): 128–41; and idem, "Women's Work and the Economic Crisis: Some Lessons from the Great Depression," in *A Heritage of Her Own,* ed. Nancy F. Cott and Elizabeth H. Pleck (New York: Simon & Schuster, 1979), p. 532.

30. See Winifred D. Wandersee, *Women's Work and Family Values, 1920–1940* (Cambridge: Harvard University Press, 1981), esp. pp. 27–54, 103–17.

31. William H. Chafe, "Looking backward in Order to Look forward," in *Women and the American Economy,* ed. Juanita Kreps (Englewood Cliffs, N.J.: Prentice Hall, 1976), p. 17.

32. See Wandersee, *Women's Work,* pp. 111–117.

33. John Modell, Frank Furstenberg, and Douglas Strong, "The Timing of the Marriage in the Transition to Adulthood, 1860–1975," *American Journal of Sociology* 84, supplement (1978); and Andrew Cherlin, *Marriage, Divorce, Remarriage* (Cambridge: Harvard University Press, 1981), pp. 8–12, 19–21.

34. Easterlin, "American Population since 1940."

35. Norman Ryder, "Recent Trends and Group Differences in Fertility," in *Toward the End of Growth: Population in America,* ed. Charles F. Westoff (Englewood Cliffs, N.J.: Prentice Hall, 1973), p. 61; see also Judith Blake, "Coercive Pronatalism and American Population Policy" (paper prepared for the commission on Population Growth and the American Future, 1972).

36. Rubin, "Thinking Sex," pp. 269–70; see also Allan Bérubé, "Marching to

a Different Drummer," in *Powers of Desire: The Politics of Sexuality*, ed. Ann Snitow, Christine Stansell, and Sharon Thompson (New York: Monthly Review Press, 1983); D'Emilio, *Sexual Politics*; idem, "Gay Politics, Gay Community: San Francisco's Experience," *Socialist Review*, no. 55 (vol. 11, no. 1; January–February 1981).

37.   Eileen Applebaum, "Women in the Stagflation Economy," in *Reaganomics in the Stagflation Economy*, ed. Sidney Weintraub and Marvin Goodstein (Philadelphia: University of Pennsylvania Press, 1983), p. 38. For more recent data, see George Masnick and Mary Jo Bane, *The Nation's Families: 1960–1990* (Boston: Auburn House, 1980).

38.   Daniel Bell, *The Cultural Contradictions of Capitalism* (New York: Basic Books, 1976), pp. 33–84.

39.   Mark Poster, *Critical Theory of the Family* (New York: Seabury Press, 1978), pp. 166–205; and Masnick and Bane, *Nation's Families*, pp. 95–116.

40.   Ehrenreich, *Hearts of Men*, pp. 14–28.

41.   Ilene Philipson, "Heterosexual Antagonisms and the Politics of Mothering," *Socialist Review*, no. 66 (vol. 12, no. 6; November–December 1982).

42.   For example, see Daniel Bell, *Work and Its Discontents*, reprinted in his collection *The End of Ideology* (Glencoe, Ill.: Free Press, 1960); and Ely Chinoy, *Automobile Workers and the American Dream* (New York: Random House, 1955).

43.   Marcuse, *Eros and Civilization*, p. 50. See Paul Goodman, *Growing Up Absurd: Problems of Youth in the Organized System* (New York: Random House, 1960).

44.   Quoted in Richard King, *The Party of Eros: Radical Social Thought and the Realm of Freedom* (New York: Dell, 1973), p. 84.

45.   Chauncey, "Sexual Inversion," pp. 114–46.

46.   Ibid., p. 120.

47.   See James D. Steakley, *The Homosexual Emancipation Movement in Germany* (New York: Arno Press, 1975).

48.   Carpenter, "Intermediate Sex."

49.   For a critical discussion of this assumption, see Gagnon and Simon, *Sexual Conduct*, pp. 132–36.

50.   Barbara Ponse, *Identities in the Lesbian World: The Social Construction of Self* (Westport, Conn.: Greenwood Press, 1978), pp. 24–30; see also Gagnon and Simon, *Sexual Conduct*, pp. 99–109.

51.   John Money and Anke Ehrhardt, *Man and Woman, Boy and Girl: The Differentiation and Dimorphism of Gender Identity from Conception to Maturity* (Baltimore: Johns Hopkins University Press, 1972); see also Nancy Chodorow, *The Reproduction of Mothering* (Berkeley: University of California Press, 1978) for an analysis of the social construction of gender identity.

52.   See Esther Newton and Shirley Walton, "The Misunderstanding: Toward a More Precise Sexual Vocabulary," *Pleasure and Danger*, ed. Vance.

53.   Michel de Certeau, *The Practice of Everyday Life* (Berkeley: University of California Press, 1984), pp. 29–42.

54.   John Rechy, *City of Night* (New York: Grove Press, 1963), p. 22.

55.   Quoted in Sacha G. Lewis, *Sunday's Women: Lesbian Life Today* (Boston: Beacon Press, 1979), p. 30.

56.   See Elizabeth Lapovsky Kennedy and Madeline D. Davis, *Boots of Leather, Slippers of Gold: The History of a Lesbian Community* (New York: Routledge, 1993).

57.   William Simon and John H. Gagnon, "Sexual Scripts," *Transaction/Society*, November–December 1984.

58.   Joan Nestle, "Butch/Femme Relationships: Sexual Courage in the 1950s," *Heresies*, no. 12 (1981): 21–24.

59.   See Amber Hollibaugh and Cherríe Moraga, "What We're Rollin around in Bed with: Sexual Silences in Feminism," *Heresies*, no. 12 (1981): 58–62; reprinted in *Powers of Desire*, ed. Snitow et al., pp. 394–405.

60.   For the best account of camp and its importance in gay male culture of the 1950s and early 1960s, see Esther Newton, *Mother Camp: Female Impersonators in America* (Englewood Cliffs, N.J.: Prentice Hall, 1972). For a somewhat priggish critique of camp from an early gay liberationist perspective, see Jeffrey Escoffier, "Breaking Camp," *Gay Alternative*, no. 4 (1973): 6–8.

61.   "Notes on Camp," reprinted in Susan Sontag, *A Susan Sontag Reader* (New York: Vintage Books, 1983), p. 117.

62.   For an excellent analysis of subcultures as counterhegemonic cultural responses, see Dick Hebdige, *Subculture: The Meaning of Style* (New York: Methuen, 1979), esp. pp. 73–99.

63.   Erving Goffman, *The Presentation of Self in Everyday Life* (New York: Doubleday Anchor Books, 1959), pp. 106–40.

64.   Laud Humphries, *Tearoom Trade: Impersonal Sex in Public Places* (Chicago: Aldine, 1970). See Michel de Certeau's discussion of "tactics" versus spatial "strategies" in *Practice of Everyday Life*, especially pp. 34–39.

65.   See Allan Bérubé, "Behind the Spectre," *Body Politic*, April 1981, and idem, "The History of Gay Bathhouses," *Coming Up!* December 1984, 18; reprinted in Dangerous Bedfellows, eds., *Policing Public Sex* (Boston: South End Press, 1996). See also Ellen Klages, "When the Bar Was the Only Place in Town," in *1984 International Lesbian/Gay Freedom Day Parade Celebration* (San Francisco: 1984), pp. 39–41.

66.   Toby Marotta, *The Politics of Homosexuality* (Boston: Houghton Mifflin, 1981), esp. pp. 48–68.

67.   Mary McIntosh, "The Homosexual Role," *Social Problems* 16, no. 2 (fall 1968).

68.   See the interview with Mary McIntosh, "Postscript: The Homosexual Role Revisited," in *Making of the Modern Homosexual*, ed. Plummer, pp. 44–49.

69.   Antonio Gramsci, "Problems of Philosophy and History," in *Selections from the Prison Notebooks* (New York: International Publishers, 1971), pp. 366–67. Sartre also identified the significance of such a moment as the transition from "being-in-itself" to "being-for-itself." See Jean-Paul Sartre, *Being and Nothingness* (New York: Citadel Press, 1971), pp. 65–77.

70.   Dennis Altman, *Homosexual: Oppression and Liberation* (reprint, New York: Avon Books, 1973). Altman later published another important evaluation of the lesbian and gay movements, *The Homosexualization of America* (Boston: Beacon Press, 1983).

71.   Altman, *Homosexual*, pp. 13–41.

72.   Ibid., p. 98.

73.   Ibid., p. 94.

74.   Ibid., pp. 108–51.

75.   Ibid., pp. 234, 237.

76.   Katz, *Gay American History* (reprint, New York: Avon Books, 1978), p. 1.

77.   Gay Left Collective, *Homosexuality: Power and Politics* (London: Allison & Busby, 1980).

78.   See Kenneth Plummer, *Sexual Stigma: An Interactionist Account* (London: Routledge, 1975), and *Making of the Modern Homosexual*, the essay collection that Plummer edited, which included many of the Gay Left authors.

79.   John D'Emilio, "Capitalism and Gay Identity," in *Powers of Desire*, ed. Snitow et al.

80.   Alan Crawford, *Thunder on the Right: The New Right and the Politics of Resentment* (New York: Pantheon Books, 1980), pp. 144–64.

81.   Robert Reilly, "Homosexual Rights and the Foundations of Human Rights," *Family Policy Insights* 1, no. 3 (December 1981): 539–40.

82.   The sex/gender system is organized, according to the principle of consistency, into a plurality of autonomous practices and identities that involve age, gender, sexuality, and form of family. The breakdown of this system suggests the rise of a new sex/gender code that could be called the *combinatorial principle*. In this new code, the social relations of gender and sex will be more fluid. Thus, distinct sexualities would emerge based on permutations of the elements (not necessarily immutable elements) of the sex/gender system—for example butch heterosexual women and femme heterosexual men. The combinatorial principle of the sex/gender system would offer an ideological framework for these permutations of diverse components of sexualities and genders.

83.   Goffman, *Stigma*, p. 111.

84.   Michel Foucault, "A Preface to Transgression," in *Language, Counter-Memory, Practice* (Ithaca, N.Y.: Cornell University Press, 1977), pp. 34–36.

CHAPTER 2

1.   This essay was both very difficult and quite fun to write. I am grateful for the encouragement of Amy Gluckman and Betsy Reed, who solicited it for a collection of essays on "homo economics" and who allowed me to write such a speculative essay. The comments of Terence Kissack, Regina Kunzel, Matthew Lore, Molly McGarry, Kevin Murphy, and Michael Rothberg were, as always, extremely helpful and stimulating.

2.   Regina Kunzel suggested the term *hypercommodification* to me. It refers to the way in which mainstream corporations promote identification with brand names and the lesbian and gay communities.

3.   See Amy Gluckman and Betsy Reed, "The Gay Marketing Moment: Leaving Diversity in the Dust," *Dollars and Sense*, November–December 1993; and Grant Lukenbill, *Untold Millions: Gay and Lesbian Markets in America* (New York: HarperCollins, 1995).

4.   See the section on employment discrimination in William Rubenstein, ed., *Lesbians, Gay Men, and the Law* (New York: New Press, 1993), pp. 243–375. There is now a series of books about gay men and lesbians in the workplace. See James Woods with Jay Lucas, *The Corporate Closet: The Professional Lives of Gay Men in America* (New York: Free Press, 1993).

5.   For a survey of economic issues, see Jeffrey Escoffier, "Homo/Economics: A Survey of Issues," in *Out in All Directions: The Almanac of Gay and Lesbian America*, ed. Lynn Witt, Eric Marcus, and Sherry Thomas (New York: Warner Books, 1995). See also M. V. Lee Badgett, "Thinking Homo/Economically" (paper presented at "Homo/Economics: Market and Community in Lesbian and Gay Life," a conference sponsored by the Center of Lesbian and Gay Studies at the City University of New York, New York, May 7, 1994). On employment discrimination, see idem, "The Wage Effects of Sexual Orientation Discrimination," *Industrial and Labor Relations Review* 48, no. 4 (July 1995): 726–39; and for an early discussion, see Jeffrey Escoffier, "Stigma, Work Environment, and Economic Discrimination against Homosexuals," *Homosexual Counseling Journal* 2, no. 1 (January 1975). For a discussion of the gay market, see Gluckman and Reed, "Gay Marketing Moment," as well as Lukenbill, *Untold Millions*.

6.   D'Emilio, "Capitalism and Gay Identity," in *Powers of Desire*, ed. Snitow et al.; and Jeffrey Escoffier, "Sexual Revolution and the Politics of Gay Identity," *Socialist Review*, nos. 82–83 (vol. 15, nos. 4–5; July–October 1985).

7.   See D'Emilio, *Sexual Politics*; Kennedy and Davis, *Boots of Leather*; Esther Newton's *Cherry Grove, Fire Island: Sixty Years in America's First Gay and Lesbian Community* (Boston: Beacon Press, 1993); Gayle Rubin, "The Valley of the Kings: San Francisco's Gay Male Leather Community" (Ph.D. diss., University of

Michigan, 1994); and the recent dissertations on Philadelphia (Marc Stein, University of Pennsylvania) and San Francisco (Nan Almilla Boyd, Brown University).

8.   In reconstructing the history of gay and lesbian communities, a number of recent studies have begun to provide a portrait of gay and lesbian economic life. See Martin Bauml Duberman, *Stonewall* (New York: Dutton, 1993), especially the chapter on the Stonewall bar, pp. 181–90; Kennedy and Davis, *Boots of Leather*; Newton, *Cherry Grove*; and Rubin, "Valley of the Kings."

9.   Mancur Olson, *The Logic of Collective Action: Public Goods and the Theory of Groups* (Cambridge: Harvard University Press, 1965); Douglass C. North and Lance Davis, *Institutional Change and American Economic Growth* (Cambridge, England: Cambridge University Press, 1971); Douglass C. North, *Structure and Change in Economic History* (New York: Norton, 1981); and idem, *Institutions, Institutional Change, and Economic Performance* (Cambridge, England: Cambridge University Press, 1990).

10.   Goffman, *Stigma.*

11.   Georg Simmel, "The Secret and the Secret Society," in *The Sociology of Georg Simmel* (New York: Free Press, 1950), pp. 307–78.

12.   Georg Simmel, "The Stranger," and "The Metropolis and Mental Life," in *Sociology of Georg Simmel*, pp. 402–27.

13.   Harold Beaver, "Homosexual Signs (in Memory of Roland Barthes)," *Critical Inquiry* 8, no. 1 (fall 1981).

14.   Maurice Leznoff and William Westley, "The Homosexual Community," *Social Problems* 3 (April 1956): 257–63.

15.   These patterns of social life predated World War II. See George Chauncey, *Gay New York: Gender, Urban Culture, and the Making of the Gay Male World, 1890–1940* (New York: Basic Books, 1994).

16.   See Escoffier, "Stigma." See also ibid. For a discussion of how informal social networks play a role in landing jobs, see Mark Granovetter, *Getting a Job: A Study of Contacts and Careers* (Cambridge: Harvard University Press, 1974).

17.   Blackmail and extortion have been features of homosexual life as long as it has been stigmatized. For an account from the early twentieth century, see Edward Stevenson, *The Intersexes: A History of Similisexualism as a Problem in Social Life* (private printing, 1908; reprint, New York: Arno Press, 1975), p. 478. See also the example of police harassment in Jonathan Weinberg, *Speaking for Vice: Homosexuality in the Art of Charles Demuth, Marsden Hartley, and the First American Avant-Garde* (New Haven: Yale University Press, 1993), p. 57. Homophile publications such as *One* or the *Mattachine Review* frequently referred to the extortionist aspects of gay and lesbian life; I owe this reference to Kevin Murphy. See also the chapter on blackmail in Jess Stern, *The Sixth Man* (New York: Doubleday, 1961), pp. 176–88.

18. See the chapters on bars and cruising in Donald Webster Cory and John P. LeRoy, *The Homosexual and His Society: A View from Within* (New York: Citadel Press, 1963), pp. 105–29; and Evelyn Hooker, "The Homosexual Community," in *Sexual Deviance,* ed. John Gagnon and William Simon (New York: Harper & Row, 1967).

19. For a good, general discussion of social norms and behavior in bars, see Sherri Cavan, *Liquor License: An Ethnography of Bar Behavior* (Chicago: Aldine, 1966).

20. To read about the role of protection (as well as other topics), see Martin S. Weinberg and Colin J. Williams, "Gay Baths and the Social Organization of Impersonal Sex," *Social Problems* 23, no. 2 (December 1975): 124–36.

21. Bob Dameron, the publisher of a national gay bar guide, estimated that by 1975, between 75 and 80 percent of San Francisco's gay bars were gay owned. See Wayne Sage, "Inside the Colossal Closet," *Human Behavior,* August 1975, reprinted in *Gay Men: The Sociology of Male Homosexuality,* ed. Martin P. Levine (New York: Harper & Row, 1979).

22. Christopher Gunn and Hazel Dayton Gunn, *Reclaiming Capital: Democratic Initiatives and Community Development* (Ithaca, N.Y.: Cornell University Press, 1991), pp. 3–6.

23. For a discussion of the relationship between economic behavior and social norms, see Jon Elster, *Nuts and Bolts for the Social Sciences* (Cambridge, England: Cambridge University Press, 1989), pp. 113–23.

24. Theorists have classified such social situations under the name of "the prisoner's dilemma." In game theory, the prisoner's dilemma is about two people who are arrested and questioned separately. They cannot communicate with one another, and each must choose whether or not to betray the other. Each would seem to benefit individually from giving away the other, but if they both chose to protect each other, they would both go free. For a brief discussion of this famous game, see Elster, *Nuts and Bolts,* p. 29.

25. The argument is made in Gagnon and Simon, *Sexual Conduct,* pp. 153–54, and Kenneth E. Read, *Other Voices: The Style of a Homosexual Tavern* (Novato, Calif.: Chandler & Sharp, 1980), pp. xvii–xviii. For a discussion, see Joseph Harry and William B. DeVall, *The Social Organization of Gay Males* (New York: Praeger Publishers, 1978), pp. 151–54.

26. Richard Dyer, "Entertainment and Utopia," in *Only Entertainment* (New York: Routledge, 1992), p. 25.

27. In particular, see Karl Marx, "Economic and Philosophical Manuscripts," in *Early Writings,* ed. Quintin Hoare (New York: Vintage Books, 1975); and Carol Gould, *Marx's Social Ontology* (Cambridge: MIT Press, 1976).

28. See Francis E. Kobrin, "The Fall in Household Size and the Rise of the Primary Individual in the United States," *Demography* 13 (February 1976): 127–

38; and D'Emilio, "Capitalism and Gay Identity," in *Powers of Desire*, ed. Snitow et al.

29.   This process is analyzed and empirically tested in Martin P. Levine, "Gay Ghetto," in *Gay Men*, ed. M. Levine; and in Joseph Harry and William B. DeVall, "Urbanization and the Development of Homosexual Communities," in *Social Organization*, pp. 134–54.

30.   Even before Stonewall, gay and lesbian bar owners in San Francisco formed their own business association—the Tavern Guild.

CHAPTER 3

1.   Georg Simmel, "How Is Society Possible?" in *On Individuality and Social Forms*, ed. Donald N. Levine (Chicago: University of Chicago Press, 1971), p. 11. The imagined gay social world is a projection of the possibility of gay community, an ensemble of shared lifestyle that differs from that of the mainstream society. For a discussion of this concept in terms of "the social imaginary," see John Thompson, *Studies in the Theory of Ideology* (Berkeley: University of California Press, 1984), pp. 23–38. See Hans Joas, *Pragmatism and Social Theory* (Chicago: University of Chicago Press, 1993), p. 167, for a discussion of Cornelius Castoriadis's recognition of the social a priori. For a critical discussion of the imaginary and its relationship to Lacan's psychoanalytic theory and ideology, see Paul Smith, *Discerning the Subject* (Minneapolis: University of Minnesota Press, 1988), pp. 18–23.

2.   Simmel, "How Is Society Possible?" p. 9.

3.   Allen Young, "Out of the Closets, into the Streets," in *Out of the Closets*, ed. Karla Jay and Allen Young (New York: Douglas/Links, 1972), pp. 17–20; Edmund Bergler, *Homosexuality: Disease or a Way of Life?* (New York: Hill & Wang, 1957); Irving Bieber, *Homosexuality* (New York: Basic Books, 1962); Albert Ellis, *Homosexuality: Its Causes and Cure* (New York: Lyle Stuart, 1964); Charles Socarides, *The Overt Homosexual* (Philadelphia: Grune & Stratton, 1968); Lionel Ovesey, *Homosexuality and Pseudo-Homosexuality* (New York: Science House, 1969); Lawrence Hatterer, *Changing Homosexuality in the Male* (New York: McGraw-Hill, 1970); and Cory, *Homosexual in America*.

4.   Pierre Bourdieu, "The Social Space and the Genesis of Groups," *Theory and Society* 14, no. 6 (November 1985): 729.

5.   A parallel discourse on race also emerged in this period. Gunnar Myrdal's *The American Dilemma* (New York: Harper & Row, 1944) marked the renewed recognition of race as a social issue in American life.

6.   Alfred M. Kinsey et al., *Sexual Behavior in the Human Male* (Philadelphia: Saunders, 1948). See the useful commentaries on the Kinsey report by Morris

Ernst and David Loth, *American Sexual Behavior and the Kinsey Report* (New York: Educational Book Co., 1948); and Donald P. Geddes, ed., *An Analysis of the Kinsey Reports on the Human Male and Female* (New York: New American Library, 1954).

7.   Roger Austen, *Playing the Game: The Homosexual Novel in America* (Indianapolis: Bobbs-Merrill, 1977), pp. 93–94.

8.   For a survey of the fiction that explored homosexuality in this period, see the following studies: John W. Aldridge, *After the Lost Generation: A Critical Study of the Writers of Two Wars* (New York: Noonday Press, 1951); Austen, *Playing the Game;* and Sarotte, *Like a Brother.*

9.   Aldridge, *After the Lost Generation,* pp. 90, 99–104.

10.   Vito Russo, *The Celluloid Closet: Homosexuality in the Movies,* rev. ed. (New York: Harper & Row, 1987), pp. 120–22, 140–43; Paul Welch, "Homosexuality in America," *Life,* June 26, 1964, pp. 68–80; Tom Burke, "The New Homosexual," *Esquire,* December 1969.

11.   Kenneth Lewes, *The Psychoanalytic Theory of Male Homosexuality* (New York: Simon & Schuster, 1988).

12.   Ibid., pp. 122–73.

13.   See the essays collected in Lary May, ed., *Recasting America: Culture and Politics in an Age of Cold War* (Chicago: University of Chicago, 1989), and in Elaine May, *Homeward Bound: American Families in the Cold War Era* (New York: Basic Books, 1988).

14.   Richard Dyer, "Homosexuality and Film Noir," in *A Matter of Images,* (London: Routledge, 1993); and Frank Krutnik, *In a Lonely Street: Film Noir, Genre, Masculinity* (New York: Routledge, 1991).

15.   David Savran, *Communists, Cowboys, and Queers: The Politics of Masculinity in the Work of Arthur Miller and Tennessee Williams* (Minneapolis: University of Minnesota Press, 1992).

16.   For writing about alienation, see Eric Josephson and Mary Josephson, eds., *Man Alone: Alienation in Modern Society* (New York: Dell, 1962), which contained essays by Marx, Dostoyevsky, W.E.B. DuBois, C. Wright Mills, and James Baldwin, among others. This volume was one of my first introductions to modern social thought. Albert Camus's *The Rebel* (New York: Knopf, 1956) and Colin Wilson's *The Outsider* (Boston: Houghton Mifflin, 1956) were the other two books central to my intellectual development in the late 1950s and early 1960s.

17.   Lindner's essay on homosexuality was reprinted in the important and influential collection of sociological and psychological articles that Hendrik M. Ruitenbeek edited: *The Problem of Homosexuality in Modern Society* (New York: Dutton, 1963).

18.   Robert Lindner, *Must You Conform?* (reprint, New York: Black Cat Book, 1961), pp. 40–41.

19. Ibid., p. 42.

20. Ibid., p. 43.

21. Ibid., p. 73.

22. Ibid., p. 75.

23. For an account of sexual radicalism in the 1950s and 1960s, see King, *Party of Eros.*

24. Lindner, *Must You Conform?* pp. 123–45.

25. In contrast to Lindner's emphasis on the urgency of sexual instincts, Mary McIntosh first elaborated the social constructionist approach to homosexuality in academic sociology during this period. See her influential article "The Homosexual Role." McIntosh was very much influenced by the interactionist tradition in sociology.

26. For a useful discussion of the effects of a discursive formation on the individual, see Michel Pecheux, "The Subject-Form of Discourse in the Subjective Appropriation of Scientific Knowledges and Political Practice," in *Language, Semantics, and Ideology,* trans. Harbens Nagpal (London: Macmillan, 1982), pp. 155–70.

27. Cory, *Homosexual in America;* A. M. Krich, ed., *The Homosexuals: As Seen by Themselves and Thirty Authorities* (New York: Citadel Press, 1954); J. Mercer, *They Walk in Shadow* (New York: Comet Books, 1959); Stern, *Sixth Man;* idem, *The Grapevine: A Report on the Secret World of the Lesbian* (New York: Doubleday, 1964); Alfred A. Gross, *Strangers in Our Midst* (Washington, D.C.: Public Affairs Press, 1962); R.E.L. Masters, *The Homosexual Revolution: A Challenging Exposé of the Social and Political Directions of a Minority Group* (New York: Julian Press, 1962); Cory and LeRoy, *Homosexual and His Society;* idem, *The Lesbian in America* (New York: Citadel Press, 1964); Ruitenbeek, *Problem of Homosexuality;* Martin Hoffman, *The Gay World: Male Homosexuality and the Social Creation of Evil* (New York: Basic Books, 1968).

28. Hoffman, *Gay World,* p. 3.

29. The increase in popular sociology literature was paralleled by the growth of an academic sociology in the interactionist tradition that treated homosexuality as a social phenomenon, without moralism. Academic sociology books on the subject included Howard Becker, *Outsiders: Studies in the Sociology of Deviance* (Glencoe, Ill.: Free Press, 1963); Goffman, *Stigma;* Edwin Schur, *Crimes without Victims* (Englewood Cliffs, N.J.: Prentice Hall, 1965); Gagnon and Simon, *Sexual Deviance.*

30. For a brief history of the interactionist perspective, see Randall Collins, *Three Sociological Traditions* (New York: Oxford University Press, 1985), pp. 180–222, and Nicholas C. Mullins with Carolyn J. Mullins, *Theories and Theory Groups in Contemporary American Sociology* (New York: Harper & Row, 1973), pp. 75–104. In 1963, two of the most influential symbolic interactionist books on "deviant identities" appeared: Becker's *Outsiders* and Goffman's *Stigma.*

31.   Becker's famous definition from *Outsiders* was quoted in David Jary and Julia Jary, *The Harper Collins Dictionary of Sociology* (New York: Harper Collins, 1991), p. 263.

32.   Georg Simmel, "The Problem of Sociology," in *Essays on Sociology, Philosophy, and Aesthetics,* ed. K. H. Wolff (Columbus: Ohio State University Press, 1959), pp. 327–40.

33.   Frank Caprio, *Female Homosexuality* (New York: Citadel Press, 1954); George Henry, *All the Sexes* (New York: Rinehart, 1955); Edmund Bergler, *Homosexuality*; idem, *One Thousand Homosexuals* (Paterson, N.J.: Pageant Books, 1957); Bieber, *Homosexuality*; Ellis, *Homosexuality*; Socarides, *Overt Homosexual*; Ovesey, *Homosexuality and Pseudo-Homosexuality*; and Hatterer, *Changing Homosexuality in the Male.*

34.   Cory, *Homosexual in America*, p. 63. Cory's most extended discussion of effeminacy appears on pp. 62–64.

35.   Ibid., pp. 129–34.

36.   As a sociologist, Sagarin specialized in deviance and criminology. He completed his dissertation, "The Structure and Ideology in an Association of Deviants," in 1966. Arno Press published it in 1975.

37.   Cory, *Homosexual in America*, pp. 230–31, 258–59.

38.   Ibid., p. 264.

39.   Stern, *Sixth Man*, p. 13.

40.   Ibid., p. 16.

41.   Ibid., pp. 13–18.

42.   Ibid., p. 16.

43.   Ibid., pp. 76–92.

44.   Ibid., pp. 189–90.

45.   See D'Emilio, "Gay Politics, Gay Community."

46.   For a discussion of this process, see Pecheux, "Subject-Form of Discourse," pp. 110–29.

47.   Michel de Certeau discusses reading as an active process in *Practice of Everyday Life*, pp. 165–76.

48.   From Roland Barthes's thoughtful and suggestive essay "On Reading," in *The Rustle of Language*, trans. Richard Howard (New York: Hill & Wang, 1986), p. 35.

49.   Ibid., pp. 33–43.

50.   Ibid., pp. 42–43.

51.   James Baldwin, *Giovanni's Room* (New York: Dial Press, 1956).

52.   Somewhere during that time, I also came across an essay by liberal newspaper columnist Max Lerner called "The Gay Crucifixion," reprinted in *The Unfinished Country: A Book of American Symbols* (New York: Simon & Schuster, 1959). This, along with Baldwin, was the start of my search to learn as much as I could about homosexuality.

53. Ibid., p. 12.

54. Norman Mailer, *Advertisements for Myself* (New York: Putnam, 1959).

55. Norman Mailer, "The Homosexual Villain," in *Advertisements for Myself*, p. 194.

56. Ibid., p. 196.

57. For James Baldwin's contemptuous dismissal of Mailer's essay "The White Negro," see "The Black Boy Looks at the White Boy," in *Nobody Knows My Name* (New York: Doubleday, 1961). Then, for Eldridge Cleaver's praise of Mailer's essay and his attack on Baldwin for his homosexuality, see Eldridge Cleaver, *Soul on Ice* (New York: McGraw-Hill, 1968), pp. 97-111.

58. James Baldwin, *Another Country* (New York: Dial Press, 1962), pp. 301-2.

59. See Richard Goldstein's interview with Baldwin in Goldstein, "Go the Way Your Blood Beats," in *James Baldwin: The Legacy*, ed. Quincy Troup (New York: Simon & Schuster, 1989), p. 174. When Goldstein asked Baldwin if he felt like "a stranger in gay America," Baldwin responded: "Well, first of all I feel like a stranger in America from almost any conceivable angle except, oddly enough, as a black person. The word 'gay' has always rubbed me the wrong way. . . . I simply feel it's a world that has very little to do with me, with where I did my growing up. I was never at home with it."

60. Undoubtedly, these interests also influenced me to pursue a graduate degree in African studies.

61. Participation in consciousness-raising groups and study groups during the early years of the women's and gay movements socialized the relatively private experience of reading.

62. Barthes, "On Reading," p. 42.

63. It is necessary to remember that Baldwin's rejection of the "gay community" is always compensated for by his deep commitment to the African American historical experience.

64. Pierre Bourdieu and Loïc J. C. Wacquant, *An Invitation to Reflexive Sociology* (Chicago: University of Chicago Press, 1992), p. 45.

PART TWO

1. The distinction between the two projects of the homosexual emancipation movement is parallel to Hans Blumenberg's original distinction between the two projects of the Enlightenment in *The Legitimacy of the Modern Age* (Cambridge: MIT Press, 1983).

2. Lisa Duggan, "The Discipline Problem: Queer Theory Meets Lesbian and Gay History," *GLQ: A Journal of Lesbian and Gay Studies* 2, no. 3 (1995), reprinted in Duggan and Nan D. Hunter's collection of essays, *Sex Wars: Sexual Dissent and Political Culture* (New York: Routledge, 1995).

3.   Seidman, "Deconstructing Queer Theory," p. 118.

4.   Newton, *Cherry Grove, Fire Island*; Kennedy and Davis, *Boots of Leather*; Chauncey, *Gay New York*; Katz, *Invention of Heterosexuality*.

5.   For a sample of this work, see Lawrence Grossberg, Cary Nelson, and Paula Treichler, eds., *Cultural Studies* (New York: Routledge, 1992).

CHAPTER 4

1.   Charles Silverstein, "The Origin of the Gay Psychotherapy Movement," in *A Queer World*, ed. Martin Duberman (New York: New York University Press, 1997), pp. 358–80.

2.   Arthur Evans, *Witchcraft and the Gay Counterculture* (Boston: Fag Rag Books, 1978).

3.   *Homosexuality: Power and Politics*, edited by the Gay Left Collective, was published in 1980, and *The Making of the Modern Homosexual*, edited by Kenneth Plummer, was published in 1981.

4.   *Pleasure and Danger* was published in 1984, and *Powers of Desire* appeared in 1983.

5.   Edelman's essays are reprinted in Lee Edelman, *Homographesis: Essays in Gay Literary and Cultural Theory* (New York: Routledge, 1994).

6.   The fourth annual Lesbian, Bisexual, and Gay Studies Conference took place October 26–28, 1990.

7.   David F. Greenberg, *The Construction of Homosexuality* (Chicago: University of Chicago Press, 1988).

8.   The *Journal of the History of Sexuality* first appeared in 1990. *Sexual Politics, Sexual Communities* was published in 1983, and *Mother Camp* was published in 1985. See Estelle B. Freedman, Barbara C. Gelpi, Susan L. Johnson, and Kathleen M. Weston, eds., *The Lesbian Issues: Essays from SIGNS* (Chicago: University of Chicago Press, 1985).

CHAPTER 5

1.   See Peter L. Berger and Thomas Luckman, *The Social Construction of Reality: A Treatise in the Sociology of Knowledge* (New York: Doubleday, 1966), pp. 19–46, for a thorough discussion of the construction and use of knowledge in everyday life.

2.   Although I have long believed in the power of such contributions, I owe this sharp formulation to Ara Wilson. On the significance of *The Well of Loneliness*, see Esther Newton, "The Mythic Mannish Lesbian: Radclyffe Hall and

the New Woman," *Signs* 9, no. 4 (summer 1984). On Whitman's impact on Wilde, Symonds, and Carpenter, see Weeks, *Coming Out,* pp. 45–83.

3.   Gramsci, *Selections from the Prison Notebooks;* Stuart Hall, *The Hard Road to Renewal: Thatcherism and the Crisis of the Left* (London: Verso, 1988).

4.   The Center for Lesbian and Gay Studies, *CLAGS Directory of Lesbian and Gay Studies* (New York: Center for Lesbian and Gay Studies, CUNY, 1994).

5.   Chapter 4, "Inside the Ivory Closet," gives a sketch of the earlier attempt. See also John D'Emilio, "The Universities and the Gay Experience," in his collection *Making Trouble,* pp. 117–27.

6.   See the essays by Karl Mannheim, "The Problem of Generations," in *Essays on the Sociology of Knowledge,* ed. Paul Kecskemeti (New York: Oxford University Press, 1952); Annie Kriegel, "Generational Difference: The History of an Idea," *Daedalus: Proceedings of the American Academy of Arts and Sciences* 107, no. 4 (fall 1978): 23–38; and Matilda White Riley, "Aging, Social Change, and the Power of Ideas," *Daedalus: Proceedings of the American Academy of Arts and Sciences* 107, no. 4 (fall 1978): 39–52. For an excellent example of generational history, see Robert Wohl, *The Generation of 1914* (Cambridge: Harvard University Press, 1979).

7.   Two books brought together some of these influences: C. Wilson, *Outsider;* and the anthology *The Beat Generation and the Angry Young Men,* ed. Gene Feldman and Max Gartenberg (New York: Greenberg Books, 1958).

8.   For two opposing testimonials on the significance of this issue, see Berman, *Politics of Authenticity,* and Trilling, *Sincerity and Authenticity.*

9.   For a critical discussion of the model implicit in this approach, see Olafson, "Authenticity and Obligation," pp. 121–75.

10.   See Ronald Bayer, *Homosexuality and American Psychiatry: The Politics of Diagnosis* (New York: Basic Books, 1981), pp. 67–101.

11.   Altman, *Homosexual;* and Kate Millett, *Sexual Politics* (New York: Doubleday, 1970).

12.   George Weinberg, *Society and the Healthy Homosexual* (New York: St. Martin's Press, 1972).

13.   For an account of the gay movement's confrontation with the psychiatric profession, see Bayer, *Homosexuality and American Psychiatry.*

14.   New York University Press has issued an anniversary edition of Jay and Young's *Out of the Closets.*

15.   "The Homosexual Imagination," special issue, *College English* 36, no. 3 (November 1974).

16.   Jonathan Ned Katz, interview by Jeffrey Escoffier and David Hathwell, in *Gay Alternative,* no. 6 (1974).

17.   First appearing in the *Body Politic,* a Canadian gay journal, their work was eventually published in book form: Steakley, *Homosexual Emancipation Movement;* and D'Emilio, *Sexual Politics.* See also John Lauritsen and David

Thorstad, *The Early Homosexual Rights Movement, 1864–1935* (New York: Times Change Press, 1974).

18.   McIntosh, "Homosexual Role." In the same volume, see the interview with Mary McIntosh, pp. 44–49. See also Carole S. Vance, "Social Construction Theory: Problems in the History of Sexuality," in *Which Homosexuality? Essays from the International Conference on Lesbian and Gay Studies,* Dennis Altman et al. (London: Gay Men's Press, 1989).

19.   Erving Goffman explored the discursive formation of identities and social interaction. See Goffman, *Stigma.*

20.   Foucault, *History of Sexuality,* vol. 1, *Introduction.*

21.   For essays on the feminist debates about pornography by two important activists, see Duggan and Hunter, *Sex Wars.*

22.   Steven Epstein, "Gay Politics, Ethnic Identity: The Limits of Social Constructionism," *Socialist Review,* nos. 93–94 (vol. 17, nos. 3–4; May–August 1987); and see Diana Fuss's essay "The Question of Identity Politics" in her book *Essentially Speaking: Feminism, Nature, and Difference* (New York: Routledge, 1989). For a cross section of the debate, see Edward Stein, ed., *Forms of Desire: Sexual Orientation and the Social Constructionist Controversy* (New York: Routledge, 1992).

23.   Radicalesbians, *The Woman-Identified Woman* (Somerville, Mass.: New England Free Press, 1970); and Jill Johnston, *Lesbian Nation: The Feminist Solution* (New York: Simon & Schuster, 1973).

24.   Adrienne Rich, "Compulsory Heterosexuality and Lesbian Existence," *Signs* 5, no. 4 (1980); and Catherine MacKinnon, "Feminism, Marxism, Method, and the State," *Signs* 7, no. 3 (spring 1982).

25.   John Boswell, "Revolutions, Universals, and Sexual Categories," *Salmagundi,* nos. 58–59 (fall 1982–winter 1983); and Will Roscoe, "Making History: The Challenge of Gay and Lesbian Studies," *Journal of Homosexuality* 15, nos. 3–4 (1988).

26.   Judy Grahn, *In a Mother Tongue* (Boston: Beacon Press, 1984).

27.   Simon LeVay, *Queer Science: The Use and Abuse of Research into Homosexuality* (Cambridge: MIT Press, 1996), pp. 11–40.

28.   Simon LeVay, "A Difference in Hypothalamic Structure between Homosexual and Heterosexual Men," *Science* 253 (August 30, 1991): 1034–37; see also Dean Hammer and P. Copeland, *The Science of Desire: The Search for the Gay Gene and the Biology of Behavior* (New York: Simon & Schuster, 1994); and Chandler Burr, *A Separate Creation: The Search for the Origins of Sexual Orientation* (New York: Hyperion Books, 1996).

29.   Simon LeVay, *The Sexual Brain* (Cambridge: MIT Press, 1993); Simon LeVay and Elizabeth Nonas, *City of Friends: A Portrait of the Gay and Lesbian Community in America* (Cambridge: MIT Press, 1995); and LeVay, *Queer Science.*

30.   LeVay, *Queer Science,* pp. 195–209.

31.   Adrienne Rich, "Disloyal to Civilization: Feminism, Racism, Gynepho-bia," in *On Lies, Secrets, and Silence* (New York: Norton, 1979), p. 229. See also Elizabeth V. Spelman, *The Inessential Woman: Problems of Exclusion in Feminist Thought* (Boston: Beacon Press, 1988), for an exploration of the relation of racial difference to feminism.

32.   Audre Lorde, *Sister Outsider: Essays and Speeches* (Trumansberg, N.Y.: Crossing Press, 1984).

33.   Cherríe Moraga and Gloria Anzaldúa, eds., *This Bridge Called My Back* (New York: Kitchen Table / Women of Color Press, 1981), pp. 105–6. See also Norma Alarcon, "The Theoretical Subject(s) of *This Bridge Called My Back* and Anglo-American Feminism," in *Making Face, Making Soul, Hacienda Caras,* ed. Gloria Anzaldúa (San Francisco: Aunt Lute, 1990).

34.   Tomas Almaguer, "Chicano Men: A Cartography of Homosexual Identity and Behavior," *Differences: A Journal of Feminist Cultural Studies* 3, no. 2 (summer 1991).

35.   Essex Hemphill, ed., *Brother to Brother: An Anthology of Writings by Black Gay Men* (Boston: Alyson Publications, 1991).

36.   Kobena Mercer has several excellent discussions of these issues in *Welcome to the Jungle: New Positions in Black Cultural Studies* (New York: Routledge, 1994), particularly in his introduction and in "Black Art and the Burden of Representation." See also my essay on representation, "The Limits of Multi-culturalism," which is now chapter 9 in this volume.

37.   Kobena Mercer, "Black Britain and the Cultural Politics of Diaspora," in *Welcome to the Jungle,* p. 21.

38.   K. Mercer, "Black Art," pp. 234–36.

39.   Robert F. Reid-Pharr, "The Spectacle of Blackness," *Radical America* 24, no. 4 (April 1993).

40.   Paul Gilroy has explored these transnational exchanges in *The Black Atlantic: Modernity and Double Consciousness* (Cambridge: Harvard University Press, 1993); see especially p. 85.

41.   See Kobena Mercer's essays, especially "Black Britain" and "Diaspora Culture and the Dialogic Imagination," in *Welcome to the Jungle.*

42.   Joseph M. Carrier, "Gay Liberation and Coming Out in Mexico," in *Gay and Lesbian Youth,* ed. Gilbert Herdt (Binghamton, N.Y.: Haworth Press, 1989); and Almaguer, "Chicano Men."

43.   Moraga and Anzaldúa, eds., *This Bridge Called My Back;* and Gloria Anzaldúa, *Borderlands / La Frontera: The New Mestiza* (San Francisco: Spinsters, 1987).

44.   Many such accounts are included in *A Lotus of Another Color: An Unfolding of the South Asian Gay and Lesbian Experience,* ed. Rakesh Ratti (Boston: Alyson Publications, 1993). In this volume, see especially the coming-out narratives, pp. 167–293; the interview with Urvashi Vaid, pp. 103–12; and the discussion

of this history in Nayan Shah, "Sexuality, Identity, and the Uses of History," pp. 116–18.

45.   Ukiko Hanawa, "Guest Editor's Introduction," *Circuits of Desire*, special issue of *positions: east asia cultures critique* 2, no. 1 (spring 1994): viii.

46.   Henry Louis Gates discusses these issues in response to Isaac Julien's film *Looking for Langston*. See Gates, "The Black Man's Burden," in *Black Popular Culture*, ed. Gina Dent (Seattle: Bay Press, 1992), pp. 75–84, as well as Julien's essay "Black Is, Black Ain't: Notes on De-essentializing Black Identities," in the same volume, pp. 255–63. Ross Posnock explores these issues; see Posnock, "Before and after Identity Politics," *Raritan* 15, no. 1 (summer 1995): 95–115. See also Scott Bravmann, "Telling (Hi)stories: Rethinking the Lesbian and Gay Historical Imagination," *OUT/LOOK: National Lesbian and Gay Quarterly*, spring 1990, 68–75; idem, "Queer Historical Subjects," *Socialist Review* 25, no. 1 (1995): 47–68.

47.   Yingling, *Hart Crane*, p. 25.

48.   For background on these developments, see Patrick Brantlinger, *Crusoe's Footprints: Cultural Studies in Britain and America* (New York: Routledge, 1990). See also these influential works on cultural studies, the new historicism, and related topics: H. Aram Veeser, ed., *The New Historicism* (New York: Routledge, 1989); and Grossberg et al., eds., *Cultural Studies*.

49.   A good sampling of the work of this new generation can be found in several anthologies: Ronald R. Butters, John M. Clum, and Michael Moon, eds., *Displacing Homophobia* (Durham, N.C.: Duke University Press, 1990); Diana Fuss, *Inside/Outside: Lesbian Theories, Gay Theories* (New York: Routledge 1991); Henry Abelove, Michele Aina Barale, and David M. Halperin, eds., *The Lesbian and Gay Studies Reader* (New York: Routledge, 1993).

50.   Beaver, "Homosexual Signs," 104.

51.   Eve Kosofsky Sedgwick, *Epistemology of the Closet* (Berkeley: University of California Press, 1990), p. 1. See also her recent essays collected in *Tendencies* (Durham, N.C.: Duke University Press, 1993).

52.   Judith Butler, *Gender Trouble: Feminism and the Subversion of Identity* (New York: Routledge, 1990), pp. 147–49. See also her collection of essays, *Bodies That Matter: On the Discursive Limits of "Sex"* (New York: Routledge, 1993).

53.   See Douglas Crimp with Adam Rolston, *AIDS Demo Graphics* (Seattle: Bay Press, 1990); Crimp, ed., *AIDS*; and Tessa Boffin and Sunil Gupta, eds., *Ecstatic Antibodies* (London: Rivers Oram Press, 1990).

54.   Walt W. Odets, *In the Shadow of the Epidemic* (Durham, N.C.: Duke University Press, 1996); and Gabriel Rotello, *Sexual Ecology: AIDS and the Destiny of Gay Men* (New York: Dutton, 1997).

55.   Steven Epstein, *Impure Science: AIDS, Activism, and the Politics of Knowledge* (Berkeley: University of California Press, 1996).

56.   Crimp, ed., *AIDS*; and Crimp with Rolston, *AIDS Demo Graphics*.

57.   Cindy Patton, *Sex and Germs: The Politics of AIDS* (Boston: South End Press, 1985); idem, *Inventing AIDS* (New York: Routledge, 1990); idem, *Fatal Advice: How Safe Sex Education Went Wrong* (Durham, N.C.: Duke University Press, 1996).

58.   Paula A. Treichler, "AIDS, Homophobia, and Bio-Medical Discourse: An Epidemic of Signification," in *AIDS*, ed. Crimp, pp. 31–70; and idem, "AIDS, Gender, and Biomedical Discourse: Current Contests of Meaning," in *AIDS: The Burdens of History*, ed. Elizabeth Fee and Daniel M. Fox (Berkeley: University of California Press, 1988), pp. 190–266.

59.   Fee and Fox, eds., *AIDS*; the same editors later assembled *AIDS: The Making of a Chronic Disease* (Berkeley: University of California Press, 1992). See also Catherine J. Kudnick, "One Epidemic, Many Histories," *Socialist Review* 21, no. 2 (April–June 1991): 165–70.

60.   Epstein, *Impure Science*; idem, "Moral Contagion and the Medicalizing of Gay Identity: AIDS in Historical Perspective," *Research in Law, Deviance, and Social Control* 9 (1988): 3–36.

61.   Patton's books are cited above. See Simon Watney, *Policing Desire: Pornography, AIDS, and the Media* (Minneapolis: University of Minnesota Press, 1987); idem, *Practices of Freedom: Selected Writings on HIV/AIDS* (Durham, N.C.: Duke University Press, 1994). See also Amber Hollibaugh, "Lesbian Leadership and Denial in the Age of the AIDS Epidemic," in *Women Resisting AIDS: Feminist Strategies of Empowerment*, ed. Beth Schneider and Nancy Stoller (Philadelphia: Temple University Press, 1994); idem, "Seducing Women into 'A Lifestyle of Vaginal Fisting,'" in *Policing Public Sex*, ed. Dangerous Bedfellows; and Amber Hollibaugh and Carmen Vasquez, "The Myth of Invulnerability: Lesbians and HIV Disease," *Focus* 8, no. 9 (1994).

CHAPTER 6

1.   Two writers have explored this subject very suggestively: Mary Douglas, *How Institutions Think* (Syracuse, N.Y.: University of Syracuse Press, 1986); and, in many essays, Pierre Bourdieu. See in particular Bourdieu's essay "Social Space," 723–44.

2.   See Carlos Munoz, Jr., *Youth, Identity, Power: The Chicano Movement* (London: Verso, 1989).

3.   For discussions of nationalism and its cultural politics, see Benedict Anderson, *Imagined Communities: Reflections of the Origin and Spread of Nationalism* (London: Verso, 1983); and the essays in Homi K. Bhabha, ed., *Nation and Narration* (New York: Routledge, 1990).

4.   For example, the environmental movement has stimulated new concep-

tions of the interdependence between human life and nature in scientific disciplines. It has also stimulated the elaboration of new forms of spirituality, such as "deep ecology" with its religious conception of human responsibility to nature, or the belief in Gaia as the spiritual unity of nature. See Will Wright, *Wild Knowledge: Science, Language, and Social Life in a Fragile Environment* (Minneapolis: University of Minnesota Press, 1992), for an examination of some of these issues.

5. For a discussion of one study, see Chris Bull, "Mom's Fault," *Advocate: The National Gay & Lesbian Newsmagazine*, August 24, 1993, 30–33.

6. I have adapted these terms somewhat loosely from Foucault. The terms *power effects* and *truth effects* both result from any discursive operation that creates power/knowledge. See in particular Michel Foucault, "Truth and Power," in *Power/Knowledge: Selected Interviews and Other Writings, 1972–1977* (New York: Pantheon Books, 1980), pp. 108–33. Barry Smart discusses the relation between Foucault's conception of power/knowledge and Gramsci's concept of hegemony; see Smart, "The Politics of Truth and the Problem of Hegemony," in *Foucault: A Reader,* ed. David Couzens Hoy (Oxford: Blackwell, 1986), pp. 157–74.

7. I derived this distinction from a similar one that Richard Rorty made in "Solidarity or Objectivity?" in *Objectivity, Relativism, and Truth* (Cambridge, England: Cambridge University Press, 1991), pp. 21–34. I do not mean, however, to equate "legitimacy" with "objectivity."

8. We have few sociological discussions of authority. There are, of course, the classic contributions by Max Weber in his essays on bureaucracy and charisma. See Hans Gerth and C. Wright Mills, eds., *From Max Weber: Essays in Sociology* (New York: Oxford University Press, 1946). For more recent discussions, see Richard T. De George, *The Nature and Limits of Authority* (Lawrence: University of Kansas Press, 1985); and Robert Dahl, *After the Revolution? Authority in a Good Society,* rev. ed. (New Haven: Yale University Press, 1990).

9. See Sedgwick, *Epistemology of the Closet;* and Michelangelo Signorile, *Queer in America: Sex, Media, and the Closets of Power* (New York: Random House, 1993).

10. For example, literary works deeply rooted in the camp sensibility include the plays of Oscar Wilde and the poetry of Frank O'Hara. On the latter, see Bruce Boone, "Gay Language as Political Praxis: The Poetry of Frank O'Hara," *Social Text,* no. 1 (winter 1979): 59–92; and Rudy Kikel, "The Gay Frank O'Hara," in *Frank O'Hara: To Be True to a City,* ed. Jim Elledge (Ann Arbor: University of Michigan Press, 1990).

11. Susan Sontag, "Notes on Camp," in *Against Interpretation* (New York: Farrar, Straus & Giroux, 1966); and Newton, *Mother Camp.* One early discussion

of camp as an indigenous form of vernacular commentary appeared in Christopher Isherwood's novel *The World in the Evening* (New York: Noonday Books, 1954).

12.   For an exploration of the ways in which vernacular knowledge is translated into the disciplinary knowledge of anthropology, see the essays in James Clifford and George E. Marcus, eds., *Writing Culture: The Poetics and Politics of Ethnography* (Berkeley: University of California Press, 1986).

13.   David Bergman, "Strategic Camp: The Art of Gay Rhetoric," in *Gaiety Transfigured: Gay Self-Representation in American Literature* (Madison: University of Wisconsin Press, 1991), pp. 103–21.

14.   In New York, Michael Callen and Richard Berkowitz also drew on their vernacular knowledge of gay men's sexuality to propose new forms of safer sex. They published a series of pieces in a New York gay newspaper and as pamphlets. See "We Know Who We Are," *New York Native*, November 8–21, 1992; idem, *How to Have Sex in an Epidemic* (New York: From the Front Publications, 1983).

15.   Steven Epstein, "Nature versus Nurture and the Politics of AIDS Organizing," *OUT/LOOK: National Lesbian and Gay Quarterly*, fall 1988, 46–53. See also Patton, *Inventing AIDS*.

16.   Michael Callen's book *Surviving AIDS* (New York: Harper Collins, 1990) is a survey of the vernacular knowledge about the long-term survival of people with AIDS. Patton's *Inventing AIDS* is a study of power and truth effects in the construction of AIDS knowledge.

17.   For documentation of the impact that AIDS activists and community intellectuals have had on medical research and federal policy, see Bruce Nussbaum, *Good Intentions: How Big Business and the Medical Establishment Are Corrupting the Fight against AIDS* (New York: Atlantic Monthly Press, 1990); and Steven Epstein, "Democratic Science? AIDS Activism and the Contested Construction of Knowledge," *Socialist Review* 21, no. 2 (April–June 1991). For an exploration of the influence of activist-artists on AIDS education and political mobilization, see Crimp with Rolston, *AIDS Demo Graphics*.

18.   Pierre Bourdieu, "Social Space and Symbolic Power," in *In Other Words: Essays toward a Reflexive Sociology* (Stanford, Calif.: Stanford University Press, 1990), especially pp. 134–39.

19.   For a detailed discussion of the relationship between the university as an institution of cultural legitimation and intellectuals outside the university, see Pierre Bourdieu, "The Market of Symbolic Goods," *Poetics* 14 (April 1985): 13–44.

20.   Alvin W. Gouldner, *The Future of Intellectuals and the Rise of the New Class* (New York: Oxford University Press, 1979), esp. pp. 28–43.

21.   See, for example, a number of the interviews and lectures in Foucault,

Power/Knowledge. See also Basil Bernstein, *Class, Codes, and Control: Theoretical Studies towards a Sociology of Language* (New York: Schocken Books, 1975).

22. Basil Bernstein's work offers an illuminating exploration of disciplinary knowledge. See particularly "On the Classification and Framing of Educational Knowledge," "Class and Pedagogies: Visible and Invisible," and other essays in part 2 of *Class, Codes, and Control,* vol. 3, *Towards a Theory of Educational Transmissions* (London: Routledge, 1975).

23. See the excellent book on this topic by John Guillory: *Cultural Capital: The Problem of Literary Canon Formation* (Chicago: University of Chicago Press, 1993).

24. See Jerry Herron, *Universities and the Myth of Cultural Decline* (Detroit: Wayne State University Press, 1988); the essays in Darryl J. Gless and Barbara Herrnstein Smith, eds., *The Politics of Liberal Education* (Durham, N.C.: Duke University Press, 1992), particularly the essay by Eve Kosofsky Sedgwick, "Pedagogy in the Context of an Antihomophobic Project."

25. For a discussion of these issues, see John D'Emilio, "Part Two: Remaking the University," in *Making Trouble,* pp. 117–78.

26. For another take on the relation between lesbian and gay studies and the university's power/knowledge regime, see Eve Kosofsky Sedgwick's discussion of the university's representational economy: Kosofsky, "Gender Criticism," in *Redrawing the Boundaries: The Transformation of English and American Literary Studies,* ed. Stephen Greenblatt and Giles Gunn (New York: Modern Languages Association of America, 1992), pp. 294–98.

27. See my discussion of the exclusion of community intellectuals from mainstream public spheres in Jeffrey Escoffier, "Pessimism of the Mind: Intellectuals, Universities, and the Left," *Socialist Review* 18, no. 1 (January–March 1988), reprinted in this book as chapter 7.

28. Sedgwick, "Gender Criticism," pp. 297–98.

29. "Rethinking the Public Sphere: A Contribution to the Critique of Actually Existing Democracy," in *Habermas and the Public Sphere,* ed. Craig Calhoun (Cambridge: MIT Press, 1992), pp. 109–42.

30. See Foucault, "Intellectuals and Power," in *Language, Counter-Memory, Practice.* Disciplinary intellectuals and community intellectuals sometimes work within different theoretical paradigms. The disciplinary intellectual working within the norms of disciplines such as cultural studies and the social sciences is usually committed to the theory that identity is socially constructed. In contrast, the community intellectual, who is often an autodidact and who works outside the university, frequently thinks in terms of authenticity and an essentialist concept of identity. For a partial explanation, see S. Epstein, "Gay Politics," pp. 9–54.

31. Antonio Gramsci, "Formation of the Intellectuals," in *Selections from the Prison Notebooks,* pp. 5–14.

CHAPTER 7

1.   Richard Reeves, "How New Ideas Shape Presidential Politics," *New York Times Magazine,* July 15, 1984; and idem, *The Reagan Detour* (New York: Simon & Schuster, 1985), pp. 9–14, 23–32.

2.   One of the first books about the deteriorating state of intellectual life was Neil Postman, *Amusing Ourselves to Death: Public Discourse in the Age of Show Business* (New York: Viking Press, 1985).

3.   Thomas Byrne Edsall, *The New Politics of Inequality* (New York: Norton, 1984); see especially the chapter on the politicization of the business community, pp. 107–40. See also Sidney Blumenthal, *The Rise of the Counter-Establishment: From Conservative Ideology to Political Power* (New York: Times Books, 1986).

4.   See Stephen H. Balch and Herbert I. London, "The Tenured Left," *Commentary,* October 1986. This belief was a major theme of conservative editors at *The Nation*'s "Conference on Journals of Critical Opinion." See Garry Adams, "Insults Fly at Editors' Conference," *Oakland Tribune,* April 20, 1985; also see the report by *Socialist Review* editors in their sustainer's newsletter, the *Public Sphere,* June 1985. This dogma is also documented in Adam Gussow, "Joseph Epstein and Company: The Rise of the Literary Right," *Boston Review* 9, no. 2 (March–April 1984): 7–10.

5.   Edwin McDowell, "The Making of a Scholarly Best Seller," *New York Times,* November 17, 1987; Michael Hirschorn, "Bestselling Book Makes the Collegiate Curriculum a Burning Public Issue," *Chronicle of Higher Education* 34, no. 3 (September 16, 1987): A1.

6.   Lionel Trilling, "On the Teaching of Modern Literature," in *Beyond Culture* (New York: Harcourt Brace Jovanovich, 1965), p. 23.

7.   Ibid., p. 23; D. Bell, *Cultural Contradictions of Capitalism,* pp. 40–41; Irving Kristol, "The Adversary Culture of Intellectuals," *Encounter,* October 1979, reprinted in Irving Kristol, *Reflections of a Neoconservative* (New York: Basic Books, 1983), pp. 27–42; Joseph Schumpeter, *Capitalism, Socialism, and Democracy* (New York: Harper & Row, 1942), pp. 145–55.

8.   Allan Bloom, *The Closing of the American Mind: How Higher Education Has Failed Democracy and Impoverished the Souls of Today's Students* (New York: Simon & Schuster, 1987).

9.   Bloom claims that "Heidegger's teachings are the most powerful intellectual force of our times." Ibid., p. 312.

10.   Hirschorn, "Bestselling Book," p. A22.

11.   Bloom, *Closing of the American Mind,* pp. 47–137.

12.   Ibid., p. 147.

13.   Ibid., pp. 151–52.

14.   Ibid., pp. 217–26.

15. Ibid., p. 260.

16. Ibid., pp. 311–14.

17. Leo Strauss, *Natural Right and History* (Chicago: University of Chicago Press, 1950).

18. I was an undergraduate at St. John's College in Annapolis, Maryland, where the curriculum consists solely of the Great Books Program (that is, there are no electives, only seminars and tutorials devoted to reading "great books"). Its faculty often took the attitude that social thought after Machiavelli was hopelessly corrupt. When I studied at St. John's, many (but by no means most) of the influential faculty members were students of Leo Strauss. Mortimer Adler, Allan Bloom, and Strauss were frequent guest lecturers at St. John's.

I am deeply ambivalent about the Great Books approach. I disliked the conservative educational philosophy that framed the St. John's program, but I benefited enormously from its disavowal of specialized training as prerequisite to reading important books. The Great Books Program actually teaches students how to study intellectual subjects in an interdisciplinary way. It can also inculcate a certain textual dogmatism.

19. Everett C. Ladd and Seymour Martin Lipset examine evidence showing that whereas university professors are more liberal (45 percent liberal, 30 percent conservative, 20 percent moderate) than the population at large, academics' convictions range across the political spectrum. See "Professors Found to Be Liberal but Not Radical," *Chronicle of Higher Education*, January 16, 1978.

20. Russell Jacoby, *The Last Intellectuals: American Culture in the Age of Academe* (New York: Basic Books, 1987). See chapters 2 and 3: "The Decline of Bohemia," and "On the Road to Suburbia: Urbanists and Beats."

21. On the cultural radicals of the early 1900s, see: Christopher Lasch, "Randolph Bourne and the Experimental Life," in *The New Radicalism in America, 1889–1963: The Intellectual as Social Type* (New York: Knopf, 1965); Arthur Frank Wertheim, *The New York Little Renaissance: Iconoclasm, Modernism, and Nationalism in American Culture, 1980–1917* (New York: New York University Press, 1976); and Edward Abrahams, *The Lyrical Left: Randolph Bourne, Alfred Stieglitz, and the Origins of Cultural Radicalism* (Charlottesville: University of Virginia Press, 1986). On the New York intellectuals, see James Gilbert, *Writers and Partisans* (New York: Wiley, 1968).

22. In just two years—1986 and 1987—at least eight books in addition to Jacoby's *Last Intellectuals* appeared on public intellectuals; four alone (not counting memoirs or biographies) are about the New York intellectuals. The eight books are: Terry A. Cooney, *The Rise of the New York Intellectuals: Partisan Review and Its Circle, 1934–1945* (Madison: University of Wisconsin Press, 1986); Alexander Bloom, *Prodigal Sons: The New York Intellectuals and Their World* (New York: Oxford University Press, 1986); Howard Brick, *Daniel Bell and the Decline of Intellectual Radicalism: Social Theory and Political Reconciliation in the 1940s*

(Madison: University of Wisconsin Press, 1986); Alan M. Wald, *The New York Intellectuals: The Rise and Decline of the Anti-Stalinist Left from the 1930s to the 1980s* (Chapel Hill: University of North Carolina Press, 1987); one about New York as an intellectual capital—Thomas Bender, *New York Intellect: A History of Intellectual Life in New York City, from 1750 to the Beginnings of Our Own Time* (New York: Knopf, 1987); one on leftist intellectuals of the World War I period—Abrahams, *The Lyrical Left*; and two literary theoretical explorations of the intellectual's role—Paul A. Bove, *Intellectuals in Power: A Genealogy of Critical Humanism* (New York: Columbia University Press, 1986); and Jim Merod, *The Political Responsibility of the Critic* (Ithaca: Cornell University Press, 1987).

23. I say *neo*intellectuals so that we can discuss them as a group but also because they share a critical stance toward the 1960s model of political culture and social movements.

24. For evidence of this development, see Gregg Easterbrook, "Ideas Move Nations," *Atlantic Monthly*, January 1986, 66–80; and Joseph G. Peschek, *Policy-Planning Organizations: Elite Agendas and America's Rightward Turn* (Philadelphia: Temple University Press, 1987). Blumenthal, *Rise of the Counter-Establishment*, also documents this trend.

25. Although it is a little dated now, see Randall Rothenberg, "The Neoliberal Club," *Esquire*, February 1982.

26. Chuck Lane, "The Manhattan Project," *New Republic*, March 25, 1985, 14–15.

27. See Jan Clausen, *A Movement of Poets: Thoughts on Poetry and Feminism* (Brooklyn: Long Haul Press, 1982) for an interesting analysis of poets' role in leading the women's movement.

28. See Harold Cruse, *The Crisis of the Negro Intellectual* (New York: Morrow, 1967)—one of the all-time great histories of intellectuals.

29. Cornel West, "The Dilemma of the Black Intellectual," *Cultural Critique*, no. 1 (fall 1985); Martin Kilson, "Paradoxes of Blackness: Notes on the Crisis of Black Intellectuals," *Dissent*, winter 1986, 70–78; Greg Tate, "Cult Nats Meet the Freaky Deke: The Return of the Black Aesthetic," *Village Voice*, Voice Literary Supplement, December 1986, 5–8.

30. Kilson, "Paradoxes of Blackness," p. 74, and West, "Dilemma of the Black Intellectual," p. 112. Greg Tate also makes this point in "Cult Nats." In his plea for a "popular poststructuralism for black culture," Tate argues that there "are artists for whom black consciousness and artistic freedom are not mutually exclusive but complementary, for whom 'black culture' signifies a multicultural tradition of expressive practices" (p. 7).

31. Kilson, "Paradoxes of Blackness," p. 77.

32. Esther Newton, "Academe's Homophobia: It Damages Careers and Ruins Lives," *Chronicle of Higher Education*, March 11, 1987, 104.

33. Lisa Duggan, "History's Gay Ghetto: The Contradictions of Growth in

Lesbian and Gay History," in *Presenting the Past: Essays on History and the Public,* ed. Susan Porter Benson, Stephen Brier, and Roy Rosenzweig (Philadelphia: Temple University Press, 1986), pp. 281–91.

34.   One of the earliest articles that brought together lesbians who had studied the history of sexuality was Deirdre English, Amber Hollibaugh, and Gayle Rubin, "Talking Sex," *Socialist Review,* no. 58 (July–August 1981). Both Amber Hollibaugh and Gayle Rubin were members of the San Francisco Lesbian and Gay History Project. The two most influential anthologies of feminist writings on sexuality include pieces by veterans of the lesbian and gay history projects: Allan Bérubé, Amber Hollibaugh, John D'Emilio, Joan Nestle, and Gayle Rubin.

35.   Bérubé, "History of Gay Bathhouses," pp. 15–19. A longer version of this piece was submitted as an exhibit in court cases in New York City, San Francisco, and Los Angeles.

36.   Gouldner, *Future of Intellectuals,* pp. 28–43.

37.   "The culture of critical discourse" is not without value as a set of norms for intellectual discourse, but adopting its norms can inhibit intellectuals' participation in the hurly-burly of the public sphere.

38.   Both Victor Navasky, "The Role of the Journal of Critical Opinion," and Ilene Philipson, "On Critical Journals," appear in *Socialist Review,* nos. 82–83: 15–29.

CHAPTER 8

1.   Warner, ed., *Fear of a Queer Planet,* p. xii.

2.   Cindy Patton, "Tremble Hetero Swine," in *Fear of a Queer Planet,* ed. Warner, p. 173.

3.   Sedgwick, *Epistemology of the Closet;* Butler, *Gender Trouble;* idem, *Bodies That Matter.*

4.   Sedgwick, *Between Men.*

5.   Laclau and Mouffe, *Hegemony and Socialist Strategy;* and Slavoj Žižek, *The Sublime Object of Ideology* (London: Verso, 1989).

6.   Patton, "Tremble Hetero Swine," pp. 166–67.

7.   Ibid., p. 173.

8.   Berlandt and Freeman, "Queer Nationality."

9.   Douglas Crimp, "Right on, Girlfriend!" in *Fear of a Queer Planet,* ed. Warner, pp. 300–320.

10.   Sedgwick, *Epistemology of the Closet,* p. 1.

11.   Warner, introduction to *Fear of a Queer Planet,* pp. xxi–xxv.

12.   For Gayle Rubin's discussion of the sex/gender system and its "heteronormativity," see "Traffic in Women."

13.   Warner, ed., *Fear of a Queer Planet*, pp. ix–x, xxiii–xxiv.

14.   Marcuse, *Eros and Civilization*; Brown, *Life against Death*; Gilles Deleuze and Felix Guattari, *Anti-Oedipus: Capitalism and Schizophrenia* (Minneapolis: University of Minnesota Press, 1983); idem, *A Thousand Plateaus* (Minneapolis: University of Minnesota Press, 1987).

15.   Anthony Giddens, *The Transformation of Intimacy: Sexuality, Love, and Eroticism in Modern Societies* (Stanford, Calif.: Stanford University Press, 1992), pp. 13–16, 28, 144–47; idem, *Modernity and Self-Identity: Self and Identity in the Late Modern Age* (Stanford, Calif.: Stanford University Press, 1991).

16.   Rubin, "Traffic in Women."

17.   See the discussion of sublimation in Marcuse, *Eros and Civilization*, pp. 206–12.

18.   James Davison Hunter, *Culture Wars: The Struggle to Define America* (New York: Basic Books, 1991).

19.   Foucault, *History of Sexuality*, vol. 1, *Introduction*, pp. 15–50, 83–85.

PART THREE

1.   Gayle Rubin sketches long-term historical "sexual transformations" in her influential essay "Thinking Sex." My 1985 essay "Sexual Revolution and the Politics of Gay Identity," which is now chapter 1 in this book, draws on her work. In John D'Emilio and Estelle Freedman, *Intimate Matters: A History of Sexuality in America* (New York: Harper Collins, 1988), esp. pp. 300–325, the authors also identify the sexual revolution as a long-term historical process.

2.   On the link between strategy and cultural politics, see Barbara Epstein, *Political Protest and Cultural Revolution: Nonviolent Direct Action in the 1970s and 1980s* (Berkeley: University of California Press, 1991), pp. 18–20.

3.   "All reification is a forgetting," according to Max Horkheimer and Theodore Adorno, *Dialectic of Enlightenment* (New York: Continuum, 1972), p. 230. As Theodore Adorno noted, although society encompasses individual subjectivity, it is also "objective because, on account of its underlying structure, it cannot perceive its own subjectivity, because it does possess a total subject and through its organization thwarts the installation of such a subject." See page 33 of the introduction and page 74 of "Sociology and Empirical Research" in Theodore W. Adorno et al., *The Positivist Dispute in German Sociology* (New York: Harper & Row, 1976).

4.   Dollimore explores the "perverse dynamic" in *Sexual Dissidence*, pp. 103–30; and Bersani takes up this line of thinking in *Homos*.

5.   K. Mercer, *Welcome to the Jungle*, pp. 21–22, 233–58.

CHAPTER 9

1.   In its original form, this essay was a talk I delivered at Ohio State University, Columbus, on February 26, 1991, during Lesbian, Gay, and Bisexual Awareness Week. For revisions to this version, I am particularly indebted to Barbara Epstein, Leslie Kauffman, and Ilene Philipson. I would also like to thank the Socialist Review Bay Area Collective for their comments.

2.   For one of the best explorations of nationalism and the cultural politics it inspires, see B. Anderson, *Imagined Communities.*

3.   I owe this point to L. A. Kauffman.

4.   See Stokely Carmichael and Charles Hamilton, *Black Power: The Politics of Liberation in America* (New York: Vintage Books, 1967), and Robert L. Allen, *Black Awakening in Capitalist America* (New York: Doubleday, 1969).

5.   See Robin Morgan, ed., *Sisterhood Is Powerful* (New York: Random House, 1970); and Munoz, *Youth, Identity, Power.*

6.   Fred Block, *Postindustrial Possibilities: A Critique of Economic Discourse* (Berkeley: University of California Press, 1990).

7.   Horace M. Kallen, "Democracy versus the Melting Pot," *Nation,* 1915; Randolph Bourne, "Transnational America," published originally in the *Atlantic Monthly,* July 1916; reprinted in Randolph Bourne, *The Radical Will: Selected Writings, 1911–1918,* ed. Olaf Hansen (New York: Urizen Books, 1977). Whether people from different races and with diverse sexualities can live together in the same society is an important theme in James Baldwin's work. See his essay *The Fire Next Time* (New York: Dial Press, 1963) and his fiction, especially *Another Country* (New York: Dial Press, 1962). British-Pakistani writer Hanif Kureishi has self-consciously taken up Baldwin's line of thought in his screenplays and essays, such as "The Rainbow Sign," in *My Beautiful Laundrette and The Rainbow Sign* (London: Faber & Faber, 1986), and *Sammy and Rosie Get Laid* (New York: Penguin Books, 1988).

8.   See Georg Simmel, *Conflict and the Web of Group Affiliations* (New York: Free Press, 1955), pp. 125–95.

9.   Moraga and Anzaldúa, eds., *This Bridge Called My Back;* Alarcon, "Theoretical Subject(s)," pp. 356–69.

10.   Cherríe Moraga, *Loving in the War Years* (Boston: South End Press, 1983); Anzaldúa, *Borderlands;* Audre Lorde, *Zami: A New Spelling of My Name* (Trumansberg, N.Y.: Crossing Press, 1982).

11.   See the discussion of "heteroglossia" in the novel, poetry, and other cultural forms in M. M. Bakhtin, *The Dialogic Imagination* (Austin: University of Texas Press, 1981), pp. 259–331.

12.   Kureishi, "Rainbow Sign," pp. 30–31.

13.   Ibid., p. 31.

14.   Ben H. Bagdikian, "Cornering Hearts and Minds: The Lords of the Global Village," *Nation* 248, no. 23 (June 12, 1991).

15.   Barbara Epstein, " 'Political Correctness' and Collective Powerlessness," *Socialist Review* 21, nos. 3–4 (July–December 1991).

16.   See the articles on the politics of multiculturalism and the OutWrite conferences by Andrea Lewis, "Who's Afraid of Edward Albee?" and by Lisa Hall, "Chockful of Irony," in *OUT/LOOK: National Lesbian and Gay Quarterly*, no. 14 (fall 1991).

17.   Louise Sloan, "Beyond Dialogue," *San Francisco Bay Guardian*, literary supplement, March 1991, 3–5.

18.   Bernice Johnson Reagon, "Coalition Politics: Turning the Century," in *Home Girls: A Black Feminist Anthology,* ed. Barbara Smith (New York: Kitchen Table/Women of Color Press, 1983), pp. 356–68.

19.   This line of thought owes something to the writings of Bakhtin, *Dialogic Imagination;* V. N. Volosinov, *Marxism and the Philosophy of Language* (Cambridge: Harvard University Press, 1973); and Jurgen Habermas, "What Is Universal Pragmatics?" in *Communication and the Evolution of Society* (Boston: Beacon Press, 1979).

CHAPTER 11

1.   This essay emerged from my despondency after the Right's victory in the November 1994 elections, but it was also inspired by the political and theoretical originality of Lisa Duggan's and Nan Hunter's individually and jointly written essays. I want to thank Chris Bull, Amber Hollibaugh, Loring McAlpin, Esther Newton, and Michael Rothberg for their comments on earlier versions of this essay. I owe special thanks to Matthew Lore, my companion in conversations about so many things, for his comments, encouragement, and company as I wrote this essay. I'm afraid that I never would have written it without David Trend's encouragement (and persistent but gentle nagging).

2.   See J. Hunter, *Culture Wars.* For a view of these issues from the Left in the United Kingdom, see the essays in Jeffrey Weeks, ed., *The Lesser Evil and the Greater Good: The Theory and the Politics of Social Diversity* (London: Rivers Oram Press, 1994).

3.   Todd Gitlin, *The Sixties: Years of Hope, Days of Rage* (New York: Bantam, 1987).

4.   See Josh Gamson, "Silence, Death, and the Invisible Enemy: AIDS Activism and Social Movement 'Newness,' " *Social Problems* 34, no. 6 (October 1989).

5.   For a history of the Religious Right, see Sara Diamond, *Spiritual Warfare: The Politics of the Christian Right* (Boston: South End Press, 1989); and Dallas A.

Blanchard, *The Anti-Abortion Movement and the Rise of the Religious Right: From Polite to Fiery Protest* (New York: Twayne, 1994).

6.   For an assessment of the Religious Right's effect on U.S. politics, see E. J. Dionne, *Why Americans Hate Politics* (New York: Simon & Schuster, 1991).

7.   Irving Kristol, "My Cold War," *National Interest* (spring 1993), p. 86.

8.   For a thorough analysis of the family values agenda, see Judith Stacey, *In the Name of the Family: Rethinking Family Values in the Postmodern Age* (Boston: Beacon Press, 1996), particularly pp. 52–82.

9.   Duberman, *Stonewall*.

10.   Arlene Stein, "Three Models of Sexuality: Drives, Identities, and Practices," *Sociological Theory* 7, no. 1 (1989).

11.   Randy Shilts, *The Mayor of Castro Street* (New York: St. Martin's Press, 1983).

12.   Alice Echols, *Daring to Be Bad: Radical Feminism in America, 1967–1975* (Minneapolis: University of Minnesota Press, 1989).

13.   The conservative antigay rhetoric has used marketing research on gay and lesbian purchasing power to argue that gay men and lesbians are a privileged and economically powerful group that has no need of civil rights protections. For a critique, see M. V. Lee Badgett, "Beyond Biased Samples: Challenging the Myths on the Economic Status of Lesbians and Gay Men," in Amy Gluckman and Betsy Reed, eds., *Homo Economics: Capitalism, Community, and Lesbian and Gay Life* (New York: Routledge, 1997), pp. 65–72.

14.   For the political, medical, and cultural context, see the essays by Douglas Crimp and Paula Treichler in Crimp, ed., *AIDS*. For some historical and political background on GMHC, see Philip Kayal, *Bearing Witness: Gay Men's Health Crisis and the Politics of AIDS* (Boulder, Colo.: Westview Press, 1993).

15.   See Shilts, *Mayor of Castro Street*.

16.   Larry Kramer, *Reports from the Holocaust*, rev. ed. (New York: St. Martin's Press, 1995).

17.   Douglas Crimp, "How to Have Promiscuity in an Epidemic," in *AIDS*, ed. Crimp.

18.   See Crimp with Rolston, *AIDS Demo Graphics* (Seattle: Bay Press, 1990).

19.   See Eric Rofes, "Gay Liberation versus AIDS: Averting Civil War in the 1990s," *OUT/LOOK: National Lesbian and Gay Quarterly* (spring 1990); also see Crimp's discussion of these issues in his article "Right on, Girlfriend!"

20.   See the special section on Queer Nation with articles by Allan Bérubé and Jeffrey Escoffier, Alexander Chee, Steve Cossen, and Maria Maggenti in *OUT/LOOK: National Lesbian and Gay Quarterly*, no. 11 (winter 1991): 12–23; Lisa Duggan, "Making It Perfectly Queer," *Socialist Review* 22, no. 1 (January–March 1992): 11–31. See also Warner's introduction to *Fear of a Queer Planet*, pp. vii–xxxi, and Berlandt and Freeman, "Queer Nationality."

21.   The broadside "Queers Read This: I Hate Straights" is reprinted in Mark Blasius and Shane Phelan, eds., *We Are Everywhere: A Historical Sourcebook of Gay and Lesbian Politics* (New York: Routledge, 1997), pp. 773–80.

22.   For an extensive exploration of this issue, see Larry Gross, *Contested Closets: The Politics and Ethics of Outing* (Minneapolis: University of Minnesota Press, 1993).

23.   Sloan, "Beyond Dialogue," 3.

24.   See Warner, introduction to *Fear of a Queer Planet*.

25.   Lisa Duggan, "Queering the State," *Social Text*, no. 39 (1994): 1–14.

26.   For a comparable discussion of racial politics, see Howard Winant, "Postmodern Racial Politics in the United States: Difference and Inequality," *Socialist Review* 20, no. 1 (January–March 1990): 121–47.

27.   Hunter's analysis is discussed in Duggan, "Queering the State"; see also Nan D. Hunter, "Identity, Speech, and Equality," *Virginia Law Review* 79, no. 7 (October 1993).

28.   Badgett, "Wage Effects." For a general survey of economic issues, see Escoffier, "Homo/Economics."

29.   Michael Nava and Robert Dawidoff, *Created Equal: Why Gay Rights Matter to America* (New York: St. Martin's Press, 1994), p. 112.

30.   Bruce Bawer, "The Road to Utopia," *Advocate*, September 20, 1994, 80. Both a detailed critique of the lesbian and gay movement and a detailed working out of the "moderate" strategy appear in Kirk and Madsen, *After the Ball*; see also Bawer, *Place at the Table*.

31.   I owe this point to Matthew Lore.

CONCLUSION

1.   "Gay Rights Laws Can't Be Banned, High Court Rules," *New York Times*, May 21, 1996, p. 1; excerpts from the Court's decision on p. A20.

2.   Ibid., p. A20.

3.   See Chris Bull and John Gallagher, *Perfect Enemies: The Religious Right and the Gay Movement and the Politics of the 1990s* (New York: Crown, 1996).

4.   On the impact of the Helms amendment and the Religious Right on AIDS prevention education, see Duggan and Hunter, *Sex Wars*, pp. 134–37; and the essays by Ephen Glenn Colter, "Discernibly Turgid: Safer Sex and Public Policy," in *Policing Public Sex*, ed. Dangerous Bedfellows; and Hollibaugh, "Seducing Women."

5.   See Bull and Gallagher, *Perfect Enemies*, pp. 1–38.

6.   Michel Foucault made this general point more than twenty years ago in *Discipline and Punish* (New York: Pantheon Books, 1977), pp. 222–23.

7.   Michel Foucault, "Politics and Reason," in *Politics, Philosophy, Culture: Interviews and Other Writings, 1977–1984*, ed. Lawrence D. Kritzman (New York: Routledge, 1988), pp. 57–85, see especially p. 67. This consists of the published version of Foucault's Tanner Lectures on Human Values delivered at Stanford University on October 10 and October 16, 1979. See also the discussion of Foucault by Jean L. Cohen and Andrew Arato in their important book *Civil Society and Political Theory* (Cambridge: MIT Press, 1992), especially pp. 263–65 and pp. 290–91.

8.   Michael Walzer, "The Civil Society Argument," in *Dimensions of Radical Democracy: Pluralism, Citizenship, Community*, ed. Chantal Mouffe (London: Verso, 1992); see especially pp. 97–102. In the same volume, see also Kirstie McClure, "On the Subject of Rights: Pluralism, Plurality, and Political Identity," esp. p. 115.

9.   Poet Frank O'Hara refused such forms of transcendence for these structures. See Yingling, *Hart Crane*, pp. 130–31.

10.   See Tony Kushner, "On Pretentiousness," in *Thinking about the Longstanding Problems*, p. 78, and in the same volume, "A Socialism of the Skin (Liberation, Honey!)," pp. 19–32.

11.   Gramsci, *Selections from the Prison Notebooks*, pp. 229–40, 245–64; and Chantal Mouffe, "Hegemony and the Integral State in Gramsci: Towards a New Concept of Politics," in *Silver Linings: Some Strategies for the Eighties*, ed. George Bridges and Rosalind Brunt (London: Lawrence and Wishart, 1981), pp. 167–87.

INDEX

Compositor:	Binghamton Valley Composition
Text:	Palatino
Display:	Snell Roundhand Script, Bauer Bodoni, Grotesque Extra Condensed (Monotype)
Printer and Binder:	Maple-Vail Book Manufacturing Group